Gender issues in clinical psychology

Clinical psychology has traditionally ignored or marginalised gender issues. It tends to see the individual subject as gender neutral, and ignores many aspects of the individual, both as client and as practitioner. *Gender Issues in Clinical Psychology* argues that if clinical psychology is to work for both men and women, gender issues must be acknowledged and resolved.

The contributors, leading researchers and practitioners in the field of clinical psychology, look at the position of women and men as practitioners, as objects of the scientific gaze, and as clients of the clinical psychologist. They argue that, by ignoring gender, clinical psychology perpetuates gender stereotypes and the oppression of women. Focusing on different aspects of clinical practice and organisation, including child sexual abuse, family therapy, forensic psychology and individual feminist therapy, the contributors demonstrate that it is vital that gender issues are incorporated into clinical research and practice and offer examples of theory and practice which do not marginalise the needs of women.

Gender Issues in Clinical Psychology will be essential reading for clinical psychologists and those in allied professions such as social work, counselling, psychiatry and medicine.

Jane M. Ussher is Lecturer in Psychology at the University of Sussex. **Paula Nicolson** is Lecturer in Medical Psychology at the University of Sheffield.

Gender issues in clinical psychology

Edited by
Jane M. Ussher and Paula Nicolson

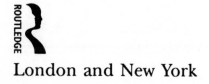

London and New York

First published 1992
by Routledge
11 New Fetter Lane, London EC4P 4EE

Simultaneously published in the USA and Canada
by Routledge
a division of Routledge, Chapman and Hall, Inc.
29 West 35th Street, New York, NY 10001

Laserprinted by LaserScript, Mitcham, Surrey
Printed and bound in Great Britain by Biddles Ltd, Guildford and
Kings Lynn

British Library Cataloguing in Publication Data
A catalogue reference for this title is available from the British Library

Library of Congress Cataloging in Publication Data
Gender issues in clinical psychology/edited by Jane M. Ussher and
    Paula Nicolson.
    p. cm.
    Includes bibliographical references and index.
    1. Clinical psychology. 2. Feminist psychology. 3. Women
    psychologists. 4. Women Mental health. I. Ussher, Jane M., 1961– . II.
    Nicolson, Paula.
    [DNLM: 1. Attitude of Health Personnel. 2. Gender Identity.
    3. Psychology, Clinical. 4. Stereotyping. WM 105 G325]
    RC467.G46   1992
    616.89′023dc20
    DNLM/DLC
    for Library of Congress   91-25284
                                                                      CIP

ISBN 0–415–05485–0
       0–415–05489–6 (pbk)

Contents

Illustrations

TABLES

FIGURE

Contributors

Jan Burns works half-time as a clinical psychologist in the area of learning difficulties for Bradford Health Authority and half-time as a lecturer on the Leeds University training course in clinical psychology. She is author of a number of publications in the area of women and learning difficulties, forensic psychology and the psychology of women.

Stephen Frosh is a senior lecturer in psychology at Birkbeck College, University of London and Clinical Psychologist in the Child and Family Department of the Tavistock Clinic, London. He is the author of several books on psychoanalysis, child sexual abuse, and psychology. He is currently working on a book on masculinity, due for publication in 1993.

Sue Holland is a London community clinical psychologist who has worked in the mental health field for 25 years, including the Tavistock Clinic (NHS) and the Battersea Action and Counselling Centre (voluntary sector). She is concerned with addressing issues of race, class and gender in mental health and is herself Anglo-Indian. She currently works as a consultant psychologist for Wycombe district psychology service.

Paula Nicolson is a lecturer in psychology in the Medical School at Sheffield University. Her research interests are women and sexuality, post-natal depression, and equal opportunities in medical education. Her books include (with Jane Ussher) *The Psychology of Women's Health and Health Care* (Macmillan 1992).

Anne Peake has worked as an educational psychologist since 1976, always in posts which had an inter-agency brief, in Education and

Social Services. She is currently Principal Psychologist for Oxfordshire Social Services, working with children and families.

Rachel E. Perkins is a lesbian, a feminist, and works as a clinical psychologist at Springfield University Hospital with individuals who have severe disabilities. She has published a number of papers and chapters on the issue of women with severe disabilities.

Janet Sayers is Senior Lecturer in Psychology at the University of Kent and also works part-time as a psychoanalytic psychotherapist. Her books include *Mothering Psychoanalysis* (Hamish Hamilton 1991).

Jane M. Ussher is a clinical psychologist, lecturing in psychology in the School of Cultural and Community Studies at Sussex University. Her books include *The Psychology of the Female Body* (Routledge 1989), *Women's Madness: Misogyny or Mental Illness?* (Harvester Wheatsheaf 1991) and with Christine Baker *Psychological Perspectives on Sexual Problems: New Directions in Theory and Practice* (Routledge 1992).

Arlene Vetere has a split post, working half-time at the University of Reading in the Department of Psychology lecturing on the psychology of family life, and half-time as a clinical psychologist in the Paxton Family and Young Persons Unit in Reading where she practises and teaches family therapy.

Gilli Watson is a community clinical psychologist working in the area of mental health in the Department of Clinical and Community Psychology, Exeter Health Authority.

Jennie Williams has worked as a feminist psychologist since the 1970s. Initially she worked as a researcher concerned with the connections between sexual inequality and mental health, then as a clinical psychologist in services for people with severe psychiatric disabilities. She now works at the Institute of Social and Applied Psychology at the University of Kent as a lecturer in Mental Health/Service Development Consultancy.

Introduction

Clinical psychology is a profession still in its infancy, some might claim its adolescence, having only emerged as a recognised professional grouping in the post World War II era. Whilst other groups such as medics can trace their history, their professional rivalries and their current practices and politics back for centuries, sometimes choosing to underplay the role of the barber surgeons and alchemists who were their forefathers (sic), and emphasise their scientific roots in the writings of Hippocrates, clinical psychologists lean on the relatively recent foundations of the experimental psychologists of the early twentieth century. As descendants of those who pioneered testing and psychometrics, the early clinical psychologists acted in a limited sphere, operating very much under the umbrella of the medics, plying their craft as experts in psychometric testing and limited behavioural interventions. Yet in the late twentieth century all of this has changed, as clinical psychology has developed and grown into a profession of 'scientist practitioners', skilled in many different arenas, and operating at a number of levels of intervention often independent from any other professional grouping.

This history of clinical psychology is an interesting one, and central to any consideration of gender issues. For as the development of medicine was inherently a male enterprise (Ehrenreich and English 1978), so was the development of clinical psychology. The early researchers, the early practitioners, were male, and the rhetoric and ethos of the profession was developed from a very patriarchal perspective – mirroring the discourse within psychology as an academic discipline. The gender of client groups has traditionally been ignored, or is seen as irrelevant – the gender of the clinical psychologist possibly more so. For clinical psychologists are, and always have been, aware of their roots as applied scientists, and as scientists are determined to be objective, rational and neutral, their own gender irrelevant, the object of their expert gaze viewed 'dispassionately and impartially' (Management Advisory Service to the NHS 1989: 43). So whilst research and practice in clinical psychology has burgeoned over the last fifty years, with the profession seemingly going from strength to strength and looking forward to a healthy future in the next century, there has been a startling omission of any discussion of gender issues within either the professional or research literature. This is despite the fact that the profession (in Britain at least) is predominantly female. Also despite the fact that those with whom the clinical psychologist works, either as colleague or as client, are predominantly female. This omission of gender can no longer go unchecked.

This volume is intended to redress the balance, to act as a catalyst for debate, as well as a clear demonstration of the need for examination of gender issues by clinical psychologists working in all areas – not just those offering therapy to individual women, the area which first comes to mind in any discussion of gender and clinical psychology. For whilst many individual feminist therapists have attempted to address gender issues in their practice, the role of therapist is only one of many for the clinical psychologist, and it is notable that consideration of gender is absent in these other spheres.

For whilst the early clinical psychologists carried out assessments or interventions on a one-to-one basis level with clients, this is not the case for the new breed of scientist practitioners. Clinical psychologists are not simply therapists, or testers, or researchers, as the popular stereotype may suggest – they are expected to be able to utilise a whole gamut of skills and work on a number of different levels. The clinical psychologist is both a scientist (researcher) and practitioner (clinician) – often combining the roles, but more frequently specialising in one model of working. Equally, clinical psychologists have varying degrees of involvement with client groups, from working in an advisory or consultation capacity, to direct one-to-one work with individuals or groups, involving assessment, therapeutic intervention and support, and recent documentation (i.e. Management Advisory Service to the NHS 1989) has advised that individuals specialise in one level of working. It has been argued that at the beginning of a professional career the clinical psychologist will work at the level of individual clinical intervention with individuals of families, moving to consultation, or to organisation and management of services as part of a career progression. If this model of practice is universally adopted, what is essential is that clinical psychologists do not forget the need to discuss gender issues as they progress – only considering them in one-to-one therapy with a woman.

One of the reasons for the current interest in gender, and in particular in women, in clinical psychology has been the change in the gender structure within the profession itself, as illustrated by Paula Nicolson in Chapter 1. This attention given to gender in psychology is reinforced by the growing interest in feminist psychology, and in the psychology of women, evidenced by both the formation of the Psychology of Women Section of the British Psychological Society in 1988, and a rapidly expanding literature on the subject in the form of books and journal articles. It is clear who is behind this movement – the women who are over-represented at the bottom of the hierarchy, not the men who hold the reins of power. For whilst women now dominate in terms of sheer numbers in clinical psychology, they are not in the majority in terms of their access to power within the profession. Many parallels can be made between the position of women and the balance of power in clinical psychology and in other professions. Unfortunately, psychology does not come out of this analysis as an exemplary case of a profession wedded to equal opportunities or to attending to the interests of women, as Paula Nicolson demonstrates.

As applied scientists, clinical psychology as a profession is committed to research, as evidenced by the insistence on the status of clinical psychologists as 'scientist practitioners'. The literature on gender issues in science is one of the more interesting consequences of the feminist involvement in academic disciplines previously dominated by men, and the application of these arguments to science and research in clinical psychology is discussed by Jane Ussher in Chapter 2. There is now a strong body of work attesting to the sexing of science and the association between masculinity and the rational scientist, femininity and nature. This has serious implications in view of the criticisms levied at positivism, the model of scientific research adopted by the majority of clinical psychologists at present, which may result in a denial of the importance of issues of gender, of politics or the social reality of many women's lives in clinical psychology.

The different chapters in this volume illustrate how gender issues should be incorporated into research and practice at a number of levels of working, and with different client groups. Thus at the consultation or organisational level, clinical psychologists plan and organise services in the health service. Sue Holland, in Chapter 3, discusses her work in a neighbourhood psychotherapy and social action project for women, a particular project which could be said to encompass all levels of working – and which certainly addresses gender issues head on, providing a model of practice for many others. In this work, Sue Holland incorporates issues of gender, class, age and ethnicity – and works alongside women rather than as an expert imparting knowledge from above. Her work illustrates the reality of incorporating critical theory and practice in a way which works for women, and clearly demonstrates that those organising services, working alongside other professionals and client groups, can acknowledge gender.

The role of consultation with other practitioners is increasingly a major role for clinical psychologists – acting in an advisory capacity, imparting skills and supervising case work. Anne Peake illustrates this practice very clearly in Chapter 4 in her discussion of a consultation service in the area of child abuse. She has discussed the working of the service in detail, and as such provides a welcome insight into the practical reality of running a successful consultation service. Her inclusion of detailed statistics on both professionals who use the child abuse consultation service, and on the survivors and perpetrators of abuse provides a convincing case for the need to place gender issues in the centre of the child sexual abuse agenda. The abusers are invariably men, and those sexually abused predominantly female. Yet as Anne Peake demonstrates, a considerable percentage of children sexually abused are male – a fact which remains unacknowledged in the main. As the number of cases of child sexual abuse being reported increases yearly, at a rate which is outstripping the service provision, this type of consultation service is obviously serving an essential function. It is interesting that it is women who use it.

The role of clinical psychology in the definition and categorisation of problems and in the provision of interventions for individuals at an institutional level is an area fraught with controversy, as Jan Burns illustrates in Chapter 5. In a discussion of gender issues in forensic psychology, the categorisation of women as mad and men as bad provides an insight into both our assumptions about what is 'normal' behaviour for women and men, and the response of institutions to the subsequent classification. As women are deemed mad and men bad for similar types of behaviour, the ethics of clinical intervention in the context of forensic and psychiatric settings may be called into question.

Equally, so may intervention with families, as gender stereotypes are often employed in the assessment and treatment within family therapy. Intervention with families was heralded in the 1960s and 1970s as a positive move away from pathologising individuals, and acknowledging the role of the system and society in any suffering. But it is not so simple, as Arlene Vetere illustrates in her lucid account of the practice of family therapy by clinical psychologists. Both women and men may be both judged and treated within models which employ restrictive gender and limited gender stereotypes: a salutary lesson for many. Arlene Vetere employs a feminist perspective to understand family dynamics, and to develop models of practice which are empowering for the family – rather than restrictive for the woman.

Yet the feminist perspective is not the only one which can be employed in an acknowledgement of gender and family therapy. For whilst he uses the work of French feminists, such as Irigaray, in his chapter on masculine ideology in therapy, Stephen Frosh essentially adopts a psychoanalytic perspective in order to examine the dynamics of working as a male therapist in family therapy. Speaking as the 'only male voice' in this volume, Stephen Frosh offers a reevaluation of the masculine position in psychological therapy – and offers suggestions for practice which allows the acknowledgement of sexual difference in a way which is empowering for both women and men.

Empowerment is a central theme of Rachel Perkin's chapter on her work with socially disabled clients – those unable to cope with the demands of everyday life without help and support. From a radical feminist perspective, and using individual client work as a model of practice, she examines the way in which psychology has been misused to disempower women with severe disablements, through both diagnosis and treatment. She criticises the institutionalisation advocated by the early psychologists as vociferously as the supposedly positive practice of community care now advocated by practitioners and politicians. Her chapter provides a powerful argument vilifying clinical psychology as it is traditionally practised for being both patriarchal and heterosexist – an argument which has implications way beyond the client group central to her discussion.

Yet there are other ways of working with individuals which acknowledge gender which are equally convincing. Janet Sayers, in Chapter 9, discusses feminism, psychoanalysis and psychotherapy, incorporating an analysis of the work of Freud, Lacan and Winnicott in her arguments. She believes that Lacanian therapy can facilitate the exposure of the illusions and sexual inequalities fostered within patriarchy, allowing women and men to develop in a way which acknowledges the similarities and differences of our sexual and social being. In this way feminism and psychoanalysis can both work together to provide insight and illumination of difficulties for individuals.

It is the different ways in which feminist practice has been incorporated into therapy that Gilli Watson and Jennie Williams examine in Chapter 10. Through a discussion of the historical development of feminist therapy in the 1970s, as a reaction to the 'male-serving ideologies' inherent within mental health practices, Watson and Williams provide a convincing case for the need to develop a new knowledge base for feminist practice in therapy. They look at both assumptions and the process of therapy, focusing on issues of power and abuse. Yet this is not a disheartening account, for whilst present mental health practices are deconstructed, their reconstruction does offer hope for the future.

This is one of the major criticisms which can be levied at feminist critiques of psychology – that they deconstruct without appearing to reconstruct: we are always ready to point out the weaknesses in current practices, but not always so ready to provide solutions. There is no one simple answer which will provide a model for fledgling clinical psychologists who wish to acknowledge gender in their work to follow (see Ussher 1991 for a discussion of this). Yet the contributors in this volume do offer many different models of work, across a range of client groups. Whilst Sue Holland provides a positive model for service development and organisation, Anne Peake for consultation, Arlene Vetere and Stephen Frosh for family therapy, the final three chapters in this volume provide positive suggestions for work with individuals. They take a different perspective – each is valuable, and constructively acknowledges the problems in traditional practices when gender is a consideration. These reconstructions need to be seen alongside the critical deconstructions, in order for clinical psychology to move forwards.

CONCLUSION

This volume cannot stand alone – it must be seen as a part of a wider discussion of gender issues in mental health practices, a discussion which has too often focused on psychiatry. Clinical psychologists often complain that they are confused with their psychiatric colleagues, and may therefore see themselves as exempt from some of the criticisms traditionally levied at psychiatrists by feminists critics. The contributors in this volume no longer allow this immunity from scrutiny to be tenable. Equally, the views expressed here within must be seen in the light of analyses of gender issues in psychology as a whole – the analysis of clinical psychology is only one strand in a much larger debate. This is not a debate only of concern to feminists, and as this volume illustrates, it is not only the feminist voice which is speaking out for change in clinical psychology. And this is a change which must occur, for if clinical psychology is to work for both women and men, at the many different levels, and for the myriad of client groups who may benefit from the skills of the clinical psychologist, we must acknowledge gender issues. The contributors to the volume provide examples of how this may be done. Yet this is merely the start – many more will hopefully follow. This book cannot be seen as the final word on this subject; it is a starting point, hoping to provoke discussion. There are many groups of clients we have not considered – this is not in any way an all-inclusive sample. There are many ways of working and ways of thinking we have not included. If this book provokes those who work in other ways, with other client groups, who hold different views to think about and write about their experiences, and thus becomes simply part of a wider discussion of gender in clinical psychology rather than being a lone voice, it will have succeeded.

REFERENCES

Ehrenreich, B. and English, D. (1978) *For Her Own Good: 150 Years of the Experts' Advice to Women.* New York: Anchor Doubleday.

Management Advisory Service to the NHS. (1989) *Review of Clinical Psychology Services.*

Ussher, J. M. (1991) *Women's Madness: Misogyny or Mental Illness?* London: Harvester Wheatsheaf.

Chapter 1

Gender issues in the organisation of clinical psychology

Paula Nicolson

Introduction

> Despite the preponderance of women as consumers of mental health services, frequently used texts for counselling and psychotherapy focus no specific attention on the particular needs of women clients (Fabrikant, 1974). Only a minority of training facilities make any attempt to train students to provide adequate services to women (Kenworthy, 1976). The difference in client responses to male and female therapists are seldom discussed: most texts are written as if all therapists were male.
>
> (Howell and Bayes 1981: xi)

These points raised in an American text on women and mental health draw together crucial dilemmas currently alive in the organisation of British and American clinical psychology training and practice. Women as clients, trainees and practitioners of clinical psychology are subordinate to men and it comes as no surprise that recent efforts to highlight sexual inequality as a key issue on clinical training courses led to reports of:

> difficulties addressing these issues at a time when the profession is increasingly staffed by women but headed by men. Some course organisers avoided talking about sexual inequality in training and identify the 'real issue' as how to attract more men into the profession. It was also evident that many female trainees felt that it was illegitimate and risky to talk about sexual inequality in the context of hierarchical relationships with male trainers and supervisors.
>
> (Williams and Watson 1991: 1)

In this book we explore the full spectrum of gender inequality at all levels of the profession. In this chapter, in particular, I examine and explain the inherent sexism in the structure of clinical psychology practice. To do so, I identify sexist practices in the discipline of psychology as a whole.

Psychology has traditionally been a male-dominated discipline at all levels of the profession and scholarship. Since the beginning of the 1980s, however, there has been a perceptible shift in the gender balance so that in 1989 around 79 per cent of first year UK undergraduate students were female (see Morris, Holloway and Noble 1990).

This has several implications for gender relations and the debate on gender in psychology provides fascinating insight into the way psychology as a whole, and clinical psychology in particular, is organised. The fact that undergraduates in psychology are now more likely to be female than was the case ten years ago, has provoked responses from the psychological community that distinguish it in a negative way from other professions (see Hansard Society 1990). While the focus of other professions appears to be on promoting equal opportunities and encouraging women to seek promotion, in psychology the perceived problem is the absence of men.

> The gender imbalance amongst psychology applications, with four-fifths of first year psychologists being female is an issue that needs addressing. Is it that psychology is particularly attractive to female applicants or are potential male applicants deterred for some reason?
>
> (Morris, Cheng and Smith 1990b: 10)

There is no evidence to suggest that the previous absence of women provoked any such interest at all!

Gender appears to become an issue when the male dominance of a profession might be threatened, and in the current climate of equal opportunities reforms in even the most traditional disciplines, the resistance to the 'ecology' by the international psychology communities requires investigation.

Despite this, women have not been totally discouraged from moving beyond first degree level to take clinical psychology qualifications (see Tables 1.1, 1.2, 1.3 and 1.4) and PhDs. In 1987 53.3 per cent of all USA doctorates awarded in psychology went to women (APA 1988) (cf 22.7 per cent between 1920 and 1974 and 36.9 per cent in 1978) and half of those currently achieving psychology PhDs in the UK are women (Squire 1989).

Such trends have produced a mixed bag of responses from feminist 'applause' to 'qualification' by both women and men manifesting severe anxiety about the cause and the effect of these patterns.

Table 1.1 Membership of the British Psychological Society's Division of Clinical Psychology* (May, 1989, BPS Records)

	Females	*Males*
N = 2,037	1, 152 (56.55%)	885 (43.45%)

* Membership of the DCP is restricted to those with a BPS recognised qualification in Clinical Psychology (from: Morris, Holloway and Noble 1990)

Table 1.2 Sex of applicants to the Clearing House for Clinical Psychology Postgraduate Courses in the UK

	1988	*1989*	*1990*
Male	195	196	163
Female	580	618	566

Table 1.3   Intake of students in England between 1980 and 1987

	1980	*1981*	*1982*	*1983*	*1984*	*1985*	*1986*	*1987*
Male	21	23	23	28	26	24	36	31
Female	41	52	52	66	63	60	73	85
Total Intake	62	75	75	94	89	84	109	116

Source: Management Advisory Service to the NHS 1989

Table 1.4 UK students on clinical psychology training courses 1990: sex of final year students

	Females	Males
Birmingham	18	1
East London	6	2
East Anglia	4	2
Edinburgh	5	5
Exeter	10	3
Glasgow	8	1
Institute of Psychiatry	–	–
Lancashire	5	2
Leeds	6	5
Leicester	10	5
Liverpool	11	5
Manchester	6	2
Newcastle	–	–
North Wales	4	0
North West Thames	–	–
Oxford	–	–
South West	–	–
South East Thames	6	2
South Wales	11	4
Surrey	12	2
UCL	–	–
Wessex	3	2

Source: J. Williams, University of Kent

Although the increase in women PhD recipients is a positive development, serious questions have been raised about psychology becoming a female dominated profession with the loss of prestige and financial remuneration usually evident in such situations. Although this pattern – the devaluation of female intensive occupations – has been well documented, the exact cause(s) or progression is not conclusively known.

(APA 1988: 9)

In clinical psychology in the UK (Table 1.1) although there are slightly more women members of the BPS Division of Clinical Psychology (DCP) the proportions are more 'equitable' than either the number of applicants to training courses would suggest (Williams and Watson 1991) (see Tables 1.2, 1.3 and 1.4) or the expressed interest of undergraduates in seeking future clinical training (Marshall and Nicolson 1990). Although not all clinical psychologists are BPS members and thus these figures should be used with caution, Barden *et al.* (1980) found that most NHS clinical psychologists are in fact Division members.

In the USA, however, there are fewer women APA members with clinical qualifications than there are men and these women are slightly more likely to have a doctorate (which is strongly encouraged) than their counterparts in the UK (see Table 1.5).

Table 1.5 Membership of the American Psychological Association's* subfield of clinical psychology and qualifications

Doctoral		Masters and Others		All degrees	
Total	% female	Total	% female	Total	% female
21,747	33.1	1,967	28.2	24,099	34.7

*Membership of the APA requires a doctoral degree in psychology or evidence of proficiency in psychological scholarship

Source: APA 1988

The debates within clinical psychology referring to the enthusiasm of women to join the profession reveal reactionary attitudes which are contrary to both equal opportunities and Government/EC policy:

Almost all current trainees are female. The trend towards an increasingly female intake was first commented on in an article by Humphrey and Haward (1981) in which they said, 'if this trend were to continue there may well be cause for concern'. The trend has indeed continued and I believe there is cause for concern. First, there is the practical problem of a nearly all-female profession providing services to men. If the situation were reversed I am sure there would be numerous letters of complaint from women and quite rightly so. However, the problems of a female dominated profession are not just the mirror image of a male dominated one. Whilst the BPS adheres to a non-sexist policy, the world at large is not necessarily so enlightened. National pay rates for women are significantly below those for men. Predominantly the female professions are lower in status and pay than predominantly male professions. Compare a nurse, teacher or occupational therapist with a surgeon, accountant or barrister.

As pay and status in clinical psychology have fallen, so men are no longer being attracted into the profession but as the profession becomes increasingly all-female, so it will become harder to persuade general managers, mostly male, to improve pay and status: a downward spiral of a declining profession.

(Crawford 1989: 30)

These attitudes are tragic as well as retrogressive. Crawford (1989) admits that the competition for training places is highly competitive, therefore the assumption must be that only the most able women and men are accepted. The places are filled by very able women, but there is clear evidence that they are not reaching positions of power in clinical psychology which represents a sad wastage of human talent and severely deprives the profession and service users (see Table 1.3). Further, the staff/trainers on professional courses reflect a gender imbalance in favour of men as the trainers with women as trainees – corresponding with the female–male ratio in academic psychology overall (Kagan and Lewis 1990b).

In order to understand and explain why the gender imbalance in favour of males is sustained, it is necessary to look beyond openly sexist challenges such as that of Crawford (1989). They are but the tip of the iceberg leading investigations as to why women's opportunities are curtailed up a blind ally! It is not these open expressions of 'gender war' but the covert discriminatory practices that occur everyday at all levels of the profession that produce inequalities. That they are often so embedded in social norms that they occur without most people being aware of them as sexism is part of the fabric of western applied and academic psychology.

The notable absence of gender as an issue in the two influential UK reports on clinical psychology (MAS 1989; MPAG 1990) provide indices of this sexism. The very exclusion of gender discussion when there is quite clearly a balance of power in favour of men is an effective means of making women invisible.

The debate about how far explicit inclusion of gender is problematic for women is an intriguing one. It is the uncontested view of the authors of all the chapters in this book that ignoring gender in any context where there are clear issues of power imbalance is equivalent to enabling men to maintain the balance in their favour. The rhetoric employed to prevent feminist scrutiny (as opposed to the sexist assertions about gender balance quoted above) penetrate both female and male consciousness so that women achieving success are often the fiercest advocates of 'gender neutrality'. That is, they favour gender blindness over explicit equal opportunities. But exactly who operates gender blindness? When men's backs are to the wall, as when 'too many' women are perceived to be entering the discipline, gender is raised as a topic for discussion by men to disadvantage women. Gender neutrality as a strategy, covertly operates to the advantage of men and only men. Evidence and examples presented below will justify this assertion.

WOMEN'S VISIBILITY IN CLINICAL PSYCHOLOGY

The UK figures on occupancy of promoted posts (Table 1.6) make it clear that women outnumber men at the lower status and lower paid end of the profession and are thin on the ground in Top Grade posts with an interesting 'cross-over' point at Principal level.[1] It may be argued that this is a function of age and, as the large cohort of women at basic/senior grade gain more experience, then a more equitable proportion will obtain Top Grade position. However, everyone who is suitably qualified and experienced becomes a senior as in fact the basic grade is equivalent to a two year training post. It is decisions about promotions that are significantly weighted in favour of men.

Table 1.6 Grades of clinical psychologists in the UK (1988)

	Basic grade	Senior grade	Principal	Top grade
Men	c 160 whole-time	c 220 (25 part-time)	200+ (+ c 5 part-time)	150+
Women	c 320 whole-time	c 320 (50 part-time)	200− (c 10 part-time)	50

Source: MPAG, 1990

The age breakdown suggests that staff in Top Grade posts tend to be over 30 years of age with most being between 35 and 44 years while most basic and senior grade clinical psychologists are under 35 years (MPAG 1990). Does this mean that women will get to the top if they serve their time? The gender profile for intake on courses since 1980 has favoured women so that, as the bulk of trainees in the early 1980s were between 21 and 25 years (MAS 1989), women should have become more visible by now in the higher grade posts if all things were equal. Clearly they are not.

A recent study of stress in the profession has suggested that following promotion to Principal Grade there is a dramatic dip in stress for men, and an equaly dramatic increase in stress for women (Cushway 1991). The implications of this had not been analysed by the researcher, but certainly suggest extreme differentials of pressure which need further consideration.

How far is the organisation of clinical psychology obscuring overt and covert sexism? If it is, what form does it take and what responsibility should members of the profession have for this, and in what ways, if any, should such a practice be reversed? In order to explore this further, I consider firstly how far gender is an issue in psychology as a whole and then examine the position of women and men in related professions, in management and other top jobs.

GENDER AND SEXISM IN THE ORGANISATION OF PSYCHOLOGY

The relatively recent genesis of division 35 of the APA (focusing on the psychology of women) and the Psychology of Women Section of the BPS has had two main effects. Firstly, the spotlight has fallen upon gender issues in the organisation of psychology internationally, so that in Australia, New Zealand, Israel, Canada, Argentina and Italy, there are identifiable groups of psychologists actively engaged in studying gender issues (Wilkinson 1990a). Secondly, there is a developing, visible and potentially influential literature on the psychology of women and gender/power relations (see for example Burns 1990).

It is through these twin developments that it becomes possible to place clinical psychology under rigorous scrutiny and conduct a systematic analysis of all the levels at which gender is salient in the profession (see all chapters in this volume).

The profession of psychology in the USA and UK (countries from where the most detailed statistics are available) is clearly one in which men are in positions of power and authority. It is not therefore surprising or radical to state that women are likely to be overlooked for appointment and promotion. The thorny issue of sexism in psychology, however, has been marginalised so that it is rarely debated outside feminist psychology groups (for example, Burman 1990; Williams and Watson 1991) although with some recent exceptions in a mainstream, but low status publication (Ussher 1990; Wilkinson 1990b).

The questions raised in relation to gender and discrimination are complex and need to address structural, interpersonal, conscious and unconscious influences which operate to maintain the balance of power and authority in favour of men.

There are three indices which will be employed to gauge the level to which the gender–power imbalance in the discipline of psychology.

(1) The award of professional fellowships for contributions to the discipline, recognised as outstanding by peers.
(2) The proportion of female to male academic staff, particularly those at professorial and other senior levels.
(3) The gender ratios on committees which govern the professional associations, although this again is not simply a question of frequency. Some committees and roles on committees are clearly more influential than others.

These three indices are important because they are measures of what is valued and who values it within the profession. This applies to awards as well as the appointment to senior academic or influential committee posts. High status people become opinion leaders and agenda setters: not only for the content of the discipline, but for the qualities required in others being groomed for power and influence.

DISTINGUISHED CONTRIBUTIONS AND AWARDS

In the USA (in 1988) only 17.7 per cent of APA Fellowships had been awarded to women, whereas 50.9 per cent of Associates were women (see Table 7). Minimum qualification for APA membership is a doctoral degree or its equivalent, and a Fellowship is awarded to members on presentation of evidence of unusual and outstanding contribution or performance in the the field of psychology. Associate members need to meet two sets of criteria. They must have completed two years of graduate work in psychology at a recognised graduate school, and be engaged in work or graduate study that is primarily psychological in character or must have received a masters degree in psychology from a recognised school/university and have completed in addition one full year of professional work in psychology.

Table 1.7 1988 APA membership statistics

	Total	*Men*	*Women*	*% Men*	*% Women*
Fellows	4,005	3,299	706	82.3	17.7
Members	54,644	34,755	19,889	63.6	36.4
Associates	8,347	4,103	4,244	49.1	50.9
Total	66,996	42,157	24,839	62.9	37.1

Source: APA 1988

In the UK (in 1989) the BPS fellowship awards included 513 men compared with 73 women (see Table 7). For the BPS the criteria for fellowships is once again nomination for outstanding research or professional practice in a field of psychology.

Table 1.8 1989 BPS membership statistics

	Men	*Women*
Honorary fellow	14	3
Fellow	513	73
Associate fellow	1,870	1,143
Chartered psychologists	3,181	2,608
Graduate member	3,368	5,120
Ordinary member	69	64
Student subscriber	441	1,020
Subscriber	112	113
Foreign affiliate	97	42

Source: Morris, Holloway and Noble (1990)

Discussion of the level of membership within the BPS has been interesting. It was initiated via the recommendations in the Future of the Psychological Sciences Report (SAB 1988) which itself led to the formation of the working party on gender representation within the BPS. Although many (including the convenor of the Working Party, Wilkinson 1990b) believed this Working Party's brief was to recommend an equal opportunities package to redress the balance, the result has been a disturbing level of self-satisfied complacency:

> Even allowing for the greater proportion of male members in the older age groups, these figures for the higher membership grades show a disproportionate preponderance of males. There are many possible sources for the observed gender imbalance in the higher membership grades. The most central concern for the Society is whether its committees are discriminating against women. Evidence upon this was sought by examining the numbers of successful male and female applicants for Fellowships, as proportions of the numbers applying. During 1988 and 1989, since its inception, the Fellowship Committee had reviewed 110 applicants from males and 42 from females. Of these, 83 (75%) males and 28 (67%) females had been successful. The difference is very far from significance (X^2 [1] = 0.787, p 0.3).
>
> Morris, Cheng and Smith 1990: 409–410)

But what is significant of course is the comparatively few women to be proposed and further, of the female Fellows (sic) most are apparently 'practitioners' rather than 'scientists' and applications of psychology have lower status than academic endeavour (Sherif 1987). This has even sharper significance for the subsequent discussion of clinical psychology!

It is the nature of the Fellowship award which mitigates against equal opportunities as the procedures

> cannot be as closely prescribed as those for the other grades of membership. Election to a Fellowship involves a substantial element of peer review (by other Fellows) using criteria which are viewed to be as general guidelines rather than as a check list of achievements.
>
> (British Psychological Society 1990)

An Equal Opportunities Policy as proposed by the Hansard Commission Report (1990) by definition has to dispense with subjective and informal selection procedures (see p. 32). It is through informality that covert sexist practices are most effective and these procedures are clearly informal by definition.

It is worth pausing to reflect upon the above quotation by Morris and colleagues, as it reveals the underlying set of sexist attitudes and practices in evidence throughout the psychological community in both the UK and USA. Despite the apparent concern to discuss sex discrimination, the desire to recognise its existence and redress the balance is clearly problematic. It would appear that a simple statistical significance test is all that it takes to satisfy any nagging doubts that the BPS might be seen to be sexist. The underlying questions about why more women don't apply, and even when they do, why are a greater (even if non-significant) proportion of men are awarded Fellowships, is swept outside the legitimate discourse. Morris, Cheng and Smith (1990) appear oblivious to research work on gender inequality and equal opportunities; and to the more traditional philosophical questions about the structure of knowledge and the reproduction of power relations (Foucault 1973).

If papers such as these, focusing directly on issues of gender, are blatantly ignoring feminist critiques of science and psychology, surely this represents a powerful form of discrimination in itself? 'Mainstream' psychologists such as these, writing about issues of gender, choose to ignore and therefore marginalise the scholarship of (mainly) women psychologists and it is this marginalisation that spearheads the covert discriminatory practices (see Ussher 1990).

The academic community in psychology is the 'parent' of clinical trainees and thus practitioners, and promotes insight into the framework through which gender issues in the organisation of clinical psychology might be understood.

THE STRUCTURE OF ACADEMIC PSYCHOLOGY

The Hansard Commission (1990) shows that the proportion of women in senior academic posts in all disciplines is derisory, and in contrast to other professional areas, is not increasing. For example, women comprise only 3 per cent of professors in the UK. In Oxford and Cambridge the opening up of single-sex colleges has meant men's appointment to tenured posts in former women's colleges, but this trend has not been a reciprocal one!

In academic psychology departments in the UK and the USA, numbers of women are thin on the ground and men appear more frequently in senior positions as heads of departments, readers or professors. Kagan and Lewis (1990b) quote data from the BPS on university and polytechnic psychology (including research) departments in the UK and Eire from 1986. Women comprised only 22.2 per cent of academic psychology staff and 15.9 per cent of senior academic psychology staff, which was far less than would have been predicted from the gender ratios (i.e. more than 70 per cent of women entering the profession as undergraduates, see p .9).

There may be many reasons for this, not least of all historical circumstance in which many more men entered higher education generally until the 1960s expansion period. Detailed figures on the length of time men and women staff have been in post would be needed to clarify the impact of such historical trends. Our own data reveals a number of women in post for over twelve years, but we do not know whether they have sought – or would want – seniority. It may also be that those departments we could not include in the data have many more women in senior positions, but we see no reason why this should be so.

Whatever the reason, the fact remains that many more men practise academic psychology than women and many more men hold senior positions in academic psychology.

(Kagan and Lewis 1990b: 277–278).

The implications of this imbalance go beyond that of a simple fact that males control academic psychology and thus determine the subject matter. Female undergraduates do not obtain suitable role models, and although they may do a research degree on graduation (see APA, 1988; Squire 1989) their talents may not be recognised or actively encouraged and indeed they may be passively discouraged so as to prevent them considering the possibility of extending that into a permanent academic post in a psychology department.

Barden *et al.* (1980) have shown that among the university lecturers on clinical psychology training courses, 78.5 per cent are male and 21.5 per cent female, and it is unlikely that these proportions will have altered over the last ten years as university appointments overall have been minimal.

This imbalance also means that there are more men available for related positions of power and control such as appointment and promotion boards, professional committee membership, influential working parties, refereeing journal and conference papers, being on and running specific subsystems (for example DCP). Men therefore are more likely to be able to take a central role in policy making in clinical psychology.

There is also less possibility of young female postgraduates having a female mentor. A mentor is someone in a position of power who is prepared to be an advocate for, or specifically encourage, an individual in a junior position (Richey *et al.* 1988). The relationship is reciprocal so that in return for the mentor's encouragement, acting as a role model, helping solve problems, opening out opportunities, increasing visibility, giving feedback and so on, the protegé provides the mentor with open respect and admiration, public approval, access to different channels of communication, emotional support, intellectual stimulation and investment in the future. For these reasons, both benefit and both become more visible. Goldstein (1979) noted that academic psychology productivity was higher among those with the same sex mentors and it appears that women and men mentors operate differently according to different styles. Women tend to be more supportive, which apparently appeals more to female protegés, and male mentors apparently are more willing to challenge technical competence, which seems to appeal more to male protegés (see Richey *et al.* 1988). In academic life in particular the absence of women in senior positions makes this system work in favour of the newly appointed men.

This situation is made worse sometimes by the fact that some women who are in a position to act as mentor or role model may have a deterring effect on younger women entering the profession. The Hansard Commission suggested strongly that: 'To achieve promotion to senior jobs, women too often have to be *better* than men' (Hansard Commission 1990: 3). What this often means is that where there are visible senior women (and both clinical and academic psychology have a few!), they are often outstanding and the 'Queen Bee' syndrome has been noted in that these women themselves have been known to operate policies of exclusion against other women (see Ussher 1990).

Also the presence of these women may be used as evidence of women's achievements (for example, as in the case of the few women BPS Spearman Medal, Presidents' Awards and May Davidson Prize for clinical psychology winners). This is another means of marginalising all those other women who 'complain' about gender inequality. They can then be accused of sour grapes! If certain women are able to make it to the top, surely this means that opportunities are there for all; perhaps the problem is simply that the right women do not put themselves forward! These achievers, however, are but 'token women'. The competition at the lower rungs of the ladder for clinical psychology training places is intensive and many women achieve these over men. This suggests that there are potentially talented women being 'wasted' on their way to the top. Why?

By the sheer fact of their numbers in senior posts, men are more likely to become the generation of clinical teachers, practitioners and scientists achieving various forms of recognition, such as special prizes or Fellowships through male-dominated commit-tees. This in turns tightens the grip of the vicious male circle! Some of the many examples are the editors of psychology journals and conference committees (who vet conference paper submissions). Kagan and Lewis (1990b) say that out of the 21 psychology journals they regularly consult, only two are edited by a woman and these are the *Psychology of Women Quarterly* and the *Society for Reproductive and Infant Psychology Journal.* The *British Journal of Social Psychology* has had two women editors in its history and most journals have few women even on the editorial boards (Kagan and Lewis 1990b: 279). It is worth noting here as a more optimistic note, that from 1991, there is another psychology journal, *Feminism and Psychology*, which has a woman editor, although of course this journal has a clear, and 'marginal', orientation.

In the USA psychology journals had 14 per cent of female editors or assistant editors in 1987 (which is lower than 32.8 per cent in 1976 which appears to be an exceptional year) and also few women participate as consulting review editors. The American Psychological Association's *Journal of Consulting and Clinical Psychology* has 21.2 per cent, 24 per cent and 23.71 per cent of women in these roles in 1985, 1986 and 1987 respectively. Com-paratively more women (42.86 per cent in 1987) were involved in *Psychology and Ageing* and the *Journal of Counselling Psychology* (23.71 per cent) (APA 1988). The BPS Standing Conference Committee (which is largely self-selecting) has a powerful role in deciding which papers to accept for conference presentation, has always been chaired by a man, and, currently includes 11 men and four women (British Psychological Society 1991).

GENDER REPRESENTATION ON PROFESSIONAL ORGANISATIONS

The BPS and the APA committee places overall have many more men and board chairs tend to be held by men. There have been some changes over the last twelve years. Of 352 committee places in the BPS in 1989, 74 per cent were occupied by men and 26 per cent by women. This is in part accounted for by the higher age/status of males in the profession of psychology and appears to be changing, with more places going to women (Morris, Cheng and Smith 1990). What is omitted from this discussion though is that many places are held by the same men and women due to the BPS system of cross-representation. For example in 1990, at least 10 of the 90 places were held by two individual females!

It is via these committees that the professional associations define the parameters for clinical training: by approving and reviewing courses and providing the forum for the emergence of new initiatives in clinical training (for example in the UK the discussion of taught doctoral programmes as clinical psychology qualifications). The more women there are involved on the decision-making bodies then the more likely it is that gender issues will be raised appropriately.

The picture we have so far then (albeit not a complete one) suggests that despite active change, psychology remains, and is likely to remain, male dominated. This will continue to be the case so long as women and men avoid seeing gender as an issue.

It is striking that when male preponderance in top positions is discussed, it is seen as a potential function of age and when there are more women than men at any stage (as at the current undergraduate level and applications for clinical psychology training) it is seen as a gender imbalance in need of consideration. As Morris and colleagues have said 'we need to find out why more men are not attracted to the discipline! (see p. 9 in this chapter). It seems at least of equal importance to assess why more women are not in positions of power and authority within psychology. To deny this question is in itself an act of discrimination.

PATRIARCHAL PRECEDENCE

The history and future of clinical psychology appears to be colliding in the minds of practitioners: the profession has reached a crisis point:

Reduced by a slow process of attrition to another predominantly female 'helping profession', underpayed and undervalued, employing a large number of unqualified assistants, managed by non-psychologist general managers and concerned only with seeing the maximum number of 'patients' in the time available.

(Crawford 1989: 31)

But what were its origins and in what way has the prescence of women reduced clinical psychology's status?

Despite its relative youth, the discipline of psychology (to include both the academic and professional wings) has a history that needs to be understood before the contemporary structure may be clarified. Once again it is the fact of Divison 35 of the APA and the Psychology of Women Section of the BPS as well as associated and communicating groups of (mainly) women psychologists that has stimulated documentation of early struggles of female psychologists.

Carolyn Sherif (1987), who worked successfully as an academic psychologist for 37 years, provides an historical and sociological analysis of the development of recent psychological ideas. In so doing, she draws together:

1. the ways in which women as psychologists were marginalised in the early days of the profession, and
2. how this happened alongside the marginalisation of the work they were doing to challenge particular assumptions and develop areas of research.

Neither of these factors appear to have changed. Women as psychologists were marginalised by the differential status applied to the branches of psychology in which women were most involved.

Experimental psychology, in the 1940s, achieved the highest status and very few women were involved in this work. Second in the hierarchy was mental testing, followed by developmental psychology and finally social psychology. The division between 'scientific' and 'applied' was essentially one in which the latter had far less status and more women were applied psychologists.

With the advent of war, mental testing managed to achieve its power through a USA government-led imperative in relation to selection and training for the armed services and industry. However, developmental psychology which focused very much on pre-school education was seen as far less important, and social psychology in the 1940s was an umbrella term for additional psychological pursuits such as the study of personality and clinical psychology. Women were most visible in these areas of psychology and it would certainly appear that this remains the case. Interestingly, social psychologists managed to increase their status by dissociating themselves from applied work and moving towards being experimental. Clinical psychology itself adheres to the traditional scientist-practitioner model (see Ussher's Chapter 2 in this volume) which also suggests an effort to distance itself from merely being an applied wing of psychology. However, as Sherif comments:

> The irony is that the preservation of psychology's hierarchy and the expansion of the entire enterprise was supported by those psychologists making in-roads into major institutions – educational, business, military, governmental, the growing mass media and the mental health institutions and industry – in short, the 'applied' psychologists. Without their in-road, psychology would have been 'small potatoes' in academia, but it need not have worried. The growing number of psychologists in major institutions needed the academic hierarchy to support its claims at being scientific.
>
> (Sherif 1987: 42)

Psychology appears only to have status when it is scientific or experimental and this attracts male psychologists (or possibly excludes female psychologists). Applications of the discipline (which are female dominated in numbers but male dominated in terms of power positions) seem to have lower status and although it is clinical and educational/child psychology that attract public attention and put theory into practical use, the power attributed to applied psychology falls short of the more overtly high status professions (for example, medicine) which are male dominated. When there is a hint that a profession is helping rather than scientific, then it is both lower status and appealing to women. The ghost of the scientist-practitioner has not been laid to rest, and clinical psychology research takes place by (mainly) men at high status universities (for example, in the UK at Oxford and Cambridge). This, however, is apart from training courses and very much removed from the daily knowledge demanded by clinical psychology practitioners.

How far can it be argued that clinical psychology is continuing to decline in status? Is it being 'reduced' to a helping profession because of the increased number of women or is it simply that ambitious men are so concerned with their own status that other factors preventing professional advancement (personal and structural) are blamed on the feminisation of 'their' profession?

Turtle (1990) in her account of the first women psy- chologists in Australia shows once again how the emphasis has been on women as applied psychologists. Three out of the four psychologists appointed to the Australian state public service between 1922 and 1926 were women, but this, Turtle argues is best seen as part of the greater pattern in the emergence of the 'helping professions'. The tasks that these women psychologists were to organise were connected with mental handicap and increasing literacy in pre-school children.

> It is noteworthy that in Australia, as in the United States. . .it was in the applied rather than the academic field that women made their first major impact upon psychology. During the 1920s only the University of Sydney had an independent department of the discipline, psychology being taught elsewhere within departments of philosophy; no full-time women psychology lecturers were appointed in any of these until after World War II. The difficulty women found in moving into positions of relative authority within the early academic system of psychology has of course continued: only two out of more than 60 professorial appointments in this country to date have been of women.
>
> (Turtle 1990: 252)

Once again, this has relevance to women as clinical and academic psychologists in the 1990s. The existing patriarchal hierarchy in any community or social setting precludes women gaining prestigious positions, but, ironically, in the current climate of reform, it is psychology and academia in general that seriously lag behind many of the more 'traditional' disciplines and professions.

BARRIERS TO WOMEN'S ACHIEVEMENT IN PSYCHOLOGY TODAY

The changes in women's education, wider employment opportunities and the decreased birthrate, have not scotched the barriers to women's career progression. Goldin (1990) has identified the contradictions existing between apparent opportunity and limited success in the USA and the reality of most women's experience, and particularly the ways in which the image of women's success makes the majority even more invisible.

> The share of women doctors, lawyers and other professionals is at an all time high. Women drive buses and work on construction sites; one ran for Vice President; and another made a bid for President. Women's employment milestones fill the press. Yet, each generation of Americans, at least since the mid nineteenth century, have claimed to be on the verge of an unprecedented and momentous change in the economic position of women.
>
> (Goldin 1990: vii)

Similarly, the fact of a woman prime minister in the UK for ten years, was heralded as a demonstration of equal opportunity, while in fact for most women nothing has changed. Sexism is upheld by refusal to implement changes and develop equal opportunities policies. Declarations that principles of meritocracy operate in the 1990s provide a counterforce to change.

The processes at work which prevent women's advancement are abundant in the broad profession of psychology in the UK and USA today. Questions raised by women psychologists are not being addressed. The fact of their being raised, however, enables an identification of how covert discrimination operates so:

> Can it not be argued that psychology is structured in such a way that precludes women at any advanced level, preventing women from passing through the 'glass ceiling' to a position of eminence or power?
>
> (Ussher 1990: 389)

What is the 'glass ceiling'? By definition it is an invisible barrier and can only be demonstrated through constant use of example. For instance, although the BPS convened a working party on gender representation within the Society, the recommendations were treated with complacency and even hostility. The recommendation that positive encouragement should be given to women was derided when discussed by BPS Council (according to the Chair of the Working Party). This was despite the constructive suggestions that

the Society could exert a positive influence by means of research and action, including: a data base on women in
psychology, research on women's experiences of psychology
and the undergraduate curriculum.

(Wilkinson 1990b: 413)

The interesting part of this though was the ways in which some
women claimed that any specific attention to their status and need
is both unecessary and patronising.

The suggestion that women may have distinctly different experiences of psychology from men (particularly with reference to its
formalisation in committee and conference activities) was
regarded by some members of Council as a contentious aspect
of the report.

(Wilkinson 1990b: 413)

Does this mean that women have chosen not to compete for
committee places, give conference papers, chair committees, go
for promotion, apply for Society Fellowships or take Top Grade
clinical or academic posts? Does it mean that many women are not
aware of the invisible barrier or 'glass ceiling'? It is likely that this
ceiling only becomes apparent when you hit it! No one hits it until
they are within reach of the top, and many women on the lower
rungs of the promotion ladder (and there are many in that
position) do not realise the existence of the glass ceiling because
they have not got there.

A brief 'case study'

At this point it seems appropriate to include some recent
anecdotal evidence which demonstrates covert sexism within the
BPS. By its very nature it is difficult to quantify and control for
covert discrimination and this is necessarily a personal account. My
impressions, however, were checked out and discussed with others
who were involved. A meeting of the BPS Membership and
Qualifications Board (MQB, an influential committee whose brief
includes the control of undergraduate, postgraduate professional
(including clinical psychology) course content is the example I
have chosen. I want to stress though that this is merely illustrative
of often repeated covert practices.

The occasion was the consideration of a document prepared by a small working party to explore and make recommendations for the content of the undergraduate psychology curriculum with a view to making it a good basis for professional training and research at postgraduate level. It was discussed in this instance after the publication of the Gender Representation Working Party and its discussion; more than three years since the birth of the Psychology of Women Section and a general 'gender awareness'; and alongside the genesis of the task-force set up to develop an Equal Opportunities policy for the BPS. The document put forward by the working party here, declared its objectives to include:

- the consideration of what knowledge of psychology is required as a basis for postgraduate training
- to consider how the undergraduate curriculum should adapt to developments in the discipline
- to consider access to undergraduate courses, especially from minority groups.

There were, in addition to these, eight further laudable aims.

Two major issues of concern arose from the ensuing discussion of this document. One was concern by the board members as to how far the document had failed to achieve these aims in relation to gender and cross-cultural/ethnic minority issues which were subsumed under a broad umbrella of 'social context'. It was proposed that relevant and vital developments in the disciplines were being ignored. Educational and clinical psychologists desperately needed to have the knowledge to practise non-sexist and non-racist psychology in a multi-ethnic society and several board members argued that these two professional groups were likely to undermine their own credibility unless these issues became a core part of psychology training overall.

The Chair, and some others (of professorial status) did not seem to consider these issues important. They thought that the wording of the document was adequate, and that the time had come to circulate the working party report widely within the BPS regardless of these criticisms. In other words, the criticisms that were being levelled at the document were merely marginal and could be dealt with cosmetically at a later date. However, the board membership (mainly practitioners, although not all women) insisted that the document should be returned to the working party so these issues could be fully addressed.

The second issue illuminates a manifestation of covert practices. The member of that working party who was on the MQB hesitatingly suggested that it would, or could, not take on board what were now becoming clear proposals for change. At this point, one board member suggested that others could be co-opted onto the working party (and it became clear that several MQB members had exactly the right expertise).

The Chair dismissed this and said he would talk on the phone to the (male) Chair of the working party. Again, there was resistance, but finally the Chair (after some 35 minutes and late in the afternoon) agreed not to do that, but to explore the possibility of some co-optees. What was interesting (and irritating) to the, by that time, flagging board membership was that none of the people who became prominent in the board discussion had been suggested. The final result was that the Honorary General Secretary of the BPS was to write a 'tactful' letter to the working party Chair and that behind the scenes possible co-optees would be considered.

This particular example has been employed here because it clarifies at least two covert processes which recur but may not necessarily be immediately apparent. The fact that essential ingredients (i.e. the issues of gender and race) were marginalised on the curriculum document and that this was seen as acceptable by the high status members of the board, only became a problem here because of a coincidence of people who were both committed and articulate and thus able to support each other in the challenge. The challenge to the content of the document gained momentum when the white male Chair of the board attempted to circulate the document regardless of the challenge. His suggestion of a phone conversation 'man-to-man' would normally I suspect, have passed unnoticed. The Chair's somewhat inept behaviour on this occasion enabled the challenge to have some effect. It is more frequently the case, however, that the subordinate group are less competent at the immediate task in hand and less articulate than the superordinate group and that is how covert discrimination occurs time and again on all sorts of selection boards and committees making policy.

Covert and unconscious discrimination exists within British psychology and the absence of women in positions of power is unlikely to change unless women and men are prepared to address discrimination seriously and implement institutionalised policy change. Discrimination is not only the misfortune of the women manifestly suffering from sexism (i.e. those psychologists who, for reasons of their gender, are unable, or who appear unable, to obtain promotion and awards). The profession of psychology (and in this case clinical psychology in particular) is impoverished without a consistent female voice. Two American writers on mental health service provision have made the point:

> It would appear that the mere presence of a woman, regardless of her sensitivity to women's concerns, has an impact on the way policy is developed. First, the physical presence of a woman may cause men to think more readily about how a policy will affect women. Second, the female policy maker is more likely to have a different perspective from the male simply because of differential world experiences resulting from gender.
>
> (Stringer and Welton 1984: 44)

Again even if this woman takes a 'gender blind/Queen Bee' stance, there is anecdotal evidence to suggest some degree of gender consciousness is raised. For instance, several people have commented that when talking about the British prime minister the term 'she' now comes more easily to the lips than 'he'! This is the case even though the she in question is not a feminist.

In clinical psychology, where a high proportion of service users are female (see other chapters in this volume), it is essential that women professionals have at least an equal input to the politics of the profession as well as to everyday practice.

WOMEN AT THE TOP IN THE UK: A CONTRADICTION IN TERMS?

The chapter so far suggests that within the organisation of academic and clinical psychology as well as the professional associations there is an inherent and specific sexist bias. Little reference as yet has been made to the wider social context within which this occurs or to other professions. As I now show, despite professional histories that are equally problematic and putatively more conservative, the response of other groups has often been more radical than that of the psychology profession.

The excellent Hansard Society Commission on Women at the Top (1990) specifically aimed at women in politics, but with a brief to undertake comparative work, has through their recommendations illuminated the overt and covert nature of sexist practice in organisations at all levels. They take the position that equal opportunities, far from being a liberal stance to help women, are actually an economic and social necessity. Demographic changes require the employment of more women, and women's particular experiences markedly absent at present, are necessary in various aspects of public life and in positions of authority. These arguments clearly hold for clinical psychology.

The Hansard Society Commission look beyond the immediate question of women's application for promotion and attack the social and institutional barriers which mitigate against women's achievements. It is here that the APA and BPS's complacency about, for example, the fact that few women are eligible or apply for Fellowships, may be counter attacked. The HSC say that 'The barriers to equality are general and pervasive and include: out-moded attitudes about the role of women, direct and indirect discrimination, the absence of proper child-care provision and inflexible structures for work and careers' (HSC 1990: 2).

These seem specifically relevant to the above discussion of the BPS particularly their argument that 'too often organisations who say they do not discriminate have not properly considered how their normal policies and practices affect women' (2).

There is then a complex net of processes which operate to exclude or discriminate against those who do not share the essential characteristics of a dominant élite. This means, for example, within the profession of clinical psychology that a number of factors mitigate against women who do not share the essential characteristics of their 'brothers'. The kinds of concerns that women might have in relation to service uses, planning their careers in the context of domestic/family life (in relation to both parenting and a partner who is likely to have a more senior and better paid job which takes priority), being able to cope with men as colleagues in superior and junior positions, are often very different from those of men. The image of a successful career woman as totally dedicated to work without a husband or children is no joke. An ambitious unmarried, childless, woman is more likely to share characteristics with men than with married women and women with children. But it is also no myth that many such women talk about having made a choice or sacrificing their social and emotional life for a career. Men do not have this problem – indeed they directly benefit from marriage, as they are serviced emo-tionally, socially and practically and are thus better able to cope with pressures in the work place (Parsons and Bales 1953; Bernard 1974). Hollway and Mukari's (1990) study of women in the Tanzanian civil service demonstrates some of these processes in action, particularly the subtle forms of harassment that directly and indirectly affect promotion. These range from direct verbal and sexual harassment to discomfort in attending the various 'clubs' and 'meeting places' where promotions and other decisions are traditionally coped with 'informally'.

In order to stop discrimination within the profession of clinical psychology, it is possible to take the advice of the HSC about the key organisational points where gender discrimination can be effectively addressed. They identify covert practices of discrimination operating through 'subjective and informal selection procedures, stereotypical assumptions, use of "insider" word-of-mouth, old boy networks, unnecessary age barriers and excessive mobility requirements' (see HSC 1990: 2–3). They also stress (as do Hollway and Mukari 1990) that women are discouraged by attitudes at work, including direct sexual harassment and refusal to take them seriously.

As Goldin (1990) suggests: 'Discrimination against women is manifested in a variety of ways. In its most typical form, no prescribed barriers exist. Rather, employers, employees and customers, can express their prejudice against women by preferring not to associate with them' (Goldin 1990: 160).

It may be argued that the work place is one where, through a range of subtle ploys, the proverbial glass ceiling becomes a potent reality. The HSC (1990) and Goldin (1990) suggest how informality and custom mitigate against women through indirect revelation of preferences at key stages of daily life as well as the more official indices, for example promotion and appointment boards, honours committees and so on. To be gender blind then is potentially to continue to operate according to custom and the covert processes of discrimination remain obscured from the view of men and women. Some form of legislation or reconstruction of formal rules appears necesary to counteract covert (as well as more obvious overt) discriminatory practices.

Well-qualified women should be openly and actively encouraged to apply for promoted clinical psychology practitioner posts, teaching and tutoring posts and for training committee places. Women should comprise half of selection panels and furthermore employers and professional societies should designate a proportion of promoted posts solely for women; directly reflecting the number of women in the profession. In addition, new women entrants should be groomed from the start and encouraged to see themselves in a career mode. Supportive facilities such as child care and flexible working arrangements should be mandatory and age barriers to promotion be removed. This would enable career breaks. Refresher courses for those on career breaks should be made readily available.

Women who do not share the values and concerns of men as a priority are often not taken seriously. The quotations at the beginning of this chapter in relation to clinical psychology as a devalued and female dominated profession is a clear example of that. Examples of varieties of sexual harassment and 'old boy networks' are many and often dismissed as simply anecdotes. It is only relatively recently that the interest and legitimation of the psychology of women has enabled a more systematic voice to emerge (Ussher 1990; Kitzinger and Thomas 1990; Hollway and Mukari 1990). However, the problem is that despite its rigour, much of this work remains invisible in the mainstream of psychology.

The practice of ageism within academic psychology operates against women (Nicolson and Phillips 1990). Academic psychology posts are, on the whole, only offered to those well under the age of 35, which means that a good first degree, a PhD, a clinical qualification and experience, several publications and at least one research grant award is required in order to become a clinical psychology tutor.

Any woman who has dared to have children in the course of her early years (and many choose to have them around or below the age of 30) is extremely unlikely to have been in a position to meet such demands; thus, even if she 'scrapes' an academic post by the skin of her teeth, she is unlikely ever to catch up with male colleagues when it comes to competing for professorships or prestigious awards for scientific contributions. It is very often the number of publications and the number of research awards a person has achieved that takes priority over quality.

The fact that a small proportion of women have 'made it' and provide a 'token' woman appears to satisfy the men in power within the psychology profession that they are not discriminating on grounds of gender. The career profile of the woman in question however, is more likely to be shared with the average man than the average woman. The recommendations of the HSC would help clinical psychologists to avoid wasting talent and improve the service.

If we compare the legal profession to clinical psycholgy, we can begin to see how this might work, although there are still no absolute solutions to gender inequality:

Women are in the majority among new law graduates and recently qualified solicitors more and more, are doing work which was regarded, a mere decade ago, as an exclusively male preserve. Both the Bar Council and the Law Society have taken steps to encourage equal opportunities among their members. However, serious problems remain. Ten years after admission to the Role, three times as many women as men solicitors have ceased practising. Moreover, three times as many women as men remain assistant solicitors ten years after admission. Men achieve partnerships at twice the rate of women. At the Bar women continue to find it much more difficult than men to obtain pupilages and tenancies.

(Hansard Society 1990: 7–8)

Similarly, in the press there are many visible women, but women only get two-thirds of the way up the ladder while men dominate the top (Hansard Society 1990) 'Men vastly outnumber women in any editorial conference, and women are scarcely found among the managerial reaches of the press' (Hansard Society 1990: 12). What is missing are the informal network and role models which help to change attitudes and give people more than a glimpse over the glass ceiling.

CONCLUSIONS

Women experience barriers to promotion, both overt and covert. Those in junior positions who see the possibility of future promotion are often unaware of invisible barriers until a top position becomes a possibility. Not only do women receive little encouragement to achieve high status positions in clinical psychology, but they begin to experience more stress than equivalent male colleagues (Cushway 1991). We need to explore more closely what precipitates this. It may be pressures at work or the conflicts between home and work, but an increase in stress with promotion is a negative reinforcer. Women are more likely to remain in junior or mid-level posts than men, for whom promotion is a stress reducer and therefore offers positive reinforcement. Institution-alised covert barriers such as the formal and informal old boy networks further mitigate against women's success and are alive and well in clinical psychology. Unless there are women at the top who recognise the way organisations discriminate against women then clinical psychology will not be able to claim equal oppor-tunities. These changes are only likely to occur if the institutions themselves restructure their policies and seriously evaluate their practices. This includes the admission and acknowledgement that sexism exists within psychology and clinical psychology in particular.

NOTE

1 These grades are now extinct and replaced by A and B grades with B
  equivalent to the old Top Grade.

REFERENCES

American Psychological Association (1988) *Women in the American Psy-chological Association.* Washington DC: APA.

Barden, V., Coles, P. and Lindsay, G. (1980) Promotion prospects for applied psychologists *Bulletin of the British Psychological Society,* 33: 413–418.

Bernard, J. (1974) *The Future of Marriage.* Harmondsworth: Penguin.

British Psychological Society (1990) Council Papers, unpublished.

British Psychological Society (1991) Annual conference programme, Bournemouth, 13–16 April.

Burman, E. (Ed) (1990) *Feminists in Psychological Practice.* London: Sage.

Burns, J. (1990) Women organising within psychology. In E. Burman (ed.), *Feminists in Psychological Practice.* London: Sage.

Crawford, D. (1989) The future of clinical psychology: Whither or wither?, *Clinical Psychology Forum,* 20, 29–31.

Cushway, D. (1991) Stress in clinical psychologists. Paper presented at the BPS Annual Conference, Bournemouth.

Fabrickant, B. (1974) The psychotherapist and the female patient. In W. Franks and V. Burtle (eds), *Women in Therapy.* New York: Brunner/Mazel.

Foucault, M. (1973) *The Archaeology of Knowledge.* London: Tavistock.

Goldin, C. D. (1990) *Understanding the Gender Gap.* Oxford: Oxford University Press.

Goldstein, E. (1979) Effects of same sex and cross sex role models on the subsequent academic productivity of scholars. *American Psychologist,* 34: 407–410.

Hansard Society (1990) *Report of the Hansard Society Commission on Women at the Top.* London: the Hansard Society for Parliamentary Government.

Howell, E. and Bayes, M. (eds) (1981) *Women and Mental Health.* New York: Basic Books.

Hollway, W. (1989) *Subjectivity and Method in Psychology.* London: Sage.

Hollway, W. and Mukarai, L. (1990) The position of women managers in the Tanzanian civil service, University of Bradford: Report to the CSD Government of Tanzania.

Humphrey, M. and Haward, L. (1981) Sex differences in clinical psychology recruitment. *Bulletin of the British Psychological Society,* 4: 413–414.

Kagan, C. and Lewis, S. (1990a) Where's your sense of humour? Swimming against the tide in higher education. In E. Burman (ed.), *Feminists in Psychological Practice.* London: Sage.

Kagan, C. and Lewis, S. (1990b) Transforming psychological practice. *Australian Psychologist,* 25, 3: 270–281.

Kenworthy, J. A. *et al.* (1976) Women and therapy. *Psychology of Women Quarterly,* 1: 125–137.

Kitzinger, C. and Thomas, A. (1990) Asymmetry and ambiguity in gender relations: constructing sexual harassment. Paper presented at the BPS London Conference, City University.

Management Advisory Service to the NHS (1989) *Review of Clinical Psychology Services.*

Manpower Planning Advisory Group (1990) *Clinical Psychology Project.* London: HMSO.

Marshall, H. and Nicolson, P. (1990) Choosing psychology: mature and other students' accounts on graduation. Paper presented at the BPS London Conference, City University.

Morris, P., Holloway, J. and Noble, J. (1990) Gender representation within the BPS. *The Psychologist,* 9: 408–411.

Morris, P., Cheng, D. and Smith, H. (1990) How and why applicants choose to study psychology courses at university. Report to the Association of Heads of Psychology Departments, Unpublished.

Nicolson, P. and Phillips, E. M. (1990) Ageism and academia. *The Psychologist,* 3, 9: 393–394.

Parsons, T. and Bales, R. F. (1953) *Family, Socialisation and Interaction Process.* New York: Free Press.

Richey, C. A., Gambrille, D. and Blythe, B.J. (1988) Mentor relationships among women in academe. *Affilia,* 3, 1: 34–47.

Scientific Affairs Board of the BPS (1988) *The Future of the Psychological Sciences.* Leicester: BPS.

Sherif, C. (1987) Bias in psychology. In S. Harding (ed.), *Feminism and Methodology.* Milton Keynes: Open University Press.

Squire, C. (1989) *Significant Differences: Feminism in Psychology.* London: Routledge.

Stringer, D. M. and Welton, N. R. (1984) Female Psychologists in policy making positions. In L.E. Walker (ed.), *Women and Mental Health Policy.* London: Sage.

Turtle, A. M. (1990) The first women psychologists in Australia. *Australian Psychologist*, 25, 3: 239–255.

Ussher, J. M. (1990) Sexism in Psychology. *The Psychologist*, 13, 9: 388–390.

Wilkinson, S. (1990a) Women organising in psychology. In E.Burman (ed.), *Feminists and Psychological Practice*. London: Sage.

Wilkinson, S. (1990b) Gender issues, broadening the context. *The Psychologist*, 13, 9: 412–414.

Williams, J. and Watson, G. (1991) Clinical psychology training: training in oppression? *Feminism and Psychology*, 1, 1.

Chapter 2

Science sexing psychology
Positivistic science and gender bias in clinical psychology

Jane M. Ussher

THE BIRTH OF THE SCIENTIST-PRACTITIONER

> Psychology, which till recently was known among us chiefly as a
> mental philosophy. . .has now at length achieved the position of
> a positive science. . .possessing its own methods, its own specific
> problems, and a distinct stand-point altogether its own. 'Ideas'
> in the philosophical sense do not fall within its scope; its en-
> quiries are restricted entirely to facts.
>
> *British Journal of Psychology* 1904, 1(1): 1[1]

Richard Gregory, the editor of *Nature* in the 1930s, is reputed to
have declared that 'my grandfather preached the gospel of Christ,
my father preached the gospel of socialism, I preach the gospel of
science' (Rose and Rose 1969: 261). If science is the new religion,
psychology is one of its most loyal disciples. For as this quote from
the first edition of the *British Journal of Psychology* illustrates, psychology has had a long history of adoption and whole-hearted
support for positivistic methodologies, following in the steps of the
natural sciences, which it looked to as its rightful parents. For from
the inception of the profession in the early twentieth century, it
was established as a positive science, 'built upon sedimented layers
of eugenic, objectivist and statistical assumptions. . .the bed-rock
syllabus for neophyte clinical psychologists' (Pilgrim and Treacher
1992). Furthermore, as academic psychology welded itself to
science, in an attempt to achieve status and define its unique role
as an emerging discipline, clinical psychology followed suit. The
early applied psychologists, such as Galton, Pearson, Spearman
and Burt, vigorously employed the precision of positivism in their
practices, and in so doing firmly established the status of applied
psychologists as objective researchers.[2]

The positivistic approach adopted by these early researchers has formed the blueprint for clinical psychologists ever since. The scientist-practitioners are not a dying breed, despite considerable criticisms of the validity of their approach and of its usefulness in clinical psychology[3] (i.e. Frank 1984). We may have moved on from the narrow approach advocated by the disciples of the Maudsley in the 1950s to 1970s, where psychometric assessment and behaviourism were the order of the day (Pilgrim and Treacher 1992), but professional training is still imbued with the positivistic philosophy. Whilst many individual practitioners are not wedded to 'science', the profession itself clearly is. In Britain clinical psychology is established as an 'applied science' – with status accrued from its position as a graduate profession skilled in research methodologies based on the foundation of academic (experimental) psychology. Research is seen to be an important part of the clinical psychologist's portfolio – and is invariably elevated to a status denied to the 'softer' activities, such as therapy.[4] The training of clinical psychologists places heavy emphasis on the completion of an empirical research project, and the utilisation of rigorous hypotheses-driven methodologies in clinical assessment and intervention.

In the USA, since the introduction of the Boulder model in the 1950s (Frank 1984), there has been a similar emphasis within the professional discourse on the importance of the adoption of scientific models in theory and practice. Recent literature has continued to expound upon the merits of the adoption of positivism in both clinical and educational psychology (e.g. Martens and Keller 1987; Kanfer 1989; O'Donohue 1989; Belar 1988; Vandereycken 1987; Stone 1983; Perry 1987; Hudson and King 1984; Rickard and Clements 1985), with a myriad of papers detailing specific instances which confirm the efficacy of such models for both training and practice (e.g. Overholser 1989; McGovern 1988; Halgin and Struckus 1985; Edlestein and Hawkins 1987; Jung *et al.* 1987). Science is used to provide both the academic and professional justification for clinical psychology, allowing us to rise above our fellow (sic) mental health professionals, who do not have the benefit of such 'rigorous' training, as this comment for the recent government survey of clinical psychology illustrates:

> Scientist-practitioner is the term frequently used to describe their professional approach. They are applied behavioural and

social scientists with a clinical role. Scientific method and systematic enquiry determines the way in which they practise. Hence characteristics of their approach are hypotheses testing, collection of evidence to confirm or deny a hypothesis and thorough evaluation of their intervention.

(MAS 1989: 45)

Yet this dawn of the new age of science and the ascendency of the positivistic practitioner has not been without its detractors. Strong critiques, mainly from philosophers and sociologists of science, have been levied at the assumptions underlying positivism, its methodological framework and the implications this has for both science and society (Knorr-Cetina 1981; Rose and Rose 1969; Latour and Woolgar 1979; Gilbert and Mulkay 1984). Specific critiques rejecting positivism have arisen from within disciplines such as sociology (Durkheim 1951), and psychology (Harre and Secord 1972; Gould and Shotter 1977; Ussher 1991). A further cohort of critics (Laing 1960; Szasz 1961; Sedgewick 1987; Ingleby 1982), who generally focus on critiques of psychiatry, have laid bare the dangers they perceive in applying positivistic method-ologies to mental health practices. When these are juxtaposed with the increasingly vociferous feminist analyses of gender and science (Bleier 1988; Keller 1985; J. Harding 1986; S. Harding 1986), a composite picture can be built up which seriously questions the philosophy of the scientist-practitioner in clinical psychology. And in particular the role that this philosophy and its concomitant practices plays in excluding gender issues from the professional agenda, often working against the interests of women, both as practitioners and as clients, whilst simultaneously preventing the development of forms of practice which are both reflexive and responsive to the needs of the individual. For despite the continued calls for reflexivity in psychology (Bannister 1970), it seems that unquestioned acceptance of the dominant paradigm of positivism is still the norm. In the eyes of the critics, it is this paradigm which contributes to regressive practices and policies. It is thus the limitations of positivism and the potentially deleterious effects of the scientist-practitioner model in relation to gender issues, which I will examine in this chapter.

THE PROBLEMS WITH POSITIVISM

> Traditional scientific discourses. . .encourage us to support co-
> ercive scientific claims and practices, and claims *about* science,
> that are historically mystifying and epistemologically and
> politically regressive.
>
> (S. Harding 1986: 243)

These 'traditional scientific discourses' have received much careful scrutiny and criticism, but what actually are the tenets underlying positivism which arouse such antipathy? Before attempting to
deconstruct the rhetoric of science in psychology and expose its
reactionary implications, it is worth briefly outlining what the
positivistic philosophy actually is.

Positivistic science assumes that observations can be made
rationally and objectively, without any contamination from values,
beliefs or politics. A clear distinction is made between 'facts',
which are the objects of the scientists' attentions, and 'values',
which are not. Thus 'authors of science texts write about the
importance of value-free observations through the "experimental
method"' (S. Harding 1986: 4). 'True science' is declared to be
completely value free: the scientist is a blank screen, rational,
objective, and apolitical. In fact the absence of such concepts from
the professional agenda is a central goal of the scientific exercise.
It is assumed that concepts and questions can be defined oper-
ationally, and investigated in an exact and replicable fashion.
Variables can be identified, measured and organised. Theories are
then constructed in a causal, deterministic fashion – hypotheses
are presented which can then be tested, ideally using rigorous
experimental methodologies. Thus to the positivist:

> the world is composed of facts and the goal of knowledge is to
> provide a literal account of what the world is like. The empirical
> laws and theoretical propositions of science are designed to
> provide those literal descriptions.
>
> (Knorr-Cetina 1981: 1)

One of the most basic criticisms is that a framework 'originally
devised for the sorting of microbes according to the clustering of
their objective characteristics' (Sedgewick 1987: 24) cannot be
applied to the study of human behaviour, and particularly to
clinical psychology. For the positivistic approach implicitly
assumes (Ingleby 1982: 28) that human action is no different from

the rest of nature and can be studied in an objective manner. If behaviour can only be placed in the right categories, classified in the appropriate way, it can be transformed into variables as simple to measure as those variables so beloved of the natural scientists. But is human thought or action really analogous to plate tectonics, the behaviour of microbes or DNA? For whilst we may be at least able to measure these with some objectivity (even if the theories constructed around them are also open to interpretation – see Kuhn 1962; Chalmer 1990), is this possible with human behaviour? This has been strongly rejected:

> Descriptions of. . .human activities and states of mind. . .are always subjective interpretations – subjective not in the sense that there are no criteria, but that the criteria are unstated ones, lying in the culture itself . . .[which] undermines the possibility of objective description in the human sciences generally.
>
> (Ingelby 1982: 32)

The adherence to positivism has led to a concentration on diagnosis, classification and categorisation within the mental health professions, from which clinical psychology is not immune. The taxonomic approach to psychological problems has achieved dominance, assuming that if the appropriate symptoms can be identified in correlated clusters, then an objective analysis of the problem can be provided. 'Psychological intervention' can then be applied in the same objective and systematic manner. For whilst clinical psychology would like to distance itself from the medical model, the professional and academic discourse of the two professions is still wedded to categorisation and cure. Psychologists may attempt to salve their consciences by avoiding the use of diagnostic labels, by working in the area of mental 'health', and by widening their portfolio to include interventions outside the medical arena (such as the analysis of systems) – but have their basic practices really changed? For cannot this criticism of psychiatry be equally applied to clinical psychology:

> Science is. . .viewed as the lynchpin of psychiatric practice; it is science that permits the boundary to be drawn between the normal and the pathological; it is science that creates the possibility of accurate identification of the mentally ill; it is science that provides effective methods of cure.
>
> (Busfield 1986: 17)

Is not the taxonomic approach still an essential part of clinical practice – even if it is reframed as a discussion of 'clinical formulations' which lead to testable hypotheses? But as any student of the mental health movements of the 1960s and 1970s will know, there has been a great deal of criticism of the taxonomic approach, questioning the very basis of diagnosis, its fundamental validity and reliability, accompanied by a dismissal of the 'treatments' meted out by professionals.[5] It has been strongly claimed, by a number of different authors (Sedgewick 1987; Ingleby 1981), that all diagnosis is necessarily subjective, as is evidenced by the lack of reliability between those carrying out diagnosis (Busfield 1986: 66–73).[6] Thus the supposed objectivity of the positivistic method when applied to psychological categorisation is thrown into doubt. For as Mechanic states:

> The usefulness of a diagnostic disease model depends on its level of confirmation, which in turn depends upon the reliability of the diagnosis (the amount of agreement among practitioners in assigning the diagnostic label) and its utility in predicting the course of the condition, its etiology and how it can be treated successfully.
>
> (Mechanic 1969 quoted by Baruch and Treacher 1978: 235)

Recent researchers have continued to criticise the legitimacy of diagnosis of many so-called syndromes reified within the DSM III (diagnostic and statistic manual of the American Psychiatric Association) and the ICD (international classification of diseases), leading to questioning of the very existence of syndromes such as schizophrenia (Bentall 1990), hyperactivity in children, and women's reproductive syndromes – PMS, postnatal depression and the menopausal syndrome (Ussher 1989; 1992a). It can be argued that as well as being subjective, diagnosis is heavily coloured by the values and politics of the expert, and by the service demands being made (i.e. if services are scarce professionals may chose not to recognise or diagnose a particular problem) and thus the categories adopted are often arbitrary and invalid. Yet by placing the problem within the person, under the guise of scientifically validated diagnosis and intervention, the values of the professionals, and consequently psychology's role in society, is concealed.

SCIENCE LEGITIMATING PSYCHOLOGY

A hundred years ago a speech by a public figure was incomplete without careful reference to at least one member of the Trinity of Church, Queen and Nation. Today a similar speech demands at the least its ritual blow in the direction of that indivisible pair: Science and Technology.

(Rose and Rose 1969: xi)

Given the many criticisms of positivism, and the seemingly inherent contradiction of a caring profession adhering to rigorous rational objectivity, one might beg the question, why does psychology adhere to it so ardently? One way of understanding the present positioning of positivism as the backbone of clinical psychology, is to look back to its roots in the scientific revolution taking place during the seventeenth to nineteenth centuries. More specifically, we can see the roots of the present scientific discourse in clinical psychology in the rhetoric of the Victorian psychiatrists, who in the late nineteenth century replaced the barbers turned surgeons and lay asylum keepers, defending their monopoly over their lucrative (and captive) patient population through their insistence on the primacy of the scientific dogma (Scull 1979; Ussher 1991). The assertions of the medics and psychiatrists of their almost divine right to exercise control were clearly based on their perceived expertise in the application of science as Henry Maudsley, the English psychiatrist claimed:

the observation and classification of mental disorders have been so exclusively psychological that we have not sincerely realized the fact that they illustrate the same pathological principles as other diseases, are produced in the same way, and must be investigated in the same spirit of *positive research.*

(Baruch and Treacher 1978: 35, *my emphasis*)

Throughout the late nineteenth century, society saw the transformation of the gentleman doctor into the scientific guru, science providing their passport to power, as 'science was the transcendent force to which the doctors looked to lift medicine out of the mire of commercialism and gird it against its foes' (Ehrenreich and English 1978: 69).

Yet as Scull (1979) and more recently Boyle (1990) have argued, it was not the efficacy of scientific expertise, the demonstration that science could offer anything in terms of solutions to the problems of the population, which precipitated the monopoly of these new positivistic experts. Science had not proven itself as an effective 'cure', but merely provided an effective justification for those who held executive power – those who were intent on the continued growth and development of their own monopolistic professions. So perhaps it is not surprising that the emerging profession of clinical psychology should adhere to the same scientific philosophy in order to legitimate its role. It also provides a feeling of security for the individual professional, who is bolstered by the confidence given by the scientific bag of tricks – a confidence which sometimes results in an exaggeration of one's competencies. As Pilgrim (1991: 53) notes:

> here are Hallam *et al.* (1989) boasting of the unmatchable skills of clinical psychologists. 'As trained clinical psychologists, who have received *intensive* training, supervision and accreditation, we are skilled in *all* the various therapeutic methods'.

The powers of positivism to provide such confidence in one's professional skills are unrivalled. Yet whilst science protects the profession from the wolves, and is used as a major justification for its very existence in the increasingly beleaguered National Health Service of the early 1990s (as in the MAS report 1989), it is also a means of increasing the status of clinical psychology within the hierarchy of psychology itself. Thus as a philosophy it serves the interests of the profession, not primarily the interests of the public. The economic and political changes within health provision and care which have taken place in the closing decade of the twentieth century have led to increased professionalisation and protection of professional boundaries – a closing of ranks. Science serves an important function in maintaining the status of psychology, and further empowering the experts, the individual clinical psychologists.

POWER TO THE EXPERTS

One of the more insidious implications of the positivistic paradigm is to glorify the role of the 'expert', a process which many feminists would argue is a symptom of a patriarchal system – as the experts within psychology are protecting a particular set of interests. Yet this is not openly acknowledged – or really open to analysis from those outside the system. The impenetrable language of science perpetuates its illusion of objectivity and expertise, creating a dense, jargonised world which can usually only be understood (or criticised) by those who have undergone the interminable initiation into its élite. The mystification of professional training, with its long and poorly paid induction, separates the expert and the patient (and the clinical psychologist from other non-professionally trained psychologists) and attributes to the clinical psychologist omnipotent powers – s/he becomes power incarnate. This is an analogous process to that achieved by the medics, who have been scrutinised more thoroughly. As Foucault argued:

> As positivism imposes itself upon medicine and psychiatry...the psychiatrist's power (becomes) more and more miraculous...the authority he (*sic*) has borrowed from order, morality, and the family now seems to derive from himself; it is because he is a doctor that he is believed to possess these powers...and it was thought, and by the patient first of all, that it was in the esotericism of his knowledge that the doctor had found the power to unravel insanity; and increasingly the patient would accept this self-surrender to a doctor both divine and satanic.
>
> (Foucault 1967: 275, *my emphasis*)

The attribution of these 'divine and satanic' powers to the clinical psychologist and the subsequent mystification of authority, the 'reification of a magical nature' (Foucault 1967: 276) ensures that knowledge, power and control cannot be held by the lay person, and most certainly not by the 'patient'. It thus acts to disqualify the views or interventions of those outside the hallowed confines of the 'caring professions'. It is this process which can result in the denial of meaning in the utterances of those with mental health problems and the disqualification of patient lobbying groups (e.g. Plumb 1990). Science acts to define what is normal; it defines who has the right to expertise, whose knowledge is taken seriously, and it defines what factors are to be considered on the clinical psychology agenda. Yet the notion of the objective scientist-practitioner who determines this agenda has come under increasing scrutiny, as the whole con- cept of neutrality is deemed to be a fallacy.

THE MYTH OF THE NEUTRAL SCIENTIST

Successful practitioners of the scientific method must ruthlessly suppress all extraneous factors, particularly intrusions of an emotional kind, and so allow themselves to be guided by logic and facts alone to arrive at their assumed goal of genuine knowledge and truth about nature.

(Easlea 1986: 136)

This confidence in the existence of the unemotional and neutral observer, the researcher or practitioner who believes he or she is 'unbiased and distanced from the emotional bullets of politics' (Tizard 1990: 436) is used as a justification for the ascendancy of the experts and their continued control of the reins of power. Yet it is a false assumption, acting as a smoke-screen for the reality of the profession's interventions. As Pilgrim and Treacher (1992) have argued 'psychologists. . .play a highly political role in terms of the management of the population, whilst at the same time dis-owning such a role by pointing to their "disinterested" scientific training and credentials'. Prilleltensky (1989: 800) argues:

> Psychology is instrumental in maintaining the societal status quo by (a) endorsing and reflecting dominant social values, (b) disseminating those values in the persuasive form of so-called value free scientific statements, and (c) providing an asocial image of the human being, which in turn portrays the individual as essentially independent from socio-historical circumstances.

Thus the very notion of objectivity can be seen to be a 'white-wash' (Ingleby 1982) and the public claim that professionals and scientists are 'disinterested, universalistic, altruistic' often contrasts sharply with the 'private face' of a profession (Atkinson and Delemont 1987: 96). Thus the very assertion that 'objective' clinical psychology can exist has been challenged, and the very notion of positivism seen as political, as Kovel has outlined:

> The notion of [positivism] also has a political power, since what is repressed. . .is that which considers the person as an active social agent, defined by what class, community and history have for him.

(Kovel 1982: 86)

The object of the clinical psychologist's attention, whether it be an individual, group or community is not a value free 'variable' able to be fitted into some neat experimental design, or examined and explained within a set of testable hypotheses. Each individual, each group, is shaped by many forces, historical, social and political – factors which are invariably absent from the positivistic agenda, and therefore deemed to be immaterial. The positivistic assessment can therefore only be partial, and invariably biased by the foundations of the science itself, a reflection of the interests of the ruling élite in the profession. For as one commentator notes:

> Contemporary analysts recognise that, whatever their intentions, scientists are the products of their society and time, and their construction of social reality is shaped by the world view and values of the culture in which they are reared. These belief systems can influence all phases of the research in which scientists engage, from choice of problem to interpretation of results.
>
> (Spence 1985: 1,285)

This assertion that any current set of theories, the current *Zeitgeist* in scientific thought, is not based solely on objective reality but on the interests of the proponents of any given theory, and the accumulated mass of evidence they produce to support their views, was most clearly argued by Kuhn (1962). He argued that scientific revolutions are not merely dependent on the discovery of a new theory, or on the validity of any given theory, but largely on the political and social forces which combine to produce society's 'best' theory. New theories or paradigms replace old when the growing dissension from those caught in the 'suspended revolution' (Healy 1990) becomes too powerful to ignore. Yet despite the acknowledgement of these issues by many individual scientists, it is still the case that 'the dominant culture ignores the uncertainty of scientific knowledge and presents an authoritarian view of scientific truth' (Fee 1988: 43). In order to continue to prosper, individual scientists and professionals have to ignore or discount certain evidence which would contradict their own perspective. In fact according to some observers, there are 'certain biases built into experimental design and data interpretation which lead the scientist to retain theories despite disconfirming evidence' (Grover 1981: 17). Psychology is as guilty of this blinkered approach as any other discipline. It defines its narrow agenda – ignoring issues which don't fit in with the interests of the dominant group. Thus 'if research findings confirm what people want to hear, the findings tend not to be scrutinised carefully' (Tizard 1990: 440). If the results contradict the *Zeitgeist* of the day they will be less likely to be accepted for publication (Kitzinger 1990a; Ussher 1992b). This has implications for research, clinical practice, and policy making, for research which goes against the grain of the current ideology of practice is disregarded:

> All knowledge is framed within a particular intellectual paradigm, which indicates what is relevant. . .Clarke and Clarke (1976). . .showed in great detail that because of the hold of the [psychoanalytic] paradigm in the US and Britain, alternative interpretations of a wide range of studies were not sought and contradictory evidence was ignored or dismissed.
>
> (Tizard 1990: 439)

Those who hold the reins of power in psychology, those who shape the profession and the academic discourse, are no more immune from politics than any other mere mortal, despite their claims to the contrary. In fact their very assertions of objectivity could be seen as political, for they ascribe false legitimacy and the status of 'truth' to theories and practices which are based on the particular perspective of the (usually white, male, middle class) positivistic psychologist. For the existence of the neutral scientist is a myth, as has been demonstrated in every branch of science, whether it be theoretical or applied. The choice of research material, the questions asked, the paradigms adopted and the interpretations made are all affected by the perspective of the researcher.[7] Clinical psychology cannot pretend to be exempt from such criticism, whilst basking in the power and prestige which the myth delivers. For this power is potentially invidious, the more so for its very hypocrisy. For as Namenwirth contends:

> In truth, scientists are no more protected from political and cultural influence than other citizens. By draping their scientific activities in claims of neutrality, detachment, and objectivity, scientists augment the perceived importance of their views, absolve themselves of social responsibility for the applications of their work, and leave their (unconscious) minds open to political and cultural assumptions.
>
> (Namenwirth 1988: 29)

So the very refusal of psychology to be reflexive, to examine its position within the dominant discourse which shapes society, to consider factors such as sexism, heterosexism, class oppression or racism (Ussher 1990; Kitzinger 1990b; Howitt and Owusu-Bempah

1990), allows it to be used for more insidious purposes. To be used as an agent of social control, diverting attention away from factors outside its remit, such as social oppression, and leading certain critics to argue that 'the role psychology plays in legitimating the oppression in this society is by no means minor' (Brookes 1973: 317). And the social reality which psychology adopts is that of the dominant élite in society – the patriarchal prelates. Perhaps it is psychologists themselves who should be the object of study, as their own chosen perspectives are determining both the science they study, and the uses to which it is put. For as Prilleltensky (1989: 800) argues:

> The penetration of the reigning ideology of psychological knowledge is largely determined by the socialisation of psychologists. This, in conjunction with psychology's apparent inability to self reflect on its nonepistemic biases, has permitted its utilization for the advancement of ideological purposes.

Thus rather than being an objective paradigm, positivism acts to mystify the conditions of those deemed in need of psychological assessment or intervention, at the same time as it reifies the power of the expert, who is protected by the anonymity provided by the supposed objectivity of the positivistic scientist. And rather than being objective and neutral, it has been claimed that 'psychology has. . .[been] implicated in coercive social regulation and in reproducing social differences in favour of men, white people, Western and middle class people' (Hollway 1989: 132). Thus the policies which will be supported will be those of this dominant order, for as Harding argues:

> the epistomologies, metaphysics, ethics and politics of the dominant forms of science are androcentric and mutually supportive; that despite the deeply ingrained Western cultural belief in science's intrinsic progressiveness, science today serves primarily regressive social tendencies.
>
> (S. Harding 1986: 9)

It is not only the psychologists who carry out research who are implicated in this censoring or moulding of research – the gate-keepers to knowledge are an equally important group, for as Tizard argues, 'for every researcher there are crucial gateways through which research findings must go if they are to become known to policy makers and practitioners' (1990: 438). These gateways include those who control training courses and department-mental budgets, and thus determine practice, academic journal editors, and in the wider social arena, those in the media who disseminate the research to a wider audience. Yet in order for ideas or research results to be taken up 'there has to be some degree of match between the ideology of the researcher and the guardians of the gateways' (Tizard 1990: 439). That ideology is shaped by the gender bias in science and psychology, a bias reflected in the actions of the gatekeepers who determine policy – the fact that the science we know and use in clinical psychology has developed as a masculine enterprise.

THE SEXING OF SCIENCE

Scientific expertise, since at least the 16th century, has repeat-edly been described and discussed in the language of sexuality and gender; science and medicine have been associated with sexual metaphors clearly designating nature as a woman to be unveiled, unclothed, and penetrated by masculine science.

(Fee 1988: 44)

Science has traditionally been synonymous with masculinity, as women and science were (and are) seen as bipolar opposites (Jordanova 1989). And the whole cornucopia of beliefs and strictures which position women outside both science and the concomitant professions (Atkinson and Delamont 1987) was sub-sumed within clinical psychology when the profession aligned itself with positivism. For as S. Harding has noted 'women have been more systematically excluded from serious science than from performing any other social activity except, perhaps, frontline warfare' (1986: 31). The science that we know is that which has evolved in a patriarchal society, and thus it 'took on a decidedly masculine tone' (Namenwirth 1988: 18).

The insistence by the experts that science is a male preserve has been a recurrent theme throughout history:

The female. . .seldom reach any farther than to a sleight super-ficial smattering in any deep science.

(The Complete Midwifes Practice Enlarged, 1659)

the man of science is deficient on the purely emotional element [and that] in many regards the character of the scientific men is strongly anti-feminine; their mind is directed to facts and abstract theories, and not to persons or human interests. . .they have little sympathy with female ways of thought.

(Galton 1874[8])

When it comes to science we find women are simply nowhere. The feminine mind is quite unscientific.

(Swinburne 1902)

It is still a prevalent belief today that women are not equipped to be scientists. The metaphors of science are still consistently masculine (Weinreich-Haste 1986; Jordanova 1989) – the rational, objective, unemotional, rigorous, logical – all are associated with both masculinity, and with science. The hallmark of a scientist came to be seen as someone who carried out a 'hard and ruthless analysis of reality' (Easlea 1986: 136). Thus from the early nineteenth century scientists to the present day, science has been gendered, as Keller notes

gender ideology [was] a crucial mediator between the birth of modern science and the economic and political transformation surrounding that birth. . .neither the equations between mind, reason and masculinity, nor the dichotomies between mind and nature, reason and feeling, masculine and feminine, are historically invarient.

(1985: 44)

The 'hard/soft' dichotomy used to distinguish between science which is good, and that which is not, has masculine (if not phallic) undertones. 'Hard' research tends to be that which utilises methodologies and frameworks nearest to that of the natural sciences – that which is quantitative, experimental and objective; often literally dependant on laboratory 'hardware'. 'Soft' science is exemplified by the methods adopted by sociology, or social psychology, methods invariably scorned by the experimental psychologists. Psychology itself is an hierarchical profession, with those at the top of the tree being the so-called 'hard' experimentalists – those who wholeheartedly embraced methods developed in the natural sciences in order to understand human behaviour (Sherif 1987). Thus to avoid positioning at the bottom of the pile, methodologies which are deemed 'hard' are advocated in professional applied psychology. It has been advocated that 'Psychologists should be more mechanistic rather than less. . .

They should cut straight through the mental to the neurophysi-ological' (Rorty 1979: 217). Many would agree. As Sherif argued:

> Each of the fields and specialities within psychology sought to improve its status by adopting (as well and closely as stomachs permitted) the perspective, theories, and methodologies as high on the hierarchy as possible. The way to respectability in this scheme has been the appearance of rigour and scientific enquiry, bolstered by highly restrictive notions of what science is about.
>
> (Sherif 1987: 43)

It is no coincidence that the areas within psychology which are most populated by women are deemed 'soft': clinical psychology, social psychology, and to a certain extent, developmental psychology (see Paula Nicolson's discussion in Chapter 1). This very dichotomy clearly places women at the lower rungs of the ladder.[9]

But if men are deemed to be the ones fit (and able) to carry out hard science, where does this leave the women in clinical psychology? Often doing the donkey work, the hard, low profile, caring work, one might cynically suggest. Thus the utilisation of the hard–soft dichotomy in psychology to position research on the hierarchy of merit, has only served to obscure the real issues behind such concerns – the issues of competition, of status, of male networking and infighting. The role of science in perpetuating the dominant culture, in serving capitalism and patriarchy. I would be inclined to agree with Sherif when she perhaps cynically notes:

> Those who proclaim the hardness of their methods and their hardware the loudest are the most guilty of producing research findings with the durability of a marshmallow.
>
> (Sherif 1987: 47)

So this gendering of science in clinical psychology serves two functions. Firstly, to position women as outside the dominant group of experts, the 'real' scientists, and secondly, to define the subject matter of the profession, which is shaped by the positivistic discourse; a discourse which frequently ignores women's interests.

WOMEN IN CLINICAL PSYCHOLOGY

> The scientific enterprise itself became fused in people's minds
> with the character traits (real or imagined) of the typical
> Western, white, middle-class male. This phenomenon has made
> it difficult for. . .hiring and promotion committees to envision
> women as suitable colleagues.
>
> (Namenwirth 1988: 21)

The adoption of this particular scientific discourse in clinical psychology, based on the interests of white, middle-class men, serves
to maintain women outside the hallowed halls of power. As women
have been excluded from science, from power in the professions
(Atkinson and Delamont 1987), with only the token woman
allowed through (Ussher 1990), women are also excluded from
the powerful positions within clinical psychology. As Paula
Nicolson has argued in Chapter 1, although women are in the
majority in terms of absolute numbers, they are in the minority in
positions of power and status. The Top Grade jobs, the training
course organisers, those who control research funding and research institutions, and the journal editors are invariably male.
Both the academic gatekeepers and the gatekeepers to clinical
practice are male. The scientific discourse very effectively maintains their control. Perhaps this is why science is not allowed to
topple from its pinnacle of power, as Sherif argues:

> [Scientific psychology's] most powerful weapons against
> charges of bias have been not dazzling scientific accomplish-
> ments, but its support by elites in psychology and the larger
> society based on consensus of opinion.
>
> (Sherif 1987: 54)

Science has evolved as an enterprise suited to the male – as have
the professions, including clinical psychology. If a small number of
individual women are allowed to take up privileged positions of
power, to believe themselves members of the élite, this does not
change the basic structures or prejudices. It merely allows for lip
service to be paid to edicts for equality of opportunity. For being
successful as a scientist or as a professional is much to do with
factors beyond the control of those who are outsiders, out of the
control of women. It is not solely to do with the excellence of one's
work, or one's personal qualities, as the rhetoric of equality of
opportunity would have us believe. Yet these ways to success are

not always clear, and are not available to the uninitiated. The analogy provided by Atkinson and Delamont seems apt:

> Just as Saturn is partially obscured from us by its rings – whirling particles of dust and ice – so the real nature of much professional work is obscured from many marginal recruits (such as women and ethnic minorities). . .the rings are obscuring the habitus, while leaving the purely technical skills of the job visible.
>
> (Atkinson and Delamont 1987: 107)

There are many reasons for the imbalance of power within psychology, and I would not want to suggest that the adoption of positivism is the only one which is important. But as women have been excluded from science for centuries, and thus excluded from the professions which look to science for their lead, they are excluded from real power in clinical psychology.

Yet the scientific discourse can also have negative implications for women on the receiving end of clinical psychology – the objects of interest, those who come under the supposedly objective scientific gaze.

WOMEN AS OBJECTS OF THE SCIENTIFIC GAZE

> Psychology has nothing to say about what women are really like, what they really need and what they want, essentially because psychology does not know.
>
> (Weisstein 1973: 394)

Some of the most vociferous assaults on psychology have come from feminists attacking both the foundations on which the profession is based, and the function it serves in society. All actions of clinical psychologists, as those of other mental health professionals, have been placed under feminist scrutiny – and found wanting. The conclusion is frequently drawn that psychology is oppressive, that it 'acts to enforce the whole male structure, and ultimately forces women upon an area which, founded and documented by men, has been used against women' (Chesler 1973: 60). The male focus of psychology directs attention away from women's real oppression, merely defining their distress as personal, as symptoms which fit within the positivistic philosophy, rather than examining the wider issues facing each individual woman. Psychology, in this view, is seen as oppressive in itself, seen to have 'done little but provide a label for emotionally disturbed women, often adding to their hardships with no plan for their cure or empowerment' (Fulini 1987: xiii). The very methodology psychology adopted has been completely dismissed:

> since clinical experience and tools can be shown to be worse than useless when tested for consistency, efficacy, agreement and reliability, we can safely conclude that theories of a clinical nature advanced about women are also worse than useless.
>
> (Weisstein 1973: 402)

As the scientific discourse ignores politics, is avowedly rational, and because it is based on the interests of the patriarchal élite, it is perhaps not surprising that it ignores misogyny and sexism, and does not acknowledge the interests of women. As I have argued elsewhere (Ussher 1991), there is considerable evidence that misogyny is one of the fundamental factors underlying women's mental health difficulties. Yet this assertion is seen as political, it is not part of the scientific agenda. Is this denial not a political action in itself? There is also a growing feminist literature which attests to the gender biased assumptions underlying clinical assessment and treatment – demonstrating that psychology acts to ensure that women conform to a particular role which doesn't threaten the status quo.

Thus, for example, women who are depressed, unhappy or angry after childbirth can be pathologised and dismissed by being labelled as suffering from postnatal depression. That their behaviour might be a normal reaction to the circumstances in which they find themselves is ignored. The term 'depression' neatly categorises the woman, simultaneously denying her any right to her feelings, or any recourse to positive action which might alleviate them. Yet the other side of this double-edged sword, in which women are more likely to be pathologised for their complaints (Ussher 1991) is that women's concerns are invariably ignored, or dismissed as not being important. As Chesler argues

> most contemporary professionals (like most non-professionals) unthinkingly consider what happens to men as somehow more important than what happens to women. *Male* psychiatric illness or 'impairment' is viewed as more 'disabling' than female illness. The ghost of female expendability and 'outsideness'

haunts almost every page of psychiatric and psychological journals.

(Chesler 1973: 65)

The scientific discourse merely legitimates this process, and cloaks it with a false air of objectivity.

These factors are not merely of academic interest, or only of interest to feminists, they have direct implications for policy. For as well as supporting traditional gender roles, and maintaining the position of the researchers, positivism in psychology can result in a regressive, rather than radical or progressive social policy, as argued above. Or, in the main, have no impact on policy at all, through the concentration of research on the abstract, or the inability of research to pass through the gateways erected around it. Perhaps it is time for this to change.

BREAKING THE NARROW GRIP OF SCIENCE

It is time for psychology to wed its indubitable methodological sophistication to a concern for problems that are more molar, less artificial, more representative of real-life situations, more substantive.

(Gardner 1985: 135)

Clinical psychology is still a young profession – it can decide to tread the tried and tested path of positivism, and continue in a reactionary mode – or look outside its present blinkers, and move forwards into a more progressive mode, a mode not dependent upon 'science'. For as S. Harding has argued, 'despite the deeply ingrained Western cultural belief in science's intrinsic progressiveness, science today serves primarily regressive social tendencies' (1986: 9). One of the major regressive tendencies it serves in clinical psychology is to reinforce gender stereotypes associated with women, and to maintain the existence of a profession which is often not responsive to women's needs.

And whilst I would argue that we should scrutinise and criticise the present role which the scientific discourse underlying clinical psychology plays in marginalising gender issues, and perpetuating a form of practice which is not always sensitive to the needs of its clients, I would not want to argue that we throw the baby out with the bathwater, by either rejecting psychology itself, or by rejecting the concept of rigour and systematic practice. What we need is to develop a form of practice which is less blinkered, more reflexive.

To reframe psychology within a model of theory and practice which is not restrictive and oppressive, but unbiased, empowering and reflexive is an enormous task, and not one to be achieved without a major shift in the academic and professional discourse. But it must be done, if psychology is not to ossify and stagnate. For any applied science cannot be ruled by the abstract theorising and separation from social and political reality which passes for 'real' science. It is a dangerous contradiction to base a profession which claims expertise in the psychological domain on the restrictive criteria of 'hard' science. If it attempts to continue in this vein, it will surely become extinct.

Whilst one could fill a whole tome with suggestions for change, a consideration of directions for future concerns will have to suffice in this context. Firstly, psychology as a profession needs to be more reflexive, to consider the implications of its underlying scientific philosophy in clinical practice. If we are to continue with the scientist-practitioner model, a broader definition of 'science' within psychology needs to be accepted – adhering strictly to positivism is not always (if ever) the most appropriate course. This can take place through the publication of research examining issues which are less abstract and artificial, more wedded to the real issues facing both men and women in 'respectable' journals. This does not negate the production of abstract research or theory, or of any quantitative research – but does deprive it of its preeminent status. Psychologists should not be afraid of addressing issues which might be seen to be 'political' or research which is directly related to policy – we are all political, whether we like it or not. Thus looking at the implications of social reality on people's lives is a legitimate concern of psychologists, we cannot continue to consider the person as an abstract unit stripped of class, culture, history or gender. As I have argued elsewhere in relation to menstrual cycle research (Ussher 1992b), it must be acceptable for issues more central to the disciplines of history, politics, philosophy, anthropology and sociology to be included on the psychological agenda for the discipline to progress and survive. Psychology has been too insular as a discipline. This cannot continue to be defended, *particularly* in clinical psychology, at either the level of theory or practice.

Change should also involve the acceptance of a wider variety of methodologies in both research carried out during training, and post-qualification. Number crunching for its own sake should become a thing of the past. Training courses and accreditation bodies, such as the British Psychological Society, should broaden their criterion for acceptability of research on the way to qualification. It should be acceptable to produce research based on qualitative methodologies, research with a greater inter-disciplinary slant, or that which is more theoretically orientated – as well as the presently sanctioned narrowly positivistic research. It should also be acceptable for individuals to produce collaborative research with client groups which does not position the psychologist as the all knowing expert (see Holland, Chapter 3, in this volume for an example of this). To legitimate research which is more wedded to practice and to the needs of clients will actually ensure that individual practitioners are more likely to continue in the scientist-practitioner mode to which we are supposed to aspire – a role which many avoid at present (Haynes, Lemsky and Sexton 1987).

One might also argue that judgements of success in the profession should not be taken solely from that defined by the male model of science – promotion should not be dependent on the number of publications in 'respectable' (i.e. hard science) journals, or on the acquisition of a higher research degree. (Equally, we should avoid the tradition of the medical model wherein efficacy is measured in terms of number of cases seen or number of 'cures'.) If professional psychology is supposed to be concerned with the needs of its client groups, it cannot follow the traditional male route to scientific success, wherein individual effort is expended mainly in the interests of the individual, and his (sic) career (Keller 1985).

The aims of the positivistic scientist and that of the practitioner are frequently at odds with each other – producing conflict for the individual, and potentially a split in the profession. Many have argued that research training is irrelevant to the practitioner (Hughes 1952; Meehl 1971) and the demands of the two roles of scientist and practitioner incompatible (Albee and Loeffler 1982; Frank 1984; Halgin and Struckus 1985). The evidence that a majority of practitioners in either educational or clinical psychology do not carry out, or even read research (see Bergin and Strupp 1972; Garfield and Kurtz 1976; Steinhelber and Gaynor

1981; Head and Harman 1990) perhaps suggests that many professionals are actually ignoring narrow models of 'science' by voting with their feet.

Some might argue that clinical psychology should turn towards therapy, which is supposedly less reductionist, following in the footsteps of those who formed the Psychology and Psychotherapy Association in 1973: 'a group of psychologists pre-occupied with rescuing their trade from methodological behaviourism and empiricist definitions of psychological discourse' (Pilgrim 1991: 54). But we should beware of such simple panaceas, for as Pilgrim argues, the psychotherapists have not been immune from the same failings as their more hard-nosed scientific predecessors:

> Psychological reductionism in psychotherapeutic discourse is typically of two sorts. . .actions in their social contexts may be reduced to individual motives. . .[and] parts of a system may be considered in isolation from their wider context.
>
> (1991: 3)

There are some indications that movements are afoot within clinical psychology to recognise the need for change – recognitions that the traditional positivistic models beloved by academic psychology may not always be appropriate in professional training and practice. This is happening in other areas of applied psychology. For example, in a recent paper on the assessment training of educational psychologists, Lindsay has claimed that 'increasingly trainees have been encouraged to undertake studies which are based upon a qualitative rather than quantitative paradigm, and which attempt to respond to questions for the field' (1990: 78). Whilst others, such as Gray and Lunt, (1990: 35) have confirmed the continuity of the belief that trainee educational psychologists should see 'research as an integral part of professional training', they stress the link between research and practice, the need for research to have applicability to LEA work, and the importance of the 'dissemination of research'. This acknowledges that the professional applied psychologist is not operating in the proverbial ivory tower, and cannot ignore the direct implications of research activity on society.

The moves towards the acceptance of single case designs and qualitative research as acceptable and legitimate methodologies is a positive sign, as the welcoming of subjectivity back onto the psychological agenda (i.e. Henriques *et al.* 1984). The infusion of critical psychology and the advancement of feminist theory in psychology has also had a significant impact (see Chesler 1973; Burman 1990; Squire 1989; Ussher 1991) – challenging many existing assumptions as well as providing a positive energy for development of practices which are pro-women, rather than marginalising or pathologising. Institutional or structural changes within the health professions are also having an impact on clinical psychology, forcing a move away from rigid ways of working. For example, the development of case management as a model of working, wherein the individual is not seen as a mere psychological entity, but is considered as a person with a myriad of interrelated needs both social and psychological, is a positive step. Yet these same structural changes may work against the needs of both clinicians and their clients as market forces begin to determine the workload of the practitioner, the areas where it is worthwhile expending energy. Research of any kind, long-term work with individuals or interventions that do not easily prove successful may be squeezed out of the clinical psychologists' working remit. Gender issues may be seen as a low priority on the new market-led agenda of the health care – it is important that we as clinicians do not allow this marginalisation to occur.

These changes, and an acknowledgement and discussion of gender issues will not bring the profession into disrepute, it will not soil the hands of the scientists with politics. Many individual clinical psychologists are continuously reflexive. Many reject, or find unhelpful, the positivistic models of science. But the public discourse of the profession still maintains the adherence to positivism, perhaps out of a fear of a loss of status or a challenge to legitimacy. This is an empty fear, but rigid adherence to old ways of working could be the kiss of death for the profession. Science itself is not bad for clinical psychology, it is not inevitably bad for women. But the way it has been practised, the theories it has reified, and the individuals it has empowered, may not serve in the interests of women, or other disempowered groups. We need to do as Sherif has suggested and 'cease accepting [our] opponents' definitions of what is "scientific" and start to assess science as a human endeavour' (1987: 47), and then we may start to move towards a model of clinical psychology which is empowering for both the clinicians and the clients, and which does not deify either 'science' or the scientist-practitioner, at the expense of those who find themselves caught under the scientific gaze.

ACKNOWLEDGEMENTS

Thanks are extended to Christopher Dewberry and Jan Burns for comments on an earlier draft of this chapter, and to Helen Malson for help with preparation of the manuscript.

NOTES

1 Quoted by Pilgrim and Treacher 1992.
2 For a more complete discussion of this early history see Pilgrim and Treacher 1992.
3 In the 1970s the growing criticisms of the empirical reductionist base of clinical psychology from within, resulted in the emphasis of psychotherapy, rather than behaviourism, within the profession (Pilgrim 1991).
4 Research publications accrue a higher status for the individual in the professional hierarchy, even if clinical skills are accorded status on an individual departmental level. See Sue Holland's chapter (Chapter 3) in this volume for some discussing of this.
5 See Sedgewick (1987) for an analysis of the dissension of the anti-psychiatrists. For some of the most influential critiques in the original, see Laing (1967), Szasz (1961), Cooper (1978), Foucault (1967).
6 Symptoms are rated differentially by different psychiatrists (Kreitman 1962), or different clinical psychologists, and any given set of symptoms may be categorised under the nosological umbrella of depression, schizophrenia, or some other syndrome, depending on the person carrying out the diagnosis.
7 See Ussher 1992b for a discussion of this in relation to menstrual cycle research. See Knorr-Cetina (1981) for a discussion of this in relation to science in general.
8 Quoted by Easlea 1986: 137.
9 See Ussher 1990 for an analysis of women in psychology in general. Also see the Hansard Commission report (1990) for discussions of the marginalisation of women in the various professions.

REFERENCES

Albee, H. E., and Loeffler, E. (1982) Alleged incompatibility of research and clinical training. *The Clinical Psychologist*, 36, 1: 8–9.

Atkinson, P. and Delamont, S. (1987) Professions and powerlessness: female marginality in the learned occupations? *Sociology*, 21, 1: 105.

Bannister, D. (1970) Psychology as an exercise in paradox. In: Schultz, D.P. (ed.), *The Science of Psychology: Critical reflections.* Englewood Cliffs: Prentice-Hall, 4–10.

Baruch, G. and Treacher, A. (1978) *Psychiatry Observed.* London: Routledge & Kegan Paul.

Belar, C. D. (1988) Education in behavioural medicine: Perspectives from psychology. *Annals of Behavioural Medicine,* 10, 1: 11–14.

Bentall, R. P. (1990) The syndromes and symptoms of psychosis. In Bentall R. P. (ed.), *Reconstructing Schizophrenia.* London: Routledge.

Bergin, A. E. and Strupp, H. (1972) *Changing Frontiers in the Science of Psychotherapy.* Chicago: Aldine.

Bleier, R. (ed.) (1988) *Feminist Approaches to Science.* New York: Pergamon Press.

Boyle, M. (1990) The non-discovery of schizophrenia. In Bentall, R., *Reconstructing Schizophrenia.* London: Routledge.

Brookes, K. (1973) Freudianism is not a basis for a Marxist psychology. In P. Brown (ed.),*Radical Psychology.* London: Tavistock, 315–374.

Burman, E. (ed.), (1990) *Feminists and Psychological Practice.* London: Sage.

Busfield, J. (1986) *Managing Madness: Changing Ideas and Practice.* London: Hutchinson.

Chalmer, A. F. (1990) *What is this thing called science?* Milton Keynes: Open University Press.

Chesler, P. (1973) *Women and Madness.* London: Allan Lane.

Clarke, A. M. and Clarke, A. D. B. (1976) *Early Experience: Myth and Evidence.* London: Open Books.

Cooper, D. (1978) Being born in a family. In Brown, P. (ed.), *Radical Psychology.* New York: Harper & Row: 156–173.

Durkheim, E. (1897) *Le Suicide.* Felix Alan; English translation (1951) New York: Free Press.

Easlea, B. (1986) The masculine image of science: How much does gender really matter? In Harding, J. (ed.), *Perspectives on Gender and Science.* Sussex: Falmer Press.

Edlestein, B. and Hawkins, R. P. (1987) Clinical Training: The program at West Virginia University. *Behaviour Therapist,* Feb., 10, 2: 41–42.

Ehrenreich, B. and English, D. (1978) *For Her own Good: 150 Years of the Experts' Advice to Women.* New York: Anchor Doubleday.

Fee, E. (1988) Critique of modern science: The relationship of feminism to other radical epistemologies. In Blier, R. (ed.), *Feminist Approaches to Science.* New York: Pergamon Press, 42–56.

Foucault, M. (1967) *Madness and Civilization: a history of insanity in the age of reason.* London: Tavistock.

Frank, G. (1984) The boulder model: history, rationale, and critique. *Professional Psychology Research,* 15, 3: 417–435.

Fulini, L. (1987) All power to the people! But how? In Fuluni, L. (ed.), *The Psychopathology of Everyday Racism and Sexism.* New York: Harrington Park Press.

Garfield, S. L. and Kurtz, R. (1976) A survey of clinical psychologists: Characteristics, activities and orientations. *The Clinical Psychologist,* 28, 1: 7–10.

Gardner, H. (1985) *The New Mind's Science. A History of the Cognitive Revolution.* New York: Basic Books.

Gilbert, N. and Mulkay, M. (1984) *Opening Pandora's Box.* Cambridge:

Cambridge University Press.

Gould, A. and Shotter, J. (1977) *Human Action and its Psychological Investigation*. London: Routledge.

Gray, P. and Lunt, I. (1990) Two different worlds? The U.L.I.E. approach to integrated training in professional educational psychology. *Educational and Child Psychology*, 7, 3: 31–36.

Grover, S. (1981) *Towards a Psychology of the Scientist: Implications of Psychological Research for Contemporary Philosophy of Science*. Washington: University Press of America.

Halgin, R. and Struckus, J. (1985) Perspectives on the utility of boulder model training. *Clinical Psychologist*, 38, 3: 61–64.

Hallam, R. S., Bender, M. P. and Wood, R. (1989) Use of psychological techniques. *The Psychologist*, 2, 9, 375.

Hansard Society (1990) *Report of the Hansard Society Commission on Women at the Top*. London: The Hansard Society for Parliamentary Government.

Harding, J. (1986) *Perspectives on Gender and Science*. Sussex: Falmer Press.

Harding, S. G. (1986) *The Science Question in Feminism*. Ithaca: Cornell University Press.

Harre, R. and Secord, P. (1972) *The Explanation of Social Behaviour*. Oxford: Blackwell.

Haynes, S. N., Lemsky, C. and Sexton, R. K. (1987) Why clinicians infrequently do research. *Professional Psychology Research and Practice*, Oct., 18, 5: 5,151–519.

Head, D. and Harman, G. H. (1990) *Clinical Psychology Forum*, 25: 15–16.

Healy, D. (1990) *The Suspended Revolution: Psychiatry and Psychotherapy Reexamined*. London: Faber.

Henriques, J., Hollway, W., Urwin, C., Venn, C. and Walkerdine, V. (1984) *Changing the Subject: Psychology, Social Regulation and Subjectivity*. London: Methuen.

Hollway, W. (1989) *Subject and Method in Psychology*. London: Sage.

Howitt, D. and Owusu-Bempah, J. (1990) Racism in a British journal? *The Psychologist*, 3, 9: 396–400.

Hudson, A., and King, N. (1984) Professional training of child psychologists. *Australian Psychologist*, 19, 3: 303–310.

Hughes, E. C. (1952) Psychology: Science and/or profession. *American Psychologist*, 7: 441–443.

Ingleby, D. (1981) The politics of psychology: Review of a decade. *Psychology and Social Theory*, 2, 4–18.

Ingleby, D. (1982) *Critical Psychiatry*. Harmondsworth: Penguin.

Jordanova, L. (1989) *Sexual Visions: Images of Gender in Science and Medicine Between the Eighteenth and Twentieth Centuries*. New York: Harvester Wheatsheaf.

Jung, C. H., Bernfeld, G. A., Coneybeare, S., Fernandes, L. (1987) Towards a scientific-practitioner model of child care: Implications for understanding adolescent group psychotherapy. *Journal of Child Care*, May, 12, 1: 13–26.

Kanfer, F. H. (1989) The scientist-practitioner connection: Myth or reality? A response to Perrez. *New Ideas in Psychology*, 7, 2: 147–154.

Keller, E. F. (1985) *Reflections on Gender and Science*. London: Yale University Press.

Kitzinger, C. (1990a) The rhetoric of pseudo-science. In: Parker, I. and Shotter, J. (eds), *Deconstructing Social psychology*. London: Routledge, 61–75.

Kitzinger, C. (1990b) Heterosexism in psychology. *The Psychologist*, 3, 9: 391–392.

Knorr-Cetina, K. D. (1981) *The Manufacture of Knowledge: an essay on the constructivist and contextual nature of science*. Oxford: Pergamon Press.

Kovel, J. (1982) The American mental health industry. In Ingleby, D. (ed.), *Critical Psychiatry*. Harmondsworth: Penguin, 72–102.

Kreitman, N. (1962) Psychiatric orientation among psychiatrists. *British Journal of Medical Psychology*, 46: 75–81.

Kuhn, T. S. (1962) *The Structure of Scientific Revolutions*. Chicago: University of Chicago Press.

Laing, R. D. (1960) *The Divided Self: A Study of Sanity and Madness*. London: Tavistock.

Laing, R. D. (1967) *The Politics of Experience*. Harmondsworth: Penguin.

Latour, B. and Woolgar, S. (1979) *Laboratory Life: The construction of scientific facts*. New Jersey: Princeton University Press.

Lindsay, G. (1990) Assessment in the training of educational psychologists. *Educational and Child Psychology*, 7, 3: 74–81.

McGovern, T. V. (1988) Teaching the ethical principles of psychology. *Teaching of Psychology*, Feb., 15, 1: 22–26.

Martens, B. and Keller, H. (1987) Training school psychologists in the scientific tradition. *School Psychological Review*, 16, 3: 329–337.

MAS: Management Advisory Service to the NHS (1989) *Review of Clinical Psychology Services*.

Mechanic, D. (1969) *Mental Health and Social Policy*. Englewood Cliffs: Prentice-Hall.

Meehl, P. E. (1971) A scientific, scholarly, non-research doctorate for clinical practitioners. In R.R. Holt (ed.), *New Horizons for Psychotherapy: Autonomy as a Profession*. New York: International University Press, 37–81.

Namenwirth, M. (1988) Science seen through a feminist prism. In Blier, R. (ed.), *Feminist Approaches to Science*. New York: Pergamon Press, 18–41.

O'Donohue, W. (1989) The (even) bolder model: The clinical psychologist as metaphysician-scientist-practitioner. *American Psychologist*, 44, 12: 1,460–1,468.

Overholser, J. C. (1989) Accurate diagnosis of personality disorders: Some critical factors. *Journal of Contemporary Psychotherapy*, 19, 1: 5–23.

Perry, N. W. (1987) The new boulder model: Critical element. *Clinical Psychologist*, 40, 1: 9–11.

Pilgrim, D. (1991) Psychotherapy and social blinkers. *The Psychologist*, 4, 2, 52–55.

Pilgrim, D. and Treacher, A. (1992) *Clinical Psychology Observed*. London: Routledge.

Plumb, A. (1990) The challenge of self advocacy. Paper presented at Women in Psychology Conference, Birmingham, 1990.

Prilleltensky, I. (1989) Psychology and the status quo. *American Psychologist*, May, 44: 795–802.

Rickard, H. C. and Clements, C. B. (1985) Compared to what? A frank discussion of the boulder model. *Professional Psychology Research and Practice*, Aug., 16, 4: 472–473.

Rorty, R. (1979) *Philosophy and the Mirror of Nature*. Princeton, N.J.: Princeton University Press.

Rose, H. and Rose, S. (1969) *Science and Society*. London: Allen Lane.

Scull, A. T. (1979) *Museums of Madness: The Social Organization of Industry in Nineteenth-Century England*. London: Allen Lane.

Sedgewick, P. (1987) *Psychopolitics*. London: Pluto Press.

Sherif, C. (1987) Bias in psychology. In S. Harding (ed.), *Feminism and Methodology: Social Science Issues*. Bloomington: Indiana University Press.

Spense, J. T. (1985) Achievement American style. *American Psychologist*, 40, 1,285–1,295.

Squire, C. (1989) *Significant Differences: Feminism in Psychology*. London: Routledge.

Steinhelber, J. and Gaynor, J. (1981) Attitudes, satisfaction, and training recommendations of former clinical psychology interns: 1968 and 1977. *Professional Psychology*, 12: 253–260.

Szasz, T. (1961) *The Myth of Mental Illness: Foundations of a Theory of Personal Conduct*. London: Secker.

Stone, G. C. (1983) Proceedings of the National Working Conference on Education and Training in Health Psychology. *Health Psychology*, 2, 5 (Suppl.): 153.

Tizard, B. (1990) Research and policy: Is there a link? *The Psychologist*, Oct., 3, 10: 435–440.

Ussher, J. M. (1989) *The Psychology of the Female Body*. London: Routledge.

Ussher, J. M. (1990) Sexism in psychology. *The Psychologist*, 3, 9: 388–390.

Ussher, J. M. (1991) *Women's Madness: Misogyny or Mental Illness?* London: Harvester Wheatsheaf.

Ussher, J. M. (1992a) Reproductive rhetoric and the blaming of the body. In Nicolson, P. and Ussher, J. M. (eds), *The Psychology of Women's Health and Health Care*. London: Macmillan.

Ussher, J. M. (1992b) The demise of dissent and the rise of cognition in menstrual cycle research. In Richardson, J. (ed.), *Cognition and the Menstrual Cycle*. New York: Lawrence Erlbaum.

Vandereycken, W. (1987) The constructive family approach to eating disorders: Critical remarks on the use of family therapy in anorexia nervosa and bulimia. *International Journal of Eating Disorders*, Jul., 6, 4: 455–467.

Weinreich-Haste, H. (1986) Brother Sun, Sister Moon: Does rationality overcome a dualistic world view. In Harding, J. (ed.), *Perspectives on Gender and Science*. Sussex: the Falmer Press.

Weisstein, N. (1973) Psychology constructs the female: or the fantasy life of the male psychologist. In Brown, P. (ed.) *Radical Psychology*. London: Tavistock.

Chapter 3

From social abuse to social action
A neighbourhood psychotherapy and social action project for women

Sue Holland

My chapter will take as its focus the book's editorial statement that 'clinical psychologists are in a position to address the criticism of gender bias in mental health practice through providing innovative services which do not prejudice individual client groups' (Ussher and Nicolson 1990). Taking this further I will demonstrate that we are also in a position to address gender bias through providing innovative services which actively and positively discriminate in favour of individual client groups, for example working-class, black and minority women.

Rather than launch at this stage into a scan of the relevant but small literature, I will present a 'practitioner's notebook' account of a ten-year project in primary and secondary prevention, and protection, for women's mental health.

In setting up this programme of mental health intervention a specific policy decision was made to target a particularly under-privileged group whose psychological health and vulnerability to mental breakdown was compounded by social and economic oppression, namely, women, many of them lone parents, living on a large multi-ethnic urban council housing estate in West London.

As a professional this project has necessitated my working at all levels of the community care system from intrapsychic one-to-one psychotherapy to socio-political organising, from personal client to committee, and all the steps between. Indeed the underpinning philosophy of the project is to see the whole programme of intervention as a dynamic movement from private symptom to public action which engages both the professional and the client/patient alike (Holland 1991).

As a woman it has involved my 'living on the patch' for all of these years, and trying to balance my domestic life as a private person, wife and mother, with my role of neighbourhood (community) clinical psychologist and psychotherapist. This has been both exhilarating and stressful, requiring greater tolerance and support from my family and empathy and self-control from my clients. Somehow possession of my home address and phone number has more often been a comforter for my clients than a licence to persecute me with their unreasonable demands. Consequently, midnight emergencies have always been genuine and far more satisfactory as a solution than picking them up in the casualty department the next day.

SETTING UP THE PROJECT

The project started in 1980. By then I had not only lived in the neighbourhood for ten years – so knowing its people for their strengths as well as in their problems – but I also had ten years' experience as a clinical psychologist and community mental health 'innovator' (Holland 1979). These credentials opened the door for me into Hammersmith and Fulham Social Services Department which at the time was keen to innovate and put women's mental health on the agenda for funding. With my written proposal for action on mental illness primary prevention, Inner Area 'Urban Aid' funding was secured from the Department of the Environment.

After a three-year trial run the project had successfully achieved its three goals: providing focal psychotherapy and counselling; educational mental health promotion; and the setting up of a mutual help network of ex-clients. It was then taken into the mainstream social services funding. By this time the whole political atmosphere within the borough was becoming more favourable. Officers and councillors could be found who were strong allies in favour of promoting the mental health of women. Our own ward councillor and our local MP (both male) lobbied and negotiated effectively for the project. This process was strengthened by the project's advisory/steering group which was made up of representatives from many school, church and community organisations on the estate.

A succession of women directors and line managers within the social services hierarchy made sure that the project was seen as a precious asset to the council's services. (Remember this is the borough that prides itself on 'serving the community'.) However, despite this formal commitment the project has not been expanded beyond our small team of myself, one social worker job-sharing and a half-time administrator. It continues to be under-resourced and overworked, and kept very much on the outer fringes of the social work system. This of course has its advantages for those of our clients who mistrust 'The Welfare' and who find us more approachable in our anonymous flat on the estate.

By the mid-1980s there was a proactively feminist influence within the council infrastructure in the form of a Women's Committee. Externally, the then Greater London Council Women's Committee made it easier for our now actively campaigning ex-client group to get funds for their first attempt at setting up their own neighbourhood counselling and advocacy service: Women's Action for Mental Health (WAMH). This leap forward was aided by financial advice and feminist solidarity from Community Health Council allies outside the borough (Langridge 1986).

After the GLC was crushed, the council, through the London Residual Body, took over the funding of WAMH. This has continued up to the time of writing despite devastating cuts in other voluntary bodies (this is beginning to feel like a letter from the trenches). Knowing how to 'access' funding opportunities when they occur, together with the energy and political know-how to recruit allies, from neighbourhood to national level, is crucial to any would-be manager of a community mental health project.

But a note of caution for apprentices. Career-wise there has been limited advancement for me in such an unorthodox and pioneering set-up. Whilst other clinical psychologists advance their careers by writing articles in the professional journals about the need for a radical therapeutic psychology I find that actually doing it leaves little time to write or meet editors' deadlines (Holland 1988)!

SO WHAT IS SOCIAL ACTION PSYCHOTHERAPY?

The essence of this therapeutic model is that women who are experiencing psychological distress such as depression, and who usually just present themselves in their GP's surgery as suffering from 'nerves', are offered a ten-week contract for once-a-week focal psychotherapy. This will concentrate on particular key issues agreed between client and therapist as central to her problems. Part of the therapist's intervention will be to make links with the client's past, present and hopes for the future. Towards the end of the contract the situation is reviewed with the client and may be renewed for a further ten weeks if necessary.

For a minority of clients who may have had particularly disabling personal histories, therapy is continued over one or even two years. For example, a young incest survivor who is in the early stages of pregnancy may need to be 'held' in therapy through to the birth and early stages of mothering. But in most cases the weekly sessions are concluded after appropriate working through and acknowledgement of dependency and separation issues aroused by the ending of weekly sessions. In all cases the client is told that she may, if she wants to, contact the therapist again in the future. Follow-up or morale boosting sessions are given as appropriate. Hopefully the client will have internalised a 'good enough' (Winnicott 1965) self-and-therapist dyad with which to question and counsel herself.

Many clients have returned over the years for 'emergency' sessions as new problems or situations occurred. Sometimes they simply want confirmation that they are doing a good job of surviving 'out there'. This continuity over time, and ease of self-referral, has been an important feature of the project's neighbourhood character. Unlike most out-patient clinics, clients have been able to see the therapist over a decade. The therapy sessions aim to explore the meaning of the women's symptoms which frequently mask grief, oppression, rage and loss. This moves her on from experiencing herself as a machine/patient who has broken down, into a more knowing sense of herself and her personal histories. Usually, towards the end of this one-to-one work the woman is expressing a greater social interest in the world around her.

It is at this point that contact with our support network of women neighbourhood counsellors (Women's Action for Mental Health) may be most appropriate. This organisation of ex-clients has itself grown out of some of the earlier group work initiated by the project, which took the form of 'conscientization' (Freire 1970) or awareness-raising, around social issues and their relation to women's mental health (Holland 1988).

By way of this networking with other women helpers on the estate, each woman can discover that she is not uniquely mad, bad or alone in her private symptoms but shares common suffering and collective strengths with other women. This 'sistering' experience may release the expression of previously unrecognised desires which can now be voiced as shared desires and demands.

For example, some of the women moved away from abuse and violent sexual relationships to warmer, more satisfying ones, which in some cases were lesbian. This in turn involved them in new, painful struggles against prejudice and rejection. Similarly, the Afro-Caribbean women's history group which explored their personal stories of painful childhood separations, found they had a collective strength and resourcefulness in struggling with the racism they faced in their lives, at work, in clinics and in their children's schools (Holland 1990).

Finding this more social sense of herself reveals that demands cannot be met without confronting the social systems and structures which both meet and limit people's needs and choices, the institutionalised structures of class, gender and race being the most oppressive and constricting. It is also the most difficult stage in any programme of neighbourhood mental health.

The women reached this stage when they articulated their desire to run their own neighbourhood support, advocacy and counselling service (Women's Action for Mental Health) from a flat on the estate. Their demands were met after a difficult campaign which included their illegal occupation of the flat (Caldwell 1984). The therapeutic effect on the women involved was to enhance their self-esteem and empower them collectively. They had decided how resources on the estate should be allocated. This movement is expressed clearly and simply in our 'Four Steps' leaflet, Women and Depression (see accompanying box).

THE STEPS IN SOCIAL ACTION PSYCHOTHERAPY

Step one

PATIENTS ON PILLS Women sometimes feel so bad about themselves that they can't face their everyday life. We go to the doctor complaining of 'nerves' and get given pills to calm us down (tranquillisers) or cheer us up (anti-depressants). We then see ourselves as having a 'medical' problem. Sometimes the doctor will send us to see a psychiatrist who continues the regime of, usually stronger, mood changing drugs. We now see ourselves as a 'psychiatric case', passively expecting to be cured.

Step two

PERSON-TO-PERSON PSYCHOTHERAPY White City Mental Health Project offers women an alternative to pills. Talking to a woman therapist helps us to explore the meanings of our depression and so reveals our buried feelings, such as anger and guilt. We can then take charge of all our painful 'ghosts' from the past.

Step three

TALKING IN GROUPS Now, freed from our personal ghosts, we can get together in groups and discover that we share a common history (HER-STORY) of abuse, misuse and exploitation of ourselves as infants, as girls, as women, as working-class women, as black women . . . Now we can see, and say together, what we really want!

Step four

TAKING ACTION Having changed ourselves from patient to person, from a state of depression to self and self-other awareness, we can now use our collective voice to demand changes outside in our community . . . in our schools, our health centres, our community centres, our housing, transport, and in anything else that affects our lives.

Not all the women clients will traverse all three modes of self and social experience, as many will be content enough with the relief from symptoms and the freedom to get on with their personal lives which the individual therapy gives them. A minority will prefer to remain in the limited space of the patient self-identity and will prefer to 'keep on taking the tablets'. These card-carrying 'patients' will sometimes return years later for another go at psychotherapy when they reach new crisis points in their lives. They may then astonish us all with their radical change, suggesting that it is not so much the patient who is chronic but the psychiatric treatment.

By using this model of therapeutic intervention, depressed women can move through a series of spaces, psychic, social and political. 'Finding a space for herself' thus becomes a series of options, each more socially connected than the last, in a progression from private symptom to public action.

A very similar model of therapy has recently been proposed by clinical psychologists working in the NHS community mental health structures. For example, David Smail's (1990, 1991) 'environmentalist psychology'.

This has proved to be a particularly effective method of therapy with women whose depression stems from childhood abuse and who now experience the added social abuse of economic exploitation, racism and sexism, etc. Because this method of social action psychotherapy brings together a combination of techniques drawn from sociological, psychological and therapeutic sources, it requires a transdisciplinary approach by both its practitioners and its clients. It will not be of much comfort or interest to the clinical psychologists who wish to carve out an exclusive territory for our

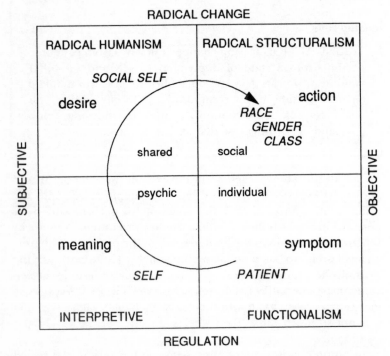

Figure 3.1   Adapted from Burrell and Morgan, 1979 and Whittington and Holland, 1985

discipline. Ownership of community mental health by clinical psychologists is no more welcome than medico-psychiatric domination. However, clinical psychologists training has given us a head start in using and moving flexibly around, if we choose to, the different paradigms of mechanistic, interpretive, humanistic and socio-structural interventions in human micro and macro systems from individual to community, from the personal to the political.

In addition, some specialist training is required to apply successfully this particular model of social action psychotherapy. I have described this more fully elsewhere (Holland 1991). Essentially it is a reflexive model of practice which assumes that what is so for the client is so for the practitioner, and both are required to change as they move through the different paradigm spaces. For example, this 'basic assumption' explains why some of my clients are now amongst my closest colleagues, a fact which other colleagues working within more formal service structures find 'unorthodox' or even – horror of horrors! – unethical.

The question of the psychological effect of injustice and inequality is not as popular an enquiry amongst clinical psychologists today as are the more glamorous fields of national disaster and post-traumatic stress disorder, and yet the cumulative effect of the daily disasters of everyday living for those who are disadvantaged, is catastrophic. Here it is not only loss of the object/person which relates to depression but the sense of having been robbed, or expropriated.

Feelings of injustice have profound psychological effects but are rarely addressed by psychologists. In contrast, some family therapists are taking a lead, and one project in New Zealand describes itself as engaged in 'Just Therapy' – a deliberate attempt to take into account the gender, cultural, social and economic context of the persons seeking help.

> Therapists have a responsibility to find appropriate ways of addressing these issues, and developing approaches that are centrally concerned with the forgotten issues of fairness and equity. Such therapy reflects themes of liberation that lead to self-determining outcomes of resolution and hope.
>
> (Waldegrave 1990)

Mental health workers of whatever professional background who choose to take a proactive role in addressing the psychological costs of inequality and injustice, whether of gender, race, class, age or disability, cannot assume that merely to be 'in the community' is in itself socially progressive. The present trends towards 'hospitalising the community' via Community Mental Health Centres and social services specialist mental health teams, using new means but old functionalist models, is a backward step in comparison with those who argue that the hospital must first be deinstitutionalised, as in the Italian democratic psychiatry movement, before an unwilling community is ready to receive ex-psychiatric patients (Tudor 1991).

But whether it is rural psychiatric hospital wards or urban housing estates, the question for clinical psychologists and other 'psy' workers is 'Do we help to sedate or to activate?' It is a fact that psychiatric hospital closure is on the agenda (however long delayed) and that much of the 'caring in the community' this requires will fall exploitatively on women. The White City Project demonstrates a way in which women users of mental health services can be helped to set up their own services which promote the idea of mental health as a community responsibility with its own social and financial rewards, whilst at the same time retaining direct access to a back-up team of professionals for advice and support. Clinical psychologists need not fear that this model will work us out of a job, but it does radically change the modes of application and the professional relationships within it.

REFERENCES

Burrell, G. and Morgan, G. (1979) *Sociological Paradigms and Organisational Analysis*. London: Heinemann.

Caldwell, S. (1984) Guardian Women *Guardian*, 25 May 1984: 12.

Freire, P. (1970) *Cultural Action for Freedom*. Harmondsworth: Penguin.

Holland, S. (1979) The development of an action and counselling service in a deprived urban area. In Meacher, M. (ed.), *New Methods of Mental Health Care*. Oxford: Pergamon, 95–106.

Holland, S. (1988) Defining and experimenting with prevention In Ramon, S. and Giannichedda, M. G. (eds), *Psychiatry in Transition: The British and Italian Experiences*. London: Pluto.

Holland, S. (1989) Women and community mental health – twenty years on. *Clinical Psychology Forum*, 22: 35–37.

Holland, S. (1990) Psychotherapy, oppression and social action: gender, race, and class in black women's depression. In Perelberg, R. J. and Miller, A. C. (eds), *Gender and Power in Families*. London: Routledge.

Holland, S. (1991) From private symptom to public action. *Psychology and Feminism*, 1, 1: 58–62.

Langridge, C. (1986) Implementation networks: the creation of a special housing needs policy. Master of Public Policy Thesis, School of Advanced Urban Studies, University of Bristol.

Smail, D. (1990) Design for a post-behaviourist clinical psychology. *Clinical Psychology Forum*, 28 August.

Smail, D. (1991) Towards a radical environmentalist psychology. *The Psychologist: Bulletin of the British Psychological Society*, 2: 61–65.

Tudor, K. (1991) One step back, two steps forward: community care and mental health. *Critical Social Policy*. 30, 3: 5–22.

Ussher, J. and Nicolson, P. (1990) Statement of editorial aims for the present issue.

Waldegrave, C. (1990) Just therapy. *Dulwich Centre Newsletter*, 1: 1–47 (Special Issue).

Whittington, C. and Holland, R. (1985) A framework for theory in social work. *Issues in Social Work Education*, 5, 1: 25–50.

Winnicott, D. W. (1965) *The Maturational Processes and the Facilitating Environment*. London: Hogarth.

Chapter 4

Consultation
A model for inter-agency work

Anne Peake

INTRODUCTION

This chapter looks at one example of a consultation model and discusses the specific contributions of psychology with a gender perspective. Consultation is defined as 'to ask advice of, to look up for information or advice, to discuss, to consider, to take measures for the advantage of, to consider jointly' (*Oxford English Dictionary*). Most professionals include consultation work as part of their role; consulting with colleagues, clients and professionals in other agencies. For some workers in specific fields of work, such as child sexual abuse, the need to consult with other agencies is now part of good practice and in fact laid down by Government guidelines, *Working Together*, (DES 1988). What is most noticeable is that the parameters of effective consultation are often not defined and the danger is that consultation will become a meaningless process which undermines the work of professionals in the field. The consultation model discussed in this chapter was developed to establish clear effective consultation.

The work demonstates two issues. Firstly, that the parameters of consultation need to be established not only for each piece of consultation work, but also for the relationship of the consultation session to the roles of professionals involved. Secondly, the centrality of gender as an issue in working in the field of sexual abuse, and as female consultants in a multi-disciplinary setting.

A Child Sexual Abuse Consultation Service (CSACS) was set up in the London Borough of Haringey in July 1986. It was based on an idea of Gerrilyn Smith, Principal Clinical Psychologist. The Service was developed and run by three women psychologists committed to a feminist understanding of the nature of child sexual abuse. It has developed into a reliable resource within the Borough, open to any professional with a concern about individual cases and/or issues related to work in the area of child sexual abuse (Smith *et al.* 1986). This chapter will provide an analysis of this one particular consultation service – but the model of practice employed could be used in many other areas of clinical psychology.

THE PARAMETERS OF CONSULTATION

Consultation as a model of work encapsulated a style of work which both fitted our feminist theoretical view of sexual abuse, and suited the demands of the work, which involves high levels of staff anxiety, confusion about roles and conflicting loyalties. As the Service has developed we have become increasingly aware of the need to develop and refine the parameters of the model of consultation. It has become clear that the parameters need to be based on specialist knowledge of the field, an awareness/commitment to local procedures, an understanding of the roles of different professionals in this work and clear expectations of the consultation process. The following parameters were established:

A regular reliable consultation service to meet professional need

Child sexual abuse is unique as a problem for professionals in terms of the extent to which it arouses professional denial, confusion and panic. It has to be pointed out that most professionals who are involved in child protection work received little or no specific preparation for such work in their initial training and that accessible practice-based in-service courses are few. Considered in such a context of a lack of training to do such personally and professionally taxing work, the wonder is that there is not more professional anxiety. Bander, Fein and Bishop (1982) point out that there are barriers to effective professional work in this field. They suggest that these include the need for shared responsibility for case management and decision-making, the need to deal with different aspects of a case simultaneously (e.g. social/legal, etc.) without a clash of priorities, and the need to provide for staff anxieties in ways which reduce the barriers between professionals.

It so happens that in Haringey there were psychologists employed by Social Services who had different but extensive experience of dealing with cases of child sexual abuse. It became clear that all three workers were being approached separately by a variety of professionals both within Social Services and from other departments such as Health and Education for advice of cases and issues to do with child sexual abuse. What was clear was that the approaches were not always well timed, for example, one would be stopped en route to the car park after a case conference to discuss one family with a colleague also at the conference who wanted to discuss another case. With one's mind full of details of the conference and switching to deal with London traffic and a next appointment, we couldn't help but feel we were not able to give our full attention to the request. What also was happening was that phone calls would come through from workers after supervision or just before a case conference when it was quite plain that their need for advice/ consultation was from their point of view pressing. Their sense of urgency and perhaps sense of lack of planning would be apparent in their persistence to reach one of us. We felt there were times when we were told only as much information before our advice was sought as would form a basis for confirming the workers own plan or lack of it, and that this was a poor basis for good consultation and improving practice.

This demand led to the development of a weekly period of time when we decided to make ourselves available to offer consultation in the work of child sexual abuse. One afternoon a week was set aside for workers to 'drop in' to discuss cases. The demand was such that we quickly needed to insist that workers telephoned to book a time, that they would be offered a maximum of one hour, and that no telephone consultations or consultations outside that time could be accepted.

The service set clear boundaries on the demands made on those offering the service

Being available to meet the need for consultation and support in the field of child sexual abuse could potentially be a recipe for our own professional demise! The cases are complex and emotionally draining, and the demand from one small London Borough so enormous that the protection of the workers running the service was clearly a necessary feature of the service. Carroll and White (1982) pointed out that the establishment of boundaries have a tremendous influence on the experience of burnout.

The service established very clear boundaries very early on in its development. These were as follows:

a) Consultations were only offered on one afternoon a week.
b) Workers had to telephone to book a time.
c) Each consultation was limited to one hour.
d) No telephone consultations were given.
e) Two workers would be in each consultation session.
f) Information brought to a session and the advice/suggestions made were written up with copies for all in the session.
g) Workers running the service met regularly to support each other and share issues which arose in particular consultations.

The above made it possible to keep some boundaries to the service. A session was always run by two workers and was organised in terms of one worker mainly running the consultation while the other worker kept a record of the work and acted as support. These two roles were rotated between the three workers.

Although the afternoons of the service were quickly full and demanding, the nature of the demands were contained by the boundaries we set and the support we offered each other. The resulting service was regular and reliable for users while being contained and an economic use of our time and skills. It thus enabled us to be quite clear and firm about our professional availability and priorities of work.

The service is run by Social Services but available to all professionals

The 1969 Children's and Young Person's Act and the 1989 Children Act which will replace it with regard to the law on child protection, both make the statutory duties of Social Services with regard to child protection quite unequivocal. The Children Act 1989 states that the welfare of children 'shall be the court's paramount consideration' and that there is a clear duty placed on a local authority where the authority has 'reasonable cause to suspect that a child who lives, or is found, in their area is suffering, or is likely to suffer significant harm ...' to 'make or cause to be made such enquiries as they consider necessary to enable them to decide whether they should take any action to safeguard or promote the child's welfare' (section 47.1). Given these statutory duties, it is important that any consultation service set up to support local authority child protection systems should be run by local authority workers aware of the procedures that bind colleagues' work.

The service was set up prior to the *Report of the Inquiry into Child Abuse in Cleveland 1987* (Department of Health and Social Security 1988). The fact that the service has always welcomed requests for consultation from colleagues in other departments and the voluntary agencies is very much in line with the recommendations of the report. These include a recognition that no single agency 'has the pre-eminent responsibility in the assessment of child abuse generally and child sexual abuse specifically', that special consideration needs to be given to working together, that prompt action in the best interests of the child should never be inhibited, and that practical issues need to be 'recognised and resolved at local level in careful discussion between respective agencies'. While no claim is made that the service is an end in itself, it does make a contribution which is locally very significant to these recommendations for inter-agency cooperation made by the Cleveland Report.

The service is separate and different from supervision/ line-management

Of the professionals who use the service, social workers are a group who have clearly defined line-management and regular case supervision offered by senior social workers. The service is not intended to cut across any such existing system of responsibility and support. Once a case is allocated to a social worker the case work responsibility is his/hers and the line-manager's. In those instances, the service is there to be taken up when workers want more information about the nature of abuse, advice about options for case management, or access to resources for work with children and families. The suggestion that a worker use the service may well be made by the line-manager and/or a consultant session may include the view that options discussed are taken back to supervision sessions for discussion. There have been inevitably instances where workers have approached the service because they have either not been able to get supervision due to staff shortages or have not felt that the supervision they have received has been what they have needed. Seniors are welcome to attend sessions with the service and we have suggested at times that a second appointment is made, at which the senior could be present so there can be a fuller

discussion of options; or we have used the record of the consultation to communicate with a particular senior, or involved the
Borough's Child Abuse Consultant where there are serious issues
of case management/procedures which have to be resolved. Such
instances are rare but demonstrate the need for the service to be
separate and different from supervision but also be available and
accessible when there is an expressed need. The service was set up
to meet the needs of workers dealing with the difficulties of work
in the field of child sexual abuse. The service was intended
specifically to offer support when workers feel confused and
anxious. The view of those setting up the service was that it is
difficult for professionals to voice confusion and anxiety in supervision to line-managers when there was an expectation that they
could cope and when the worker might feel that failure to meet
such expectations could adversely affect their career prospects. So
it was felt that a resource separate and different from line-
management would meet a need.

It is important to point out that other professions, and the
service is open to all professionals (see Table 4.2 on page 89),
don't have the same system of supervision as do social workers. For
such workers, for example teachers, the service is a resource for
information, consultation and support which doesn't exist in their
daily practice.

**The service is separate from, but complementary to the local
Child Protection Procedure**

A substantial proportion of the cases discussed with the service are
either unallocated with Social Services or are not known to Social
Services (see Table 4.5 on page 94). Quite frequently the professional using the service is not employed by Social Services and is
unaware of the authority's guidelines and the resources that exist
(see Table 4.2 on page 89). Many of the cases relate to the
suspicion of abuse, and consultation is needed before decisions
can be made about investigation, case conferences and the
registration of the children (see Table 4.8 on page 96). So one of
the useful features of the service is that it provides professionals
with the opportunity to get information about the local guidelines
for the investigation of abuse, together with the space to talk
through the ramifications of these guidelines on a particular case.
Obviously it is essential that those running the service are

completely *au fait* with the guidelines and committed to their appli- cation. For this reason it is essential that Social Services employees are involved in the establishment of any such service, and this was the case for the Haringey service.

There is an additional consideration in thinking out the rela- tionship of such a service to local authority procedures for child protection. That is that the choice of those offering consultation should not be such that subsequent investigations could be felt to be influenced, or such that they could inhibit the uptake of the service. For this reason the service has been staffed by professionals who are not themselves involved in the statutory investigation and management of child abuse, and not involved in chairing subsequent case conferences. This way the separateness from the procedures can be demonstrated in a way which is helpful to professionals and families alike. This separateness has seemed to be an encouraging factor to some users of the service. It has not been uncommon for example to have a professional say that she/he is reluctant to report the suspicions of abuse to a local Social Services team either because of past experience of the consequences of so doing or because she/he had no clear picture of what would happen in response to their concern and feared either for the child or for their own professional practice. A most common fear is one expressed by teachers, that, having reported the suspicion of abuse, Social Services will not keep them informed of the progress of the investigation and that the relationship between the teacher and the child, and the school and the family, will be irreparably spoiled; often such sequelae do occur, but it has been quite clear that teachers have valued the opportunity to discuss their views of another agency and to hear the reasons why procedures are framed and followed through for the protection of children, and to be helped to understand and come to terms with the statutory duties of Social Services in terms of child protection.

The service should provide a regular reliable consultation but not foster dependence

From within weeks of the start of the service it was quite clear that it met a professional need. The uptake of the service (see Table 4.1 on page 88) has been consistently high. One difficulty did emerge, that some workers felt the need to use the service at every stage of the case, such that issues to do with case work supervision and responsibility were becoming less clear and the service could be said to be operating to foster dependence, and deskilling the worker. The opportunity to have readily accessible consultation was obviously being valued and the sense of being helpful, was found to be very reinforcing and motivating for the service providers. So the boundary of only allowing two consultations per case was set and was helpful for both users and providers of the service. There can be obvious examples where one would need to be flexible about such a boundary, for instance where a duty social worker uses the service to discuss a referred suspected case of abuse, and the options for management of the investigation. Once investigated, it may well be that the child is able to disclose abuse. Some time later, an allocated social worker and/or residential social worker may engage in work with the child or the family which may result in different demands being made of the service, even if the case is the same.

The service should be so linked into the main work of child protection that it can feed back to local authority systems to improve practice and laid down procedures

No procedures for child protection can deal with every case and eventuality. The most rewarding feature of the service has been the way in which its work with professionals has been a way of logging instances where 'exceptions prove the rule'. These instances have provided the impetus to feed back to the system, ideas of ways in which practice and procedures can be improved. This feedback loop is best illustrated by examples.

Ideas used in sessions for the service have been developed into authority-wide systems to support professionals in work with child sexual abuse. An example of this is the system of monitoring children in schools which was developed to help teachers deal with the suspicion of child sexual abuse (Peake 1989a).

Teachers are a group of professionals who are most likely to be dealing with the suspicion of abuse. They are the only professionals who are in regular contact with children about whom they may express concerns. They are in a unique position for monitoring suspicion, for three main reasons. Firstly, their initial training as teachers includes considerable work on child development; certainly compared to social workers, whose training reflects an extremely wide focus including family work, mental health, the elderly, legal matters. The training of teachers includes an in-depth study of child development which is a helpful basis for considering children whose presenting behaviour is a focus for professional concern. Secondly, teachers are the only professionals in regular virtual daily contact with the children about whom there may be concern. So the teachers are able to make detailed observations of the children, often in a variety of situations in interactions with peers and adults. Thirdly, and most importantly, there is no other professional group, except teachers/nursery workers, who have regular daily contact with a large number of children of a given age group. So as a professional group, they are able to place their observations of children about whom there is concern in a context of training in child develop-ment and practical regular experience of the normal range of children's behaviour. The need to advise teachers on dealing with the suspicion of child sexual abuse led to the development of monitoring guidelines for young children and for children in secondary schools, with a pre-school monitoring guide being planned currently.

There have been occasions when professionals booking sessions with the service have raised issues which had not been covered by the Borough's child protection guidelines. The fact that the service has had the active interest and support of the Child Protection Consultant has been an encouraging link, for workers in the service to feed back to the Consultant and the Area Child Protection Committee (ACPC) those cases where 'exceptions have proved the rule'. A memorable example of this was a consultation requested by two head teachers from an infant and adjourning junior school. They wanted to discuss a problem which had arisen in the playground where a seven-year-old boy was displaying sexualised behaviour and being joined in this by two ten-year-old girls. The consultation was a complex one, but one clear question which needed to be addressed was why were children of such different age groups coming together to do this? One could hypothesise that all had been abused and that their sexualised behaviour, as a sequence of the abuse drew them together. We felt that one strand of this was the possibility that they had all been abused by the same person and that this explained the otherwise unusual combination of ages and over-sexualised behaviour. This session led us to consider how adequate were the authority's guide-lines for dealing with children abused by sex rings/large numbers of children abused in an extra-familial setting by one abuser. The guidelines did not adequately deal with the need of the police to be able to investigate in ways likely to bring about convictions. This session led to a central working party on procedures for dealing with sex ring investigations and the setting up of a group of experienced social workers willing, and supported by their managers and teams, to be relocated and work together with the police to investigate a sex ring should one arise, and to support the children and their families. Another example of the way in which requests for consultations have led to working groups and developments in procedures has been the fact that the service has been used over the past year to discuss three separate instances of the abuse of learning/physically disabled young adults. Most, if not all local authority guidelines do not cover the abuse of young people over 19 years of age. Yet the special vulnerability of the disabled young person, whether over age or not, suggests that there should be greater local authority protection (Burns 1992). However the current problems inherent within using the laws to protect over age mentally disabled young adults from familial abuse presents serious obstacles to this. Factors such as the difficulty in securing a conviction given, the capacity of abusers to deny what they have done (Snowden 1980), and the 'competency rule' which currently operates in the criminal courts, all stand in the way of those who would extend protection in this area. There are also problems in using legislation to protect the young person. The law with regard to guardianship provides for the local authority to intervene where mentally disabled people are a risk to themselves or others in a family, but provides less sure ground for intervention where there is the suspicion of abuse, but where the abuser denies the abuse and the young person is unable to make an informed choice.

The existence of the consultation service run by professionals who themselves carry a case load of child sexual abuse clinical work, has led to the workers who run the service developing their own expertise in ways which have been useful for the authority. The main example of this has been that all the workers of the service have made and continued to make contributions to the programme of in-service training in the field of child sexual abuse for professionals in the Borough. Demands made on the service keeps the workers alert to the range of work problems and their possible solutions in ways which inform the plan for and content of training. In addition, the workers have been able to make suggestions of resources needed such as books, videos and inter-view room equipment.

THE WORK OF THE SERVICE

The workers running the service have kept records of the work of the service. As time has passed and the work of the service has developed, it has become clear that detailed statistics provide a useful measure of the work, but also reflect professional practice in the authority to those planning policy. This is the first detailed review of the service and, as such, discusses both our work and the statistics collected to date. The review has highlighted the gaps in the details collected and these will be discussed on page 100–04.

The uptake of the service

The service has been consistently used, with few sessions remaining vacant. The fact that the uptake of the service has been so consistent, particularly given the rapid turnover of staff in the Borough, indicates it fulfils a need for professionals to have access to consultation about cases of child sexual abuse. Some sessions are cancelled or those booking do not take up the sessions, the majority of these 'failed' sessions being due to social workers having to appear in court, or sickness of staff. Most failed consultations are explained and alter-native sessions arranged. Cancelled sessions where no explanation was given beforehand or at the time are followed up by those running the service by telephone or letter.

Table 4.1 Uptake of the service

July–Dec	1986	1987	1988	1989
Number of slots available	24	140	110	92
Number booked	8	117	101	85
Number vacant	16	23	9	7
Number of cancelled/did not arrive	0	13	14	18

The details of the uptake of the service are very limited and reflect only a quantitative view of the uptake. The figures would be more interesting if they were collected alongside some qualitative data on the uptake of the service (see Discussion section on page 101). However in terms of gender, the figures provide a clear case for the need for an acknowledgement of the gender imbalances in both service users and providers, as well as in perpetrators of sexual abuse.

Who uses the service?

The Service is open to any professional working in the Borough of Haringey who has concern which relates to issues of child sexual abuse. Table 4.2 lists the professionals who could be expected to use the service.

Table 4.2 Who uses the service?

| | Total (July 1986–December 1989) | |
	Male	Female
Field Social Workers	37	157
Residential Social Worker	37	8
Child Guidance	2	8
Hospital Social Worker	–	–
NSPCC	–	9
Ed. Social Worker	7	6
Teachers/Heads	8	58
Welfare Assistants	–	1
Ed. Welfare Officers	3	7
Ed. Psychologists	–	6
School Nurses	–	–
School Doctors	–	–
General Practitioners	–	3
Hospital Doctors	–	–
Health Visitors	–	2
Nursery Officers	–	21
Juvenile Justice Team	–	–
Probation Officer	–	1
Court Welfare Officer	–	–
Others	2	28
Parents	–	1
Foster Parents	2	4
Total	98	320
Percentage	[23.45]	[76.55]

The main users of the service are social workers from a variety of settings, child guidance, NSPCC and education social workers (attached to secondary schools). Their work with families and statutory duties *vis-à-vis* child protection are such that the service needs to prioritise support and consultation for these workers. As noted earlier teachers/nursery workers are in a unique position, by virtue of their training in child development and their almost daily contact with children about whom there may be concerns, to deal with the suspicion of abuse. These workers make up the next largest group using the service. In fact sessions are often the most useful in making child protection plans when the social worker and child's class teacher come for a consultation together.

Little use is made of the service to date by health service professionals. It is interesting to hypothesise about why this is the case. It may well be that the service needs to be explained to those professionals working in health whose work would include cases of child abuse, and that increased publicity would encourage their use of the service. Certainly it has not been possible to date to 'tap into' a system for circularising health workers in the way it has been possible for social workers and teachers/nursery staff. This may well also relate to the fact that until autumn 1989 the local health department did not have a designated post of Child Protection Coordinator and so those running the service had no named person through whom to establish the service as a resource for health professionals. Subsequent service statistics may well reveal that such a post is pivotal to improving inter-departmental links. It may also be that workers in health department settings are more accustomed to working with their own hierarchies and have less experience of co-work between agencies. Guidelines from the Department of Health following the Cleveland Report (1988) have stressed the need for joint working and so the service may well be more used by health workers locally in the future.

The most remarkable feature of the figures of the professional groups who use the service is the fact that the major users of the service are female professionals. This holds for every group, every year, with the small exception of one year of use by education social workers. In fact these figures are almost entirely made up of the use of several sessions by one particular male worker. Other male workers in that group did not subsequently use the service, and when he left to work elsewhere the figures for that group of workers then reflected the preponderance of female workers using the service shown by all other professional groups each year and overall. The ratio of 4:1, female:male professional use of the service can be explained in different ways. Firstly, it may well be that the fact that the service has been run by female professionals encourages other female professionals to use the service and has some kind of discouraging effect on male professionals. Those who work with cases of child sexual abuse are all too aware of the strong feelings aroused by the work. It could be that women feel more comfortable discussing these with another woman. Secondly, due to the work of the women's movement, women have a history of getting together to discuss sexual violence, as evidenced by the Rape Crisis Centres and self-help Incest Survivors' Groups (London Rape Crisis Centre 1984). This 'history' of sharing may well be providing a facilitating context for female professionals to use the service. Thirdly, it has been suggested that the style of work of women is essentially different from that of men, in that they display more cooperation and a willingness to listen and share decision-making. It may well be that the model of consultation offered by the service is more acceptable to female than to male workers, or fourthly, that male workers devalue services which are organised by women (see Nicolson, Chapter 1 of this volume).

Ages and gender of the children discussed

The age at which children are assaulted is variously estimated depending on the way statistics are collected. The Mrazek, Lynch and Bentovin study (1981) of cases reported to professionals gives the figures in Table 4.3.

Table 4.3 Age and sex of last case seen by professionals

	Girls	*Boys*
0–5 years	12%	–
5–10 years	19%	6%
11–15 years	50%	7%
Not given	3%	3%

Source: Mrazek *et al.* 1981

This study suggests the majority of children who are assaulted are over the age of 11 years and are girls. Recent detailed clinical work suggests the picture may be different from this. Certainly the average age of the children about whom there was concern of the suspicion of sexual abuse in Cleveland was 6.9 years (Campbell 1988). This figure is much closer to the figures of the service, where approximately 60 per cent of the children about whom there is concern are under 10 years. This has implications for resources in terms of the need to prioritise work on prevention with younger children. Of the children discussed by the service, 20 per cent were pre-school. So much more needs to be done in nurseries and with families to protect these younger children, and to train staff in daily contact with the children to be aware of the vulnerability of children of this age group and the warning signs that they may show which would indicate they could be subjected to abuse.

Table 4.4 Ages/gender of children discussed

| | July 1986–December 1989 | |
	Numbers	%
Females under 5 yrs	38	15.64
Males under 5 yrs	9	3.70
Sub-Total	47	19.34
Females 5–10 yrs	67	27.57
Males 5–10 yrs	33	13.58
Sub-Total	100	41.15
Females 10–16 yrs	63	25.93
Males 10–16 yrs	11	4.53
Sub-Total	74	30.45
Females 16+ yrs	20	8.23
Males 16+ yrs	2	0.82
Sub-Total	22	9.05
Total Children	243	100

The Mrazek, Lynch and Bentovim study (1981) suggested a ratio of 85:15, girls to boys, in terms of known cases of child sexual abuse. The confidential survey of the prevalence of child sexual abuse conducted by MORI (Baker and Duncan 1985) suggests that a ratio of 60:40, girls to boys, is more likely to reflect the reality of the experience of abuse. It has been suggested that the sexual abuse of boys is under-reported. Issues underpinning the under reporting may well include attitudes towards male sexuality, boys having more freedom and thus more to lose if parents were to view them as equally at risk as girls, the implications of the stigma of abuse for the boys, boys' view of their sexuality, the effect of perceived agency roles on levels of reporting, and the power of the paedophile lobby (Peake 1989b). In the work of the service the ratio of 3:2 (Baker and Duncan 1985) is only featured in the age group 5–10 years. This may be because this age range attends school daily and has one teacher all day every day, and so is the age range where concerns about children, both boys and girls, are more likely to be noted. Thus more work needs to be done in the area of staff training to make staff aware of the levels of abuse of pre-school boys. In addition, the school context for children over 11 years with several changes of subject teachers each day, coupled with the developmental pressures on adolescent boys, are such that it is not surprising that the figures relating to concerns about boys are so low. The pressing issue is how to raise professional awareness of the abuse of boys and create a school/community context in which boys are more able to disclose abuse.

Resource implications

Only a small proportion, 15 per cent, of the concerns about children discussed with the service are not known to Social Services. Most frequently these are concerns raised by teachers and nursery workers which they want to discuss, particularly issues to do with whether they should contact Social Services and also asking what will Social Services do. Teachers are often concerned about how to deal with information which may have been given to them in confidence and they often fear that child abuse investigations will 'spoil' a relationship between the school and the family about whom there are concerns. The service provides a forum to talk out these issues and promote inter-agency cooperation.

Table 4.5 Resource implications

	July 1986–Dec. 1989 Numbers	%
Allocated cases	91	54.82
Unallocated	51	30.72
Not known to Social Services	24	14.46
Total	166	100

What is a matter for local authority resources is that a substantial proportion of those concerns known to Social Services are unallocated social work cases. In many instances, the approach to the service is made by a duty social worker as part of the decision-making process about whether the case should be allocated. The service has no figures indicating how many of these cases which it is felt should have an allocated worker do in fact get one. This could be included in a feedback exercise on the uptake of the service aimed at collecting more than simply quantitative data (see Discussion on page 101). The most worrying sessions are those where professionals approach the service primarily because the case is unallocated and unlikely to be so, because of staff shortages. The problems of staff recruitment are particularly acute in the London Boroughs. While there are not enough staff to deal with child abuse concerns, there will continue to tragedies such as Kimberley Carlile, and the scope for social workers to be involved in a preventative way with families as envisaged in the framing of 'Family Assistance Orders' (The Children Act 1989) will remain limited.

Child Protection Register

One abiding impression from the work of the service is that professionals, even allocated social workers, often have to check the precise details if a child(ren)'s names are on the Register, i.e. whether the details are 'at risk of' or 'actual', and the nature of the concerns, physical, sexual, emotional abuse or neglect. Teachers are, more often than not, not aware of these details and some inter-agency misunderstandings are due to this. Time spent in staff training and improving the proforma for record keeping could do much to clarify the need for detailed information available to those professionals with a need to know. Approximately 25 per cent of children discussed have their names on the Child Protection Register.

Table 4.6 Child Protection Register

	July 1986–Dec. 1989 Numbers	%
On the Register	36	23.38
Not on the Register	104	67.53
Not applicable	14	9.09
Total	154	100

The largest proportion of the children discussed are not on the Register, this is because the service is separate from, but complementary to, the local Child Protection Procedures (see page 83). This preponderance of children not on the Register should be a feature of the service. Often by the time when a decision has been made to register children, the case is allocated, the investigation complete and the plan of work has been discussed and decided, there is less need for consultation; where there is need for ongoing case discussions this can be adequately dealt with in regular case supervision by senior social workers (see page 82).

Placement situation for children

The overwhelming majority of the children discussed live at home. Sessions focusing on the suspicion of abuse (see Table 4.7) often feature discussions about the nature of information needed from parents/care givers and ways of involving non-abusing parents in protection plans for children.

Table 4.7 Placement situation for children

	July 1986–Dec. 1989 Numbers	%
Living in care	42	25.15
Living at home	122	73.05
Not applicable	3	1.80
Total	167	100

The concept of non-abusing parents and their involvement in the protection of their children is one which has been developed in Haringey. The Child Protection Guidelines include prioritising work with the non-abusing parent (invariably the mother, see Table 4.10) and criteria upon which to judge the capacity of the parent(s) to protect. A failure to distinguish between abusing and non-abusing parents in terms of the sequence of an investigation and assessment belies the reality of abuse, which is that more often than not one parent did not know of the abuse and initially will react with disbelief and anger. The social work task is to help the non-abusing parent understand these feelings and move to believe she can protect her own children. Prioritising this work requires a shift from family dysfunction models of child sexual abuse (Porter 1984), where the mother's role has been seen as central and often interpreted as collusive (Hooper 1989).

Nature of the concerns

The majority of the requests for a session with the service are prompted by a disclosure by a child (47 per cent) and the suspicion of abuse (28 per cent).

Anxiety about how best to use local procedures to protect children are the main features of professional concern, and thus the need for the service to be run by workers employed by Social Services and committed to the authority's procedures is essential.

Table 4.8 Nature of the concerns

	July 1986–Dec. 1989 Numbers	%
Disclosures	102	47.44
Disclosures with retraction	2	0.93
Suspicion	61	28.37
Lives with named abuser	19	8.84
Prevention work with children	8	3.72
Advice on treatment plans	10	4.65
Courses	5	2.33
Previous work	8	3.72
Total	215	100

Those using the service are asked at the beginning of a consultation why they approached the service. The table of the nature of concerns was compiled from their open-ended responses. It is important to note that this present compilation fails to make clear how many consultations touch on several concerns and to analyse the pattern of professionals' concerns. A more clear picture would be possible if categories for concerns were set up beforehand.

Abusers

For over half the consultations, the abuser is known but not a member of the same household as the child. This figure needs to be set with the fact that a high percentage of the children live at home (see Table 4.7) and that most are not on the Child Protection Register (see Table 4.6). The picture is one of a need for well-directed social work intervention which does not depend on statutory intervention.

Table 4.9 Abusers

	July 1986–Dec. 1989 Numbers	%
Living in the same household	23	14.47
Known but not the same household	81	50.94
Abusers not named	55	34.59
Total	159	100

Given the fact that many professionals use the service to discuss instances of the suspicion of abuse (see Table 4.8), it is not surprising that the figure of abusers not being named/known is so high (34 per cent). This does mean that work in the sessions needs to establish clearly based hypotheses about the risk to a child(ren) being discussed, which can be used in subsequent monitoring/investigation/assessment work.

These hypotheses need to be demonstrably clear and free from assumptions which would cloud the validity of the outcome of the work, which may at a later stage need to be presented to a court for civil or criminal proceedings. This is very difficult taxing work and the service needs feedback on how useful the sessions were for workers dealing with the suspicion of abuse.

The tie between the abusing adult and the child

The categories for the tie between the abusing adult and the children are many and, given the total number of named abusers, this means the number in each category are very small. However, some patterns do emerge. The overwhelming majority of the abusers are male: 95 per cent. This needs to be acknowledged in the theoretical model used to explain child sexual abuse, and reflected in the nature of the social work practice. The reasons for this gender imbalance are many. For example, Frosh (1988) suggests male socialisation with its features of fear of intimacy, the premium placed on force, the undervaluing of women and feminine attributes, and the splitting off of the sexual act from emotional and relationship contexts, explains the preponderance of male abusers. What is essential is that the social work team develops practice which recognises this gender difference in a way which provides children with effective protection. Ways this can be done include: reevaluating theories of sexual abuse where notions of gender are not analysed; debating the implications of the gender of the worker, i.e. the impact of male workers on help offered to abused children; the practicalities of staff allocation according to gender; encouraging more adult male survivors to speak about their experiences so that the notion of the cycle of male victim/ abuser can be challenged; and, most of all, a continued striving for equal opportunities which will ensure that the majority of positions of power and responsibility are not held by men – a fact which silences so many victims.

Another feature of the categories of abusers which demands an explanation and strategies for intervention is the proportion of abusers who are themselves children (23 per cent). The question needs to be asked from whom or from what do children learn to sexually assault other children and on what basis should there be intervention with the abusing child? Practice guidelines need to reflect the likelihood that the abusing children are themselves victims, acting out their victimisation in a confused and hurtful way. Haringey procedures lay down guidelines for having separate workers for the abusing child, whose needs are considered in a separate case conference, and whose name may also be placed on

Table 4.10 Tie between the abusing adult and the child

	July 1986–Dec. 1989 Numbers	%
ADULT FAMILY		
Father	35	29.66
Mother	2	1.69
Stepfather	9	7.63
Foster father	2	1.69
Adoptive father	–	–
Mum's boyfriend	8	6.78
Grandfather	7	5.93
Grandmother	1	0.85
Childminder's boyfriend	2	1.69
Uncle	6	5.08
Family friend	8	6.78
Residential social worker	1	0.85
CHILDREN		
Brother	10	8.47
Cousin	–	–
Male peer	15	12.71
Female peer	2	1.69
OTHER ADULTS		
Babysitter	–	–
Professional	3	2.54
Adult known to child	7	5.93
Stranger	–	–
Total	118	100

the register. There are issues about planning work with abusing children which need consideration before the grouping of children for treatment work can be undertaken (Peake 1989c). These include: the nature of the offending; the extent to which a history of abuse is known; the level of supervision needed; the extent to which treatment is seen as reducing recidivism; the way in which the juvenile justice system recorded and dealt with the offence; and the extent to which the abusing child's account of his/her behaviour matches the account of the assault by the victim. Certainly these figures of the proportion of children abusing other children suggest these issues are central to intervention with the abusing child.

DISCUSSION

The service has been running for 4.5 years and continues to date, and we feel that the consultation work has been all the more useful because the parameters were clear. It has reinforced our view of the contribution that clinical psychology has to make to establishing models of practice, including clear definitions, understanding roles, establishing expectations and analysing outcomes.

Yet our task has not always been aided by academic psychology, as the research into child sexual abuse offers little agreement and there is no shared definition of sexual abuse and no standard way to estimate the incidence of abuse. So different theoretical models remain largely untested. What is clear is that the issue of gender is remarkably absent from the main theoretical models; it has been left to feminists to look at gender as a starting point in considering why children get abused (MacLeod and Saraga 1988). Yet what every abused child knows is that abuse is about the abuse of power and the betrayal of trust and dependence, and that it is invariably men who do this to the powerless in our society – namely women and children (see Jan Burns' Chapter 5 in this volume). This abuse of power remains less apparent while the majority of positions of responsibility are held by men and the contributions and achievements of women are undervalued and denied (Miles 1988; Ussher 1991). The factors emerging from the work of the service in one London Borough point to the need for the concept of gender to be central to any theoretical explanation and policy regarding child sexual abuse. The service is run by women workers, the majority of the abuse is committed by men (95 per cent, Table 4.10), the majority of the children are girls (76 per cent, Table 4.4), and the professional service users are female (81 per cent, Table 4.2). We need to ask why do men do this, why are boys so silent about their experiences of abuse, what are the effects of sexual abuse on women and on men, and why do women constitute the major professionals who express concern by using a consultation service and by running self-help and survivors' groups?

The model also highlights practice issues for example: firstly, the figures of unallocated cases, 31 per cent, (Table 4.5), make a strong case for increased staff recruitment. The problems facing Social Services Departments in recruiting enough staff raise a range of issues such as staff pay, the need for professional support structures to boost morale and reduce turnover, and adequate funding of local authority service for those in need. This can be related to other services run by women, where issues of 'women's work' being devalued are pertinent (see Nicolson, Chapter 1 in this volume). Secondly, the young age at which some children are assaulted (Table 4.4) argues for an increased priority to be placed on prevention work with young children. This work would involve training staff in nursery settings and families to be sensitive to the warning signs of abuse in young children, funding prevention programmes in such settings, making more treatment resources available for children who are abused and adequate support for non-abusing parents, usually mothers to leave abusers and protect their children, as so many would want to do. Thirdly, if we do acknowledge the central place of gender issues in child sexual abuse then a variety of equal opportunities policy and practice tasks present themselves. These include the need to have a work-force which reflects the community in terms of gender, ethnicity and class; and is not dominated by white middle-class men in positions of power as so often is the case at present. There is a need also to question why our response to child sexual abuse does not empower more boys who are victims to speak out.

The data presented in this review has its limitations. First and foremost much of the record of the work of the service is quantitative. There is a real need to inform further with qualitative pictures of the work. For example, it would be useful to ask a sample of users of the service to provide feedback on the usefulness or otherwise of the sessions. Feedback could include asking what was helpful/not helpful about the sessions, asking workers about the resource implications of the advice given and the level to which these were resolved; for example, was the case later allocated? Could Section 1 money from Social Services' discretionary funds be used to support a protective parent? Did case-load weighting permit adequate professional time to do the work with a given case? Details of ethnicity, class and disability might inform the debate and theories about why child sexual abuse happens, as each contributes to an understanding of levels of vulnerability in children.

Thus gender is not the only issue which should be given a higher place on professional agendas. Myths, stereotypes and racism have surrounded child sexual abuse to the extent that the isolation and silence of black children have been largely ignored (Bogle 1988). In order to address this, details of the ethnicity of children discussed with this service were collected for the year 1990. Table 4.11 gives the details of the origins of the children.

Table 4.11 Ethnicity of the children discussed with the service (1990)

African	1
Asian	5
Caribbean	26
UK European	36
Other European	0
Irish	0
Greek Cypriot	0
Turkish Cypriot	4
Jewish	2
Travellers	2
Others	3
Mixed	9
Total	87

The proportions of the children in different ethnic groups reflect the mix of peoples in the borough. It has been suggested that different levels of identification of child sexual abuse in different ethnic groups, which are out of proportion to the mix of groups in a given community, reflect a lack of confidence in local child protection workers and perceived racism at both a personal and institutional level. Few Social Services departments have procedures which develop an anti-racist practice in child protection work and have the staff to represent and empower different ethnic groups.

Equally, class is an absent factor in much of the debate about service delivery, and especially protection work. One can only speculate without the information about differences in intervention or in the use of statutory powers and the treatment resources offered to families and children from different class groupings. Certainly while homelessness continues to be one great divide in our communities such that local authorities like Haringey have to make extensive use of bed and breakfast accommodation, there are likely to be distinct differences in service delivery across social classes.

Until recently little was written about the special vulnerability of disabled children and young people to sexual abuse. Details of the disability of children discussed with the service were collected for the year 1990 (Table 4.12).

Table 4.12 Disability groups of children discussed with the service (1990)

Severe learning difficulties	4
Moderate learning difficulties	7
Emotional/behavioural difficulties	0
Medical condition	3
Physical disability	0
No disability	63
Other	0
Total	77

In percentage terms these figures are quite high – more than those found in the general population, and thus they underline the very special vulnerability of disabled children. Often their disability such as an inability to speak or reduced mobility makes them more vulnerable, the lack of care and respect offered to many of the disabled means they can be viewed as less precious to the community than more able children, and the fact that so many are dependent on the care of others and perhaps in residential settings increases their vulnerability (Brown and Craft 1989).

What is clear from the work of this service is the usefulness of keeping even quite basic records of one's work and formally re-viewing these records at a given point in time. This review has done much to improve the record keeping of the service, particularly highlighting the need for qualitative data the inclusion of missing data, and the reorganisation of some data categories. It has shed light on policy and practice issues in work with child sexual abuse. It has also hopefully made a contribution to the debate about the need to include gender as central in our theoretical models and our work with children. The data contained in this chapter presents clear evidence that a consideration of gender issues should be a central part of all work in the area of child sex abuse. The consultation model is one way of working which allows us to acknowledge gender – but it can equally be central to other means.

REFERENCES

Baker, A. and Duncan, S. (1985) Child sexual abuse: a study of prevalence in Great Britain. *Journal of Child Abuse and Neglect*, 9: 457–467.

Bander, E., Fein, E. and Bishop, G. (1982) Child sexual abuse treatment: some barriers to programme operation. *Journal of Child Abuse and Neglect*, 6: 133–146.

Bogle, M. (1988) Brixton Black Women's Centre: organizing on child sexual abuse. In *Family Secrets: Child Sexual Abuse*. Special edition of *Feminist Review*.

Brown, H. and Craft, A. (1989) *Thinking the Unthinkable*. London: Family Planning Association.

Burns, J. (1992) Sexual problems with the mentally handicapped client. In Ussher, J. and Baker, C. (eds), *Psychological Perspectives on Sexual Problems: New Directions for Theory and Research*. London: Routledge.

Campbell, B. (1988) *Unofficial Secrets*. London: Virago.

Carroll, J. F. X. and White, W. L. (1982) Theory building: integrating individual and environmental factors with an ecological framework. In Paine, W.S. (ed.), *Job Stress and Burnout*. London: Sage.

Department of Health and Social Security (1988) *Child Protection: Guidance for Senior Nurses, Health Visitors, and Midwives*. London: HMSO.

Department of Health and Social Security (1988) *Report of the Inquiry into Child Abuse in Cleveland 1987*. London: HMSO.

DES (1988) *Working Together for the Protection of Children from Abuse*. Department of Education and Science, 4/88.

Frosh, S. (1988) No Man's Land?: The role of men working with sexually abused children. *British Journal of Guidance and Counselling*, 16, 1.

Hooper, C.A. (1989) Alternatives to collusion: the response of mothers to child sexual abuse in the family. In *Child Sexual Abuse*, British Psychological Society DECP Occasional Papers, vol. 6, number 1.

London Rape Crisis Centre (1984) *Sexual Violence: The Reality for Woman*. London: The Women's Press.

MacLeod, M. and Saraga, E. (1988) Challenging the orthodoxy: towards a feminist theory and practice. In *Family Secrets: Child Sexual Abuse*. Special edition of *Feminist Review*.

Miles, R. (1988) *The Women's History of the World*. London: Michael Joseph.

Mrazek, D. A., Lynch, M. and Bentovin, A. (1981) Recognition of child sexual abuse in the United Kingdom. In Mrazek P. B. and Kempe C. H. (eds), *Sexually Abused Children and their Families*. Oxford: Pergamon Press.

PGA (1989) Children's Act. Chapter 4, HMSO.

Peake, A. (1989a) An outline for monitoring young children in school. In Peake, A. and Rouf, K., *Working with Sexually Abused Children: A Resource Pack for Professionals*. London: Children's Society.

Peake, A. (1989b) Underreporting: the sexual abuse of boys. In Christopherson, J., Furness, T., O'Mahoney, B. and Peake, A., *Working with Sexually Abused Boys*. London: National Children's Bureau.

Peake, A. (1989c) Planning groupwork for boys. In Christopherson, J., Furniss, T., O'Mahoney, B. and Peake, A., *Sexually Abused Boys*. London: National Children's Bureau.

Porter, R. (ed.) (1984) *Child Sexual Abuse Within the Family*. London: CIBA Foundation, Tavistock.

Smith, G., Peake, A. and Mars, M. (1986) *Child Sexual Abuse Consultation Service*. Haringey Social Services.

Snowdon, R. (1980) Working with incest offenders: excuses, excuses, excuses. Aegis issue on Child Sexual Assault, 29, Autumn.

Ussher, J. M. (1991) *Women's madness – Misogyny or Mental Illness?* London: Harvester Wheatsheaf.

Chapter 5

Mad or just plain bad?

Gender and the work of forensic clinical psychologists

Jan Burns

INTRODUCTION

HUSBAND GETS FOUR YEARS FOR KILLING HIS WIFE

A husband who flew into a jealous rage when he saw his wife dancing and kissing other men in a nightclub was today beginning a four year prison sentence for manslaughter . . . Passing sentence judge — told Mr — his pleas had rightly been accepted, adding 'I approach this case on the basis you lost your self-control'.

The judge said Mr — had a record for violence starting in 1970 and ending in 1975 when he was jailed for one and a half years for unlawful wounding [it was later reported in the article that this was for slashing the face of his then girlfriend with a razor four times].

Because this happened a long time ago it gives me only limited concern', he said [the Judge]. But he added that by one single blow he had lost his three children for the foreseeable future and the wife he loved.

Mrs — had left her husband 17 times and been rehoused by the council four times after fearing for her safety after her husband discovered where she was.

Bradford Telegraph and Argus, Tuesday 23 November 1990

In today's society, it can be argued that the position of women has commonly been that of outside the 'norm', in other words 'deviant', with men constituting the central position of 'normality' (Henley 1985). Other more socially constructed groups, by their mere definitions, also hold deviant positions within, or more accurately on the outside of society. The two other groups to be talked about here are the 'psychiatric patient' and the 'offender'. Such positions are not only 'deviant' from how society is, or more likely how it would like to see itself, but they are viewed as deleterious and threatening to society as a whole. In an effort to further distance and understand such deviations, an explanation is frequently offered in terms of the simplistic, dichotomous notion of the individual being either 'mad' or 'bad'. A cursory glance at recent Home Office and Department of Health and Social Security statistics would suggest that most commonly women are seen as mad, whilst men are seen as bad (Home Office 1988; DHSS 1986b).

However, a contemporary theoretical view within criminology would implicate psychological factors, intertwined with social factors to account for offending behaviour, and would not be reliant upon 'badness' alone: 'a famous dictum of criminology is that society gets the crimes that it deserves' (Cameron and Fraser 1987). Likewise, it would be similarly unfashionable and simplistic to argue that the development of psychiatric problems is completely divorced from psychological and social factors, and dependent entirely upon organic aetiology.

Yet despite the more 'liberal' development of the psychiatric and criminological fields, the discourses of the penal system and mental health services are clearly and actively gendered, with subsequent different outcomes for men and women. This chapter hopes to provide a critical exploration of some of the explanations for these differences and how the examination of discursive practices might provide some alternative insights. The terminology used here reflects that used in both psychiatry and the legal system. Hence, the word 'disposal' is used to refer to how and where somebody is placed at the end of criminal proceedings. 'Deviance' is used to describe those people who do not adhere to the norm. Both are extremely value and stigma laden terms, and are not ones I would usually choose to describe real people in the real world. I use them here to endorse and typify my arguments, and would certainly argue against their usage outside of this context. In addition the word 'forensic' has a wider operational definition than commonly interpreted, and means 'as, or used in the Court of Law' (*Oxford Dictionary*, 7th Edition). Hence 'forensic psychology' refers to that psychological knowledge which may be used in the assessment and treatment of people who have in some way come under the explicit power of the law.

To further place these arguments in context it is perhaps worth giving some explanation of where clinical psycholgists fit into the current services and how psychiatric and psychological factors come into play when a crime has been committed. There are a wide variety of institutions and services that cater for people who need both psychiatric care and legal supervision. Constraints of space prevent a detailed discussion of the development and aims of these services, but Mason (1984) provides an excellent description. Clinical psychologists can also play a variety of roles within these services. They may work within a custodial institution such as in a Regional Secure Unit or a Special Hospital such as Rampton. Particularly within these two types of service the representation of psychologists is particularly strong and has had made large contributions to their development. Clinical psychologists may also work on a sessional basis with other services such as probation, hostels, and hospitals with secure units. Additionally, psychologists working within any specialities are increasingly receiving direct referrals from the courts, the police and solicitors asking for assessments and possible treatment.

However, forensic work is one area where psychology has still lagged behind psychiatry, and psychiatrists have remained the gatekeepers for the entry of psychologists. This is partially as a consequence of the Mental Health Act having the requirement that those detained under the Act have a Responsible Medical Officer, who is usually a consultant psychiatrist. In terms of the interplay between psychiatric and psychological factors this is frequently in terms of mitigating circumstances. If psychology enters, it is frequently by psychiatrists' invitation. Thus, it can still be the case, if there is to be a psychological assessment, that this is made through a referral from a psychiatrist. Occasionally, these psychological reports may then be subsumed into the psychiatric report, unless the psychologist specifically states that they would like their report to stand as it is, in full. Hence, the discourse of 'psychiatry' within the legal arena may include psychological issues, although they are not specifically referred to, and are included under the verbal umbrella of psychiatry.

Our first point of reference in examining gender differences within these systems is to take a closer look at the statistics that refer to criminal behaviour, psychiatric disorder, and subsequently the disposal of people into either the prison or the psychiatric system.

CRIMINAL STATISTICS

In 1986 the total number of men in custody in England and Wales was 48,295; for females it was 1,791 (Home Office 1988). At that time 2,304 males and 66 females were serving life sentences. In June of that year the statistics for those held in custody and their crimes was as in Table 5.1.

Clearly, the gender differences are extremely significant and pervasive across different crimes. In none of these crimes do women outnumber men. In most cases the number of men who have committed these crimes are many times the number of women who have been convicted of the same crime. On reading any criminological text which examines crime statistics, a cautionary note will always be added as such statistics are notorious for being inaccurate and open to wide and differing interpretations. Nevertheless, no matter what sort of inaccuracies have crept into

Table 5.1 Prison Statistics in England and Wales (1986)

	Males	*Females*	
Offences with immediate custodial sentence	36,743	1,229	(3.2)
Violence against the person	8,586	247	(2.8)
Murder	1,917	70	(3.5)
Other homicide and attempted homicide	991	32	(3.1)
Woundings	4,473	120	(2.6)
Assault	278	12	(4.1)
Cruelty to children	14	3	(15.8)
Other offences of violence	913	10	(1.1)
Sexual offences	2,677	15	(0.6)
Rape	1,069	6	(0.6)
Gross indecency with children	187	3	(1.6)
Other sexual offences	1,071	6	(0.6)
Burglary	7,857	57	(0.7)
Robbery	3,915	73	(1.8)

Source: Home Office 1988

The figures in brackets represents the number of women who have been convicted of the crime as a percentage of the total, male and females.

these figures, a stretch of the imagination would be needed to argue that such discrepancies are significant enough to account for this gender imbalance. Hence indisputably, men in this country are convicted of crimes many more times than women, and this holds true across all the usual types of crime.

PSYCHIATRIC STATISTICS

If we then turn to look at the gender differences in terms of admission to psychiatric hospital, and differences in diagnosis, we begin to see a contrasting profile. Again a cautionary note should be added about the difficulty of obtaining meaningful and accurate figures, and it should be remembered that these figures refer only to admissions. Nevertheless, the disparity between the sexes is thought to be even greater for those people who seek out-patient services (Ussher 1991).

Table 5.2 All admissions to mental illness hospitals and units by sex and diagnostic group

Diagnostic group	Males		Females	
All diagnoses	83,865	(361)	113,386	(465)
Schizophrenia, paranoia	15,271	(66)	14,148	(58)
Affective psychoses	8,107	(35)	16,526	(68)
Senile and presenile dementia	7,624	(33)	13,234	(55)
Alcoholic psychosis	509	(2)	266	(1)
Other psychoses	7,455	(32)	17	(44)
Neurotic disorder	4,978	(22)	10,291	(42)
Alcohol dependence syndrome	8,301	(36)	3,508	(14)
Nondependent use of alcohol	2,095	(9)	1,204	(5)
Drug dependence	1,382	(6)	806	(3)
Nondependent use of drugs	614	(3)	278	(1)
Personality and behaviour disorder	6,531	(28)	7,667	(32)
Depressive not classified elsewhere	11,740	(51)	23,469	(97)
Other psychiatric conditions	287	(1)	346	(1)
Other conditions and undiagnosed cases	8,601	(37)	10,774	(44)

Source: DHSS 1986b

Figures in brackets are rates per 100,000 population.

Clearly, if you are female you are much more likely to be admitted into psychiatric services, and probably with a different diagnosis to your male counterparts. Interestingly, apart from the diagnosis of schizophrenia and paranoia, the only other area where the number of men diagnosed as having a mental illness which exceeds the female number is under diagnoses related to alcohol or drug problems. Otherwise there are nearly twice as many women suffering from affective psychosis, neurotic disorder and depressive illnesses than men. Tables such as this yield interesting and valuable information. However, they also present very complex information, that is itself reliant upon the discursive practices at work, and therefore widely open to misunderstanding (Ussher 1991).

PSYCHIATRIC DISPOSAL OF CONVICTED PERSONS

These figures become even more interesting when we examine the link between psychiatry and the law and see which section of the population have entered both of these arenas by being detained under the Mental Health Act. As there is a large amount of complex data that can be presented here, I have been selective and present a snapshot pertinent to the topic under discussion. This is information that relates to gender, place of containment, and Sections 3 and 37 of the 1983 Mental Health Act.

Section 3 of the Mental Health Act refers to 'Admission to Treatment' and concerns those people not undergoing criminal proceedings, but who are deemed a danger to themselves or others through psychiatric illness or psychopathic disorder. This must be open to treatment, and the circumstances are such that treatment cannot be provided unless the person is detained under this Section. The duration of detention is not defined, it is reviewed after 6 months, the following 6 months, and then once every year. This is the Section that perhaps covers the old concept of having somebody 'committed' into hospital, or more recently the one used when somebody is being 'sectioned' for their own or others safety.

Section 37, commonly called a Hospital Order, relates to those individuals undergoing criminal proceeding. Hence, it refers to those people who have committed a crime, but for whom the mitigating circumstances included the presence of psychiatric illness or psychopathic disorder, which requires treatment.

However, this can never apply to murder as the sentence, life imprisonment, is mandatory. Nevertheless, in the case of psychiatric illness being present with a charge of murder the plea of diminished responsibility might be submitted and the charge dropped to manslaughter. The review procedure is similar to that of Section 3 (see Gostin 1983 for a fuller description).

From these statistics gender imbalances are again clear, although perhaps more subtle and involved, than in the crime and psychiatric statistics cited earlier. The three contexts of Special Hospital, Regional Secure Unit and Mental Nursing Home differ in the level of security and restrictions, with Special Hospitals being the most secure and Mental Nursing Homes being least secure. The number of people detained in these three settings under the Mental Health ˚Act show that men tend to be kept in more restrictive settings than women. There are also generally

Table 5.3 Those detained under Sections 3 and 37 of the Mental Health Act (1986)

Place of containment	Males	Females
Special hospitals, i.e. Rampton, Moss Side, Park Lane, Broadmoor and Carstairs		
Section 3	185	118 (39.0)
Section 37	884	173 (16.4)
Total detained under the Mental Health Act	1,376	337 (19.7)
Regional Health Authority, e.g. Regional Secure Unit		
Section 3	1,252	1,239 (49.7)
Section 37	792	152 (16.1)
Total detained under Mental Health Act	2,592	2,021 (43.8)
Mental Nursing Homes		
Section 3	48	30 (38.5)
Section 37	23	8 (25.8)
Total contained under Mental Health Act	2,266	3,075 (57.6)

Source: HMSO 1986

Those figures in brackets give the percentage of women in terms of the total, men and women.

many more men held under Section 37 of the Mental Health Act than women. However, it must also be recognised that this Section refers to those undergoing criminal proceedings, and as we have already seen many more men are convicted than females. In this way the statistics possibly reflect what might be predicted by looking at the criminal and psychiatric statistics. However, the figures involved in Section 3, where no criminal proceedings are taking place, do not reflect the psychiatric statistics in terms of a greater preponderance of women. Indeed, these figures suggest that again more men than women are held under this Section. Thus, it seems that although there may be more 'mad' women than 'mad' men generally, if men are seen as 'mad' society deserves much greater protection from them than it does from women. In other words, if men do go mad it might well be likely that they are also dangerous, and thus are burdened with the double title of mad and potentially bad.

From this point we really start to draw near to the crux of the problem, which concerns the origins of these differences. This can be conceptualised in a number of different ways, for example, man the aggressor and woman the victim. However, the fundamental question remains, are these gender differences due to the inherent biological nature of the two sexes? There has been much discussion about why there is a greater preponderance of psychiatric illness amongst women (Chesler 1973; Ussher 1991), and thus I will not enter into, or even attempt to summarise that discussion. However, this literature will necessarily be drawn upon during the examination of the main theme of this chapter, which concerns how these sexual differences are perpetuated, and how the eventual consequences are arrived at in terms of the disparity in treatment of individuals.

MAN THE AGGRESSOR, WOMAN THE VICTIM

Margaret Atwood writes that when she asked a male friend why men felt threatened by women, he replied that, 'They are afraid women will laugh at them.' When she asked a group of women why women felt threatened by men, they said, 'we're afraid of being killed.'

(Caputi 1987: 1)

The women I killed were filth, bastard prostitutes who were just standing round littering the streets. I was just cleaning the place up a bit.

(Peter Sutcliffe, quoted by Beattie 1981: 133)

It seems to be the expectation that men inherently have strong, violent emotions which they constantly have to keep under control, but which under 'unreasonable' provocation, especially sexual jealousy, can break out of control and have violent and irreversible consequences. The blame for such consequences may lie at the man's feet for losing control, but the provocation he was under is usually used, and accepted, as powerful mitigating circumstances, as in the case cited at the beginning of this chapter. Such misogyny was made clear in the 'Yorkshire Ripper' case where the 'morality' of his deeds was matched to the 'morality' of his victims, such that the prosecuting council remarked 'some of the victims were prostitutes, but perhaps the saddest part of this case is that some were not' (Hollway 1984: 21). Such misogyny can be witnessed time and time again in the reporting of male crimes, frequently in offences of rape, for example the scantily dressed hitch hiker, the woman who invites a man in for coffee, etc.

There is a strange tension and hypocrisy when one thinks of man as the one ruled by fluctuating emotions – can we envisage men as victims of their own raging hormones? This seems a strange position as women are usually the ones considered to behave as a function of their biological make-up (Ussher 1989). This mismatch between the 'sold' identity and reality is further evidenced in the the common portrayal of woman as the schemer, wily, manipulative and above all else avaricious. This stereotypical heritage has accompanied women from as early as Adam and Eve.

Tis woman that seduces all mankind, By her we first were taught the wheedling arts.

(*The Beggars Opera*, I ii by John Gay (1728))

This stands in stark contrast to the statistics which show that it is mainly men who assault, steal and deceive. The sexual discrepancy in offending is one of if not the most striking feature of criminality, yet much of criminology ignores this factor in its analysis of deviant behaviour. There is no body of literature, apart from recent feminist critiques, within criminology which offers explanations as to why women do not offend. Possible it is an uncomfortable fact to be ignored by those whom it reflects badly upon? As men constitute the majority of academics (see Paula Nicolson's Chapter 1 in this volume), together, with the androcentricity which exists in psychology and related topics, theories of criminality have been built mainly around men, with just the occasional sketchy reference to why women are under-represented in crime. Interestingly, it is usually why women are under-represented, as opposed to why men are over-representated, again positioning women as the deviant and man as the norm. I will now go on to review briefly some of the works that have actually attempted some explanation in this area.

ETHOLOGY AND THE CRIMINAL PRIMATE

One of the earliest works on female criminality was that of Lombroso and Ferrero's book *The Female Offender*, published in 1895. Their claim was that criminals are a product of degeneration to an earlier more primitive evolutionary form, and they presented evidence that male criminals had certain physical features that differentiated them from non-criminals. However, they could not find similar physical evidence to support the theory for women. Nevertheless, they did not exclude women from this evolutionary perspective. They argued that female criminals showed fewer signs of this degeneration because they were generally at at a retarded state of development compared to men in the first place. As Lombroso and Ferrero construed women as governed totally by their biology, going right back to the immobile egg and the highly active sperm, the dictated and true position of women was therefore one of passivity and conservatism. Hence any women who stepped out from that role was stripped of her passivity and was seen to be acting in a masculine way – and thus was a truly deviant women. Lombroso and Ferrero did not leave the castigation of the female sex at that but took it one step further by making the claim that as most women criminals seemed to fall into the petty offending category, their primitive development again handicapped them, making them fail even at criminality (Heidensohn 1985).

Such ideas may seem amusing and crude today, but there are certainly elements in their theory which still affect the positioning of women in our contemporary legal system. Clearly, within this theory women are both positioned within and without femininity; they are deviant because they are female, and they become even more deviant if they step out of that role – a paradoxical and no-win position.

WOMEN – THE ARCH-CRIMINALS

Otto Pollack, in his book Criminality of Women (1950) built upon this misogynist theme and offered an alternative theory by suggesting that women are under-represented in crime because they are masked by their conventional roles. For example, he suggests that the abuse of children by their mothers goes unrecorded because they have both the opportunity and power to commit and hide the crime. Such ideas remain not far from the surface today. For example, the current idea that those who have been sexually abused become abusers themselves has again turned the focus upon women for a largely male crime. If the majority of victims of sexual abusers are female, and one believes the idea that such abuse may be re-enacted by the victims themselves, then one comes very quickly to the conclusion that there may be many more sexually abusing women around than are coming through the courts. Obviously, this is a crude overstatement of a complex area, but certainly the phrase 'cycle of abuse' has become well established within the 'helping professions', if not with the public at large. In fact according to Home Office Criminal Statistics (Home Office 1985) only 0.95 per cent of sex offences were committed by women. Furthermore, those women who are guilty of unlawful sexual intercourse with children under 16 are usually aiding and abetting a male in the offence. Additionally, it is very rare for them to cite sexual gratification as a motive for their participation (O'Connor 1987).

Pollack (1950) also went on to assert that women are seen less frequently in the courts as a consequence of the legal system mainly consisting of men who take a chivalrous attitude to women offenders. Carlen (1985) claims that this last suggestion has had a lasting effect on our judicial system, with judges and magistrates arguing repeatedly that as women offenders are given so many chances, those that end up appearing in court must indeed be very bad. Carlen cites Box (1983) as presenting evidence against this assertion.

> The weight of relevant evidence on women committing serious offences does not give clear support to the view that they receive differential, and more favourable, treatment from members of the public, police, or judges.

Earlier, Klein had observed:

> Chivalry is a racist and classist concept founded on the notion of women as 'ladies' which applies to wealthy white women . . . These 'ladies', however are the least likely ever to come in contact with the criminal justice system in the first place.
>
> (Klein 1973: 5)

Carlen then goes on to quote Box again as telling a different story regarding juvenile crime.

> Juvenile courts are often transformed into stern parental surrogates who lock up their naughty daughters for behaving in ways which scarcely concealed approval when committed by sons.
>
> (Box 1983)

THE ROLE OF SOCIALISATION

More recently, writers and researchers have moved away from biological determinism to look at sex roles as offering some explanation. The suggestion is that the feminine role model which guides socialisation attenuates any aggressive drives and emphasises the development of a more passive, moral stance, mainly as a role model to the developing children (Williams 1987). Parallel to this is the suggestion that boys are rewarded by their peers for resisting authority and engaging in illegal acts. It is perhaps not just the approval of other boys that occurs, as Box above hints at, but the drive to become a real man as perceived in films, literature and TV. Indeed, it is perhaps hard to conceptualise a male hero that has not committed illegal acts and been involved in violence, from James Bond to Indiana Jones. In talking about man as the acceptable rebel, and drawing upon existential philosophers, Cameron and Frazer (1987: 59) make this comment:

> A crucial aspect of his material being is his **subjectivity**: he is not an object, that which is experienced, but an experiencer; not that which is acted upon, but an actor. He is potentially a free being, **but** he is trapped in a tight cocoon of a body, conventions and meanings, so that the moments of being and experiencing are fleeting. Even when he feels himself to be acting freely, he is acting in accordance with the norms of society; even when he looks at someone, he is also being looked at and thus objectified, made not-subject. This is the tragedy.
>
> (Emphasis in original)

From such all-embracing socialisation theories of criminality, come ideas which type-cast women as victims and delinquent men as heroes. The idea that the gender difference within criminality relates specifically to the socialisation of men and women into these particular positions seems intuitively appealing. The argument might be that women play just as an important part in criminality as men do; the part they play is just different. They are the victims of criminal acts and men are the perpetrators. Such an explanation will be backed up by reference to biology, ethology, socio-cultural factors, economics, political and psychological influences (Williams 1987).

Nevertheless, such theorising again fails to provide an explanation of criminal women, except perhaps by implicit references to the old and exclusionary idea that they must in some way be lacking in femininity. Indeed, in recent years, the emancipation of women and 'women's lib.' has on occasion been held up to account for a recent increase in criminality amongst women. For example, Adler (1981) suggests that the new female criminal is 'a free masculine spirit'. Again such an explanation very quickly falls short. For example women who tend to be active in women's liberation are usually, white, middle class and educated, whilst those women who end up in prison are frequently not white, not middle class and from underprivileged backgrounds.

The idea of delinquency being some form of hero worship has been developed into a more sophisticated theory, taking a developmental perspective, and seeing juvenile delinquency and consequentially, criminality, as having its own culture, capable of enmeshing and moulding individuals' behaviour (Whyte 1955; Thrasher 1963). Most of this work comes from American sociological studies of delinquent boys and gangs, and once again girls or women remain invisible from these descriptions of deviance. Heidensohn (1985) criticises this work from four angles. Firstly, she charges that working-class delinquency is treated as romantic and heroic, and that such deviancy becomes a 'celebration from which the powerless male intellectual draws vicarious pleasure'. Heidensohn usefully sums this up by saying 'In short it seems that the "college boys" became fascinated by the "corner boys"' (141).

This draws attention to the second criticism, that of male dominance in academic life, which has been well documented and evidenced elsewhere (e.g. Burman 1990; Nicolson's Chapter 1 in this volume). Thirdly, she suggests that delinquency and crime amongst girls and women has, due to the lower incidence, remained elusive both in terms of attracting research money, but also in terms of gaining access to the subjects of the research. Finally, Heidensohn draws upon the hegemony that exists within the central themes of the discipline of criminology. Although sex and age have always and still remain the major predictors of crime, they have not been examined to the same length as weaker predictors such as the social environment, and have failed to explain why such factors operate so much more strongly on males than females. Heidensohn offers the following as an explanation for this notable absence:

> I believe that they did not do so because they were able (as I have tried to show) to pursue an exclusive interest in male criminality in a comfortable world of academic machismo. There was for a long time no intellectual critique of this approach nor any strong social pressure because of political issues.

Finally, we are now perhaps coming to an age of not only a feminist analysis of criminology, but also feminist contributions to theory making. New ideas have developed not just from critiques of past work, but also from more politically informed and substantiated theories of social control. Thus, it seems clear these days to any 'gender-conscious' individual that to truly understand explanations of criminality they must be inextricably linked to those social forces which control behaviour. Additionally, any understanding of female pro-social behaviour and their resistance to becoming involved in criminality cannot but be understood from first 'understanding the control and oppression of women in the family, work and public space which feminist analysis offers us' (Heidensohn 1985). Heidensohn offers the bones of a theory encompassing gender in criminology that points towards some explanation of why men and women differ in the frequency and seriousness of their offences and the consequences of being caught.

carrying out deviant acts must be related to:
1. opportunity
2. time
3. space
4. scope
5. available role models
6. deviant images and stigma

Being observed, caught, cautioned or convicted will in turn depend upon how agencies of control operate and use
1. values and ideology
2. agency practices
3. formal rules and laws
4. conventional behavioural stereotypes (of race, sex etc.)
I would like to suggest that women face distinctly different opportunity situations and to some extent with agencies of control, the main point with the latter being that women face an additional series of controls. They are the one section of society whose policing has already been 'privatised', even though they have not ceased to be publicly controlled as well.

(Heidensohn 1985: 198)

MAD OR BAD?

I have described the discrepancy between the sexes in terms of the frequency and seriousness of crimes committed in society today and the androcentricity that has served to handicap adequate reflexive theory development. Prior to this I have contrasted criminal statistics with the imbalance which exists in the sphere of psychiatric disorder. Leaving the analysis of gender and psychiatric illness to others in this book, and to more specialised texts (such as Chesler 1973; Sayers 1986; Showalter 1987; Ussher 1991), I now want to draw these two themes together and look at the third which is highlighted by the statistics presented in Table 5.3 – who is called bad and who is called mad, the consequences of such labelling, and why such gender differences might come about?

Clearly, from the figures shown in Table 5.3, from what we know about the proportion of women who are deemed as having a psychiatric disorder (see Table 5.2), and the proportion of females who are offenders (see Table 5.1), women are over-represented within the figures for the psychiatric disposal of offenders. In other words, if one is female and commits an offence one is much more likely to be seen as having a psychiatric problem, and end up serving time in a psychiatric institution than if one were a man. This discrepancy cannot be accounted for merely by the higher incidence of women receiving psychiatric care than men, as the discrepancy is even larger than this (Allen 1987). In addition, given the much higher rate of men becoming involved with the law, one would expect to see a higher number of men involved in psychiatric disposals than one does. Certainly, the 364 men per 100,000 diagnosed as mentally ill (see Table 5.2) are clearly under-represented within the psychiatric disposal figures (Home Office 1988).

The consequences of this are serious and deleterious for both men and women. For men, it is likely that many are in need of psychiatric care which is certainly not recognised, nor provided. For women, the caricatured stereotype of 'madness' is perpetuated with all its sad consequences. However, this discrepancy within the statistics also shows another alarming reversal, in that more men than women tend to end up in more restrictive forms of psychiatric care than do women. Allen (1987) also found this pattern within her more extensive analysis of the statistics, and concludes:

> it can very clearly be seen that the excess of psychiatry in the disposal of female cases is not uniformly distributed across all the forms of psychiatric disposal, but is in fact concentrated at the lowest level of psychiatric involvement, in the least restrictive and most consensual forms of treatment.
>
> (Allen 1987: 7)

As any close scrutiny of Table 5.2 might suggest, this psychiatric discrepancy in gender has no explanation which is confined solely to fundamental biological differences. Those values, assumptions, myths and words that Heidensohn (1985) described as accounting for the gender imbalance within criminology are also at work to craft these differences in psychiatric diagnosis. Indeed, I would also argue that the psychiatric or otherwise disposal of convicted or potential criminals is more greatly open to such influences since two very traditional and powerful forces meet head on – that of the professions of medicine and law. I would further argue that any understanding of these influences cannot get very far without examining their discursive practices.

Discourse is about language. Language covers different levels of analysis, from the way it organises, limits or expands our internal cognitions, to the more meta-social constructs of the symbols and signs conveyed. Discourse analysis as a method in psychology examines how language conveys information, and the implications and functions that this language carries with it (see Potter and Wetherall 1987). By examining the discourse and thus defining and identifying discursive practices we are able to inject the reflexivity so often absent from previous psychological and social analysis. For to be able to identify the discourse used within a particular subject area, we must acknowledge how both the area and the user of that discourse is governed and constrained within it.

Within the discursive practices used in the legal system we see the prime example of this, where at the end of the day the verdict must always fit one of the options available with recourse to the specific law being invoked. These options are pathetically limited compared to the variation of human circumstances and situations which face them.

> Doctors and sentences cannot make just **any** decision: in any particular case they cannot even make what they perceive to be the **best** decision. They too are constrained in their social actions by the discourse that they speak but cannot own. (Emphasis in original)
>
> (Allen 1987: 112)

Any explanation of the gender imbalance both within psychiatry and the judicial system has to be at the level of the analysis of the discourse used, if we are to understand the subtleties, perpetuations and generalisations of such gender imbalances.

Although there are clear parallels between the discourses used in psychiatry and the law, their languages and processes do not dovetail comfortably to work easily alongside each other. Each has its own traditional and largely immovable classification system, which it uses to 'diagnose' what is the problem, or which law has been contravened, and set it upon the expected and usual course of treatment or action. However, on the occasions where they meet there is an uncomfortable mismatch which has required even tighter and so more restrictive terminology and classifications to bring them closely into line, thus bringing with it the requirement to fit an even wider variation of situations into an even tighter set of criteria and outcomes, and making the distance between the everyday understanding of everyday people even greater.

However, the argument being presented is that, over and above the effects of different social constructions of deviance, as detailed earlier, and the perpetuation of patriarchal oppression, etc., it is the discourse of psychiatry and law which is the active agent which enacts and perpetuates these gender imbalances. Allen, in her study of 'Gender, Psychiatry and the Judicial Decisions', provides evidence for taking this perspective.

medico-legal discourse constructs male and female subjects in divergent terms differently interpreted as evidence of male and female personalities; and in male and female cases different criteria are called into play in assessing the 'same' parameters of legal culpability, personal pathology and clinical need.

(Allen 1987: 113)

It quickly becomes clear from any of the older criminological texts which includes a section on criminal women, that offending is pathologised and described in more psychiatric terms than in their descriptions of male offending.

Pathological psychiatric deviations are much more common in delinquent girls than boys . . . Delinquent girls more often than boys have other forms of impaired physical health; they are noticed to be oversized, lumpish, uncouth, and graceless, with a raised incidence of minor physical defects.

(Cowie, Cowie and Slater 1968)

Within society as a whole, and within medico-legal matters, human behaviour is indisputably understood in gendered terms. However, Allen would argue that the dominance of patriarchy alone is not enough to account for the eventual imbalance, but it is indeed the intersection and interaction of the two broad structures of psychiatry and legislation that brings about an eventual understanding of how this discrepancy comes into being. Allen argues with great clarity that it is not the proven existence or non-existence of a psychiatric condition that is the greatest predictor of a psychiatric disposal under the law. Nor is it an insidious, collective and covert or overt decision on the part of men to position women in psychiatric terms as a part of some great patriarchal 'master-plan'. But it is such factors as the availability of psychiatric resources, the prevailing fashionable attitudes towards community-based treatments, and the pervasive gender biases that frequently dictate the final outcome. All of which mould, and in turn are moulded by, the discourse of psychiatry, psychology and the law.

Hence, within our present gendered discourses women are expected to be unstable and out of control, and as such women who offend more frequently come under the psychiatric remit. As Table 5.3 demonstrates, they are also seen as less deranged than men who come under this remit, and as such enter less restrictive facilities. Men on the other hand, being sane and rational the majority of the time, are deemed as exceptionally mad if they do manage to enter into the psychiatric services, needing very secure provision, and may also be seen as too intractable and too dangerous to be treated in anything other than the prison system. A key term that frequently enters into both psychology and the law is responsibility, and those seen as being responsible (i.e. having a nature that is not unstable and at the mercy of raging hormones) may often be seen as holding more legal culpability and deserve more retributional punishments. Those seen as holding responsibility within society are most frequently men and the values, attributions and assumptions which then follow any criminal transgressions may insidiously lead us to the agreement that they deserve punishment, as opposed to understanding and treatment in psychiatric or psychological terms.

Hence it is being argued here that such gender imbalances are the result of two strong forces, which are not mutually exclusive. First the gendered understanding of behaviour that is all pervasive. Secondly the intractable and static discourses of medicine and psychiatry, and a structure that has evolved around them from the debris of past solutions to ever-changing problems.

As Allen points out, there are a number of conclusions that can be drawn from this analysis that are particularly galling for a feminist. Firstly, that the discrepancy in psychiatric disposals for offenders can be seen as a deficiency of psychiatry in relation to male offenders rather than an excess in relation to females. Secondly, that on the whole female offenders might do rather well out of psychiatry in comparison to male offenders. However, clearly despite winners or losers there are real and important concerns surrounding the issues of psychiatry and the law. Gendered assumptions have been institutionalised through the discourses of psychiatry and the law and serve to colour the outcome of cases from their assessment to their disposal, leading to unfair and possibly dangerous consequences for the individual and society.

CONCLUSION

This sexual discrepancy in the medico-legal interface has been on the whole ignored. This is bizarre in itself, but again perhaps epitomises the absence of reflexivity in psychological accounts and explanations that focus upon highly gendered topics. Perhaps to start to shed some light on how this can come about is to again look at the discursive practices in use. We have talked about 'assumptions about gender and behaviour' – this is primarily a psychological concept. It is also from psychology that more critical, and recently feminist, analysis of gender differences originates. However, this has not as yet permeated all areas of psychology. It has only entered areas of psychology where the discourse allows it. So, for example within the area of social psychology there is rhetoric within the natural discourse of feminist analysis and social psy- chology that is shared. Words such as 'subjectivity' are common currency. There are other areas of psychology where there is no such common currency and the discourse of gender and behaviour, particularly a feminist analysis has no place in the common language of that subject, forensic psychology being one of these areas.

In support of this view I would like to present a typical example. Recently, I was asked to review a book entitled *Working with Sex Offenders: Guidelines for Therapist Selection* (O'Connell, *et al.* 1990). Now much has been written about sex, and even sex offending, in terms of gender and power relationships (e.g. Brownmiller 1985; Box 1983; Stanko 1985). Much also has been written about power and gender in terms of the therapy relationship (e.g. Sayers 1986; Hobson 1985; Ussher 1991). Nowhere throughout that whole book have the issues surrounding the sex of the therapist been mentioned. Surely, from what we already know it is clear that we cannot de-gender a therapist and say that there are no differential consequences between a male and a female therapist working with a male sex offender. Even though O'Connell *et al.* cover such topics in choosing a therapist as their 'ability to remain objective', gender of the therapist was never a question. Obviously, here remains a territory virgin to feminist analysis.

If we then place psychology, with its own patchy record of dealing with gender, within the discourses of psychiatry and the law, we hit even further problems. As already mentioned the discourses of both psychiatry and the law are precise and pre- scriptive; psychology is anything but that, and clinical psychology prides itself in its ability to provide formulations as opposed to diagnoses (Turkat 1985). Any clinical psychologist who has appeared as an expert witness will be critically aware that the discourses of psychology and the law are frequently worlds apart.

The law wants to know if a woman can be said to be 'mentally handicapped' or not, in the precise, though meaningless, terms of an IQ score, and is certainly not interested in fuzzy ideas about labelling, or being able to function independently. As psychology, particularly through sexual abuse cases and child witness work, is starting to play an increased role in the courts a more flexible role is painfully, and slowly, being negotiated.

However, what must not be forgotten is that our present psychological knowledge is flawed by androcentricity and the dogma of 'science'. It represents 'a deposit of the desires and disappointments of men' (Horney 1974: 7). The current model within clinical psychology is 'the scientist-practitioner'; Jane Ussher in this volume (Chapter 2) has succeeded well in drawing attention to the pitfalls of this approach. Yet we must remember that this currently represents the psychological 'science' that is taken into the court rooms and used to try and impress and influence judicial decision-making. Psychology in turn has to change, and we have to be conscious of its weaknesses if we are to use such knowledge prudently. This in turn must be carefully balanced with the fact that psychology still plays either no, or a very thorny, part in the interface between psychiatry and the law. Not to press for a greater use of psychological knowledge in judicial decisions is to cut off the most obvious avenue for interjecting knowledge about gender and behaviour.

Not only is a gender and/or a feminist analysis lacking from within forensic psychology, but psychology is frequently lacking from the medico-legal structures. Forensic and prison psychology are often areas shunned by feminist psychologists, as being 'mainly to do with men', and particularly about men 'who are worse' than most other men. However, this is an area ripe and rich for the study of gender differences, and if we are to practise the reflexivity which we espouse then many clues must be available both to the further understanding of the over-pathologising of women, and more frequent offending behaviour of men. Certainly, if we are to have any further analysis and even promote change in the medico-legal systems, then the discourse of forensic psychiatry needs to open its doors wider to encompass not only psychology, but also gender and feminist analysis and 'gender-conscious' psychologists need the confidence to step through that door.

REFERENCES

Adler, F. (ed.) (1981) *The Incidence of Female Criminality in the Contemporary World.* New York: University Park Press.

Allen, H. (1987) *Justice Unbalanced: Gender, Psychiatry, and Judicial Decisions.* Milton Keynes: Open University Press.

Beattie, J. (1981) *The Yorkshire Ripper Story.* London: Quartet/Daily Star.

Box, S. (1983) *Power, Crime and Mystification.* London: Tavistock.

Brownmiller, S. (1985) *Against Our Will: Men, Women and Rape.* New York: Simon & Schuster.

Burman, E. (ed.) (1990) *Feminists and Psychological Practice.* London: Sage.

Cameron, D. and Frazer, E. (1987) *The Lust to Kill.* Cambridge: Polity Press.

Caputi, J. (1987) *The Age of the Sex Crime.* London: Women's Press.

Carlen, P. (ed.) (1985) *Criminal Women.* Cambridge: Polity Press.

Chesler, P. (1973) *Women and Madness.* Harmondsworth: Penguin Books.

Cowie, J., Cowie, V. and Slater, E. (1968) *Delinquency in Girls.* London: Heinemann.

DHSS (1986a) *Mental Health Statistics for England 1986.* Booklet 11: *Legal Status of Patients.* London: HMSO.

DHSS (1986b) *Mental Health Statistics for England and Wales.* Booklet 12: *Diagnostic Data.* London: HMSO.

Gostin, L. (1983) *A Practical Guide to Mental Health Law.* London: MIND.

Heidensohn, F. (1985) *Women and Crime.* London: Macmillan.

Henley, K. (1985) Psychology and gender. *Signs: Journal of Women in Culture and Society*, 11, 1: 101–119.

Hobson, R. E. (1985) *The Forms of Feeling: The Heart of Psychotherapy.* London: Tavistock.

Hollway, W. (1984) 'I just wanted to kill a woman'. Why? The Ripper and male sexuality'. In H. Kanter *et al.* (eds), *Sweeping Statements: Writings from the Women's Liberation Movement 1981–1983.* London: Women's Press.

Home Office (1985) *Home Office Criminal Statistics 1975–1984.* London: HMSO.

Home Office (1988) *Prison Statistics in England and Wales.* London: HMSO.

Horney, K. (1974) The flight from womanhood. In J. B. Miller (ed.), *Psychoanalysis and Women.* Harmondsworth: Penguin.

Klein, D. (1973) The etiology of female crime: a review of the literature. *Issues in Criminology*, 8: 3–29.

Lombroso, C. and Ferrero, W. (1895) *The Female Offender.* London: Fisher Unwin.

Mason, P. (1984) Services for the mentally abnormal offender – an over-view. In T. Williams, E. Alves and J. Shapland (eds), *Options for the Mentally Abnormal Offender.* Issues in Criminological and Legal Psychology no. 6. Leicester: British Psychological Society.

O'Connell, M., Ledberg, E. and Donaldson, C. (1990) *Working With Sex Offenders: Guidelines for Therapist Selection.* London: Sage.

O'Connor, A. (1987) Female sex offenders. *British Journal of Psychiatry*, 150: 615–620.

Pollack, O. (1950) *The Criminality of Women*. New York: A. S. Barnes.

Potter, J. and Wetherall, M. (1987) *Discourse and Social Psychology: Beyond Attitudes and Behaviour*. London: Sage.

Sayers, J. (1986) *Sexual Contradictions*. London: Tavistock.

Showalter, E. (1987) *The Female Malady: Women, Madness, and English Culture, 1830–1980*. London: Virago.

Stanko, E. (1985) *Intimate Intrusions*. London: Routledge.

Thrasher, F. M. (1963) *The Gang*. Chicago: Phoenix Press.

Turkat, I. D. (ed.) (1985) *Behavioural Case Formulation*. London: Plenum Press.

Ussher, J. M. (1989) *The Psychology of the Female Body*. London: Routledge.

Ussher, J. M. (1991) *Women's Madness: Misogyny or Mental Illness*. Hemel Hempstead: Harvester Wheatsheaf.

Whyte, W. F. (1955) *Street Corner Society*. Chicago: University of Chicago Press.

Williams, J. (1987) *Psychology of Women: Behaviour in a Biosocial Context* (third edition). London: Norton.

Chapter 6

Working with families

Arlene Vetere

INTRODUCTION

Feminists and family therapists are both closely concerned with families. The family is central to the thinking of both groups because it mediates the values of the wider culture in which it is embedded and children first learn what it means to be male or female most often in a family context. However, feminists interested in the condition of women differ from most family theorists and therapists in the closeness with which they scrutinise family life for its impact on women. The division of labour by sex in our society ensures the family is the major beneficiary of women's labour and acts as a major source of women's identity, in particular as a mother. In addition, many feminists consider that the socially constructed role differences between men and women serve as the basis for female oppression (Eisenstein 1983) and thus the family itself has become the focus of their critical attention.

In this chapter, feminist theory and analysis will be used to inform family therapy theory and practice in the direction of greater sensitivity to the implications of the structural inequalities said to exist between men and women in families. Feminist theory has been helpful in a number of ways, for example, by articulating men and women's different experiences of self, of other/s, of life (Rich 1976); by questioning whether gender categories determine what it is possible to know; by drawing attention to the wider representation of men's experience; by placing the family in historical context (Oakley 1974) and challenging current views of family life as given (Mintz and Kellogg 1987); by recognising that women do not have as yet equality of opportunity in the work place (*Social Trends* 1990); and by calling for a re-examination of family life. Such a re-examination entails validating non-traditional sexual and living arrangements, supports an end to women's economic dependence on men, supports a redistribution of household and nurturing tasks and responsibilities, and fights for women's reproductive rights. This has major implications for how we, as clinical psychologists, work with families.

In this chapter I have a number of tasks. I shall consider both the skills necessary for the practice of gender-sensitive family therapy and the vexed question of how to train therapists. Vexed, because of the problem of self-reflexivity, i.e. we are training within a gender-bound culture so that our perceptions are to some degree gender biased.

To train gender-sensitive therapists, we need to re-think not only the relationships between men and women in the family and in wider society, but the theories we have available to explain those relationships and which thus guide our practice. In this light, I approach the next task, that of examining one of the most commonly used frameworks in family therapy, Minuchin's Structural Family Theory and Therapy (1974). (See pages 133–5 for a description of the theory.) I shall examine what place gender has in Minuchin's model of theory and practice, what assumptions are made about gender in the development and maintenance of problems, and whether gender is considered in therapeutic planning and in the therapist's use of themself in family therapy.

As we shall see, gender-sensitive family therapy is not a set of prescriptions nor techniques, but is more an awareness of the gendered constraints on men and women's perspectives and choices and how such constraints are addressed in family therapy. It does not overlook the social dominance of men in the public world, nor does it assume equality of power or opportunity in the home.

For those men and women who choose to take part in family life, gender-sensitive family therapy attempts to facilitate their participation as cooperative, equal and intimate partners. This demands that family therapists change their views of family functioning and their ways of intervening in families.

For clarity and consistency, the definitions of sex, gender and gender stereotyping put forward by Goodrich, Rampage, Ellman and Halstead (1988) will be used in this chapter. Sex is a biological category referring to maleness and femaleness. Gender is a social construct which involves assigning specified social tasks to one sex and others to the other sex. This defines what is labelled masculine and feminine in a particular society at a particular time. Gender stereotyping is a process whereby certain behaviours, attitudes and emotions are regarded as appropriate to only one sex and then acting as if these are natural differences rather than socially learned.

GENERAL SYSTEM THEORY

The major schools of family therapy have been developed under the umbrella of General System Theory (von Bertalanffy 1956). Recent feminist criticisms of family therapy for ignoring gender as an organising variable of family life have blamed General System Theory (GST) for the subsequent perpetuation of sexist beliefs and practices. Family therapists have been further criticised for their GST-induced narrow focus on the family which does not take account of the wider social and cultural influences on family life (Avis 1985; McGoldrick, Anderson and Walsh 1989; Williams and Watson 1988). However, GST does offer a framework that links the interactions of family members to the larger social system. GST can deal with hierarchical levels of subsystem, system and suprasystem; organised complexity within system levels; defining the boundaries around the system and its environment; feedback processes for promoting growth and change and maintaining stability; and describing emergent properties at more complex levels of organisation. (See Vetere (1987) for a more complete discussion of General System Theory and its application to the understanding of family life.)

Goodrich and her colleagues (1988) suggest that family therapy theorists have accepted unquestioned the prevailing gender roles. This apparent inattention to the impact of gender roles on individual family members and their family relationships is strange, particularly in a field which highlights second-order change, structure and hierarchical relationships across generations. One explanation is rooted in the history of the development of family therapy theory and the move away from individual, trait-based explanations of behaviour to a systematic, interactional view (von Bertalanffy 1968). Goldner (1985) wondered whether family therapists with their egalitarian values could not tolerate the idea that arrangements of inequality between men and women might be structurally essential to family relations, as propounded by

Parsons (1964), for example. Whatever the reasons, there is no doubt that family therapy theory has overlooked the differentials in power between men and women. For example, whilst both Haley (1976) and Minuchin (1974) use unbalancing techniques to restore the generational power balance between parents and children, they do not address power between husbands and wives.

It would seem that if family therapists have ignored wider social influences on the family and failed to analyse marriage and motherhood as potential vehicles for the oppression of women, that is a problem for family therapists, not GST. GST is a theory, an organising framework that is more or less useful. It is in the application or misapplication of the theory that the problem lies. It is very worrying that some feminist commentators do not appear to have gone back to GST to understand its structure and explanatory power before making their critiques. However, feminist analysts are correct to point out that the interpretation of some theoretical concepts and the application of some methods of therapy have assumed that men and women have equal impact on their surroundings. For example, the assumptions of circular causality, where all family members are seen to play a part in the maintenance of family problems, not only disadvantaged women but also fostered a reluctance to confront gender issues in practice. Thus in cases of spouse violence, where women are abused and victimised, therapy which relies on explanations of circular and recursive patterns of behaviour leaves no one accountable or everyone equally responsible. Yet, as we have seen, the woman may not be equal in power and resources. Some family therapists, such as Minuchin (1984), Carpenter and Treacher (1989) and O'Brien (1990) rely on linear explanations of victim and perpetrator to attribute responsibility and General System Theory to explore the options and possibilities for co-actors in relationships.

Gurman and Klein (1984) in their critique of behavioural marital therapy comment that much family therapy takes place within a family system, laden with gender bias which disfavours women. They suggest it is spurious to engage spouses in bargaining, negotiating and behavioural contracting and therefore further question whether we can have 'an objective and data-based neutrality' for our therapy. Hare-Mustin (1987) further comments 'when we alter the internal functioning of families without concern for the social, economic and political context, we are in complicity with society to keep the family unchanged'. So, to ignore gender inequalities between men and women in our therapy is both non-systemic and sexist at the family and socio-political level. Jacobson (1983) commented that 'all forms of psychotherapy are political by virtue of the fact that they have consequences for the expression and distribution of power'. Jacobson is calling for therapists to be aware of these underlying issues so they know what gender values and beliefs they are reinforcing or challenging!

STRUCTURAL FAMILY THEORY AND THERAPY

The following is a brief description of Structural Family Theory. (For a fuller discussion and critical evaluation, see Gale and Vetere (1987).)

Minuchin developed his theoretical ideas in three key publications. *Families of the Slums* (Minuchin *et al.*1967) focused on executive behaviour and leadership in inner-city single parent families; *Families and Family Therapy* (1974) details the structural model and develops the concepts of enmeshment and disengagement; *Psychosomatic Families* (Minuchin *et al.* 1978) describes patterns of conflict avoidance and resolution in parent–child interaction. Minuchin has always been aware of the effect of the socio-economic and cultural environment on individual and family functioning, as illustrated, for example, by his work with low-income single-parent mothers, promoting their competence and authority whilst addressing their unmet needs for adult companionship and support. Minuchin does not incorporate gender as a structural organising variable of family life, but his ideas have developed to become gender aware, as exemplified in the creativity and diversity of family forms applauded in his latest volume, Family Kaleidoscope (1984).

Structure refers to the family's organisational characteristics, the subsystems it contains and the rules governing interactional patterns among family members. Thus therapy aims to alter these organisational patterns, particularly where modes of communication between family members are seen to be dysfunctional, for example, when a family has difficulty in restructuring in response to a developmental or environmental challenge.

The theory has five key features:

a) the family is a system which operates through transactional patterns;

b) the functions of the family are carried out by bounded subsystems;
c) the subsystems are made up of one or more individuals, on a
permanent or temporary basis, and members can belong to
more than one subsystem, within which their roles will differ;
d) subsystems are hierarchically organised so as to regulate power
structure within and between subsystems; and
e) cohesiveness and adaptability are key features of family life.

The four subsystems typical of Western family life are the marital/
cohabitee, parental/executive, parent–child and sibling subsystems. At the apex of the family hierarchy is the marital/
cohabitee subsystem whose functions include affectional exchange
and intimacy, decision-making, role allocation in relation to
executive and economic supports and which forms the primary link
between the family and the outside world. The parental/executive
subsystem has the task of nurturing and socialising the children
with the adaptability necessary to meet developmental changes in
children and the pressures of age-related expectations from society.
Teamwork and complementarity of function are believed to be
crucial to satisfying the conflicting demands for guidance and
control on the one hand and for the encouragement of autonomy
and responsibility on the other. The parent–child subsystem is
concerned with affectional bonding and sex-role identification and
presupposes the effective functioning of marital and parental
subsystems. The sibling subsystem is an important social context in
which the child learns to cooperate, compete and resolve conflict
in preparation for later peer-related activities.

Thus for family members to meet these functional demands
they need different skills and different patterns of behaviour at
different stages in the family's life cycle. For Minuchin, the concepts of boundaries, cohesion, adaptability and power are central
to the theory and are revealed by examination of family relationships. The focus in therapy is very much on the here-and-now and
the relationship factors that maintain individual symptomatology,
rather than on the historical conditions that may have given rise to
current family distress.

Although Minuchin did not address gender issues specifically,
the theory has the structure and the language to address gender-
based arrangements in the family, for example, in the construction
and functioning of marital and parental subsystems. The focus on

current family interaction in therapy may have made it more likely that the historical origins of women's inferior position in the family (Baker-Miller 1976; Hoffman 1981) would be overlooked or that men and women would be assumed to operate from shared and equal power bases. The current interest in integrating theories and perspectives which emphasise current and past patterns of interactions provides us with a basis for specifying more clearly the impact of gender-based arrangements on individuals and their relationships (for example, the work of Wachtel and Wachtel (1986) integrating family systems theory and object relations theory). While some family therapists have been criticised for their focus on the interior of the family, there is nothing in Structural Family Theory that prohibits therapists from making theoretical and practical linkages with those significant systems that interface with the family.

For example, one typical structural family therapy intervention that has attracted considerable criticism is the use of the father to unbalance the triangle of an over-involved mother and her child and a peripheral father. The expansion in the father's role and function by involving him more in the care of the child is intended to reduce the mother's focus on the maternal and to open up new possibilities for her to function as a more differentiated, complex woman. Various commentators (for example, Walsh and Scheinkman 1989) argue that this intervention assumes that a woman, socialised primarily for a maternal role, can develop quickly alternative roles and sources of satisfaction and self-esteem in a society where her choices may be limited. However, if this criticism is taken seriously, so that the constraints inherent in the father's position are acknowledged also, it is possible to use therapy as an opportunity to explore men and women's access to and participation in public and private life in a manner which is respectful of both their needs and wishes. For example, a woman might be helped to plan time for herself each day and to be assertive in maintaining that personal boundary in the face of requests to attend to other family members' needs during that time. Or, a man might be helped to acknowledge and articulate his feelings more clearly and to learn nurturing behaviours with his children. In practice, structural therapists can combine their emphasis on instrumental problem-solving with a developing awareness of the need to elicit and share emotional responses in bringing about change in family relationships.

INTERPERSONAL POWER BASES

Jean Baker-Miller (1976) was one of the first to draw our attention to the effects on couples who accept patriarchal explanations for sexual inequality. She pointed out that the consequences for such couples were likely to be profound, such as, the needs of both partners were not mutually satisfied, unacknowledged conflict arising out of unmet needs could act as a source of resentment and distress, and the couple would not have the means to resolve these issues directly. For example, a woman's anger and frustration might be directed at her husband in the form of critical attitudes and comments, rather than realising that inequality in the relationship was the problem. Betty Friedan (1963) called this the problem that has 'no name'. Baker-Miller analysed women's use of power in the home as the means by which they influenced relationships whilst maintaining deference. She identified such covert strategies as using helplessness and weakness, manipulation of emotional tone and the application of emotional pressure. These strategies are limited in their effectiveness, define women as weak and do not facilitate mutual respect between men and women. Baker-Miller was careful to point out that a focus on women's power in the home ignores the fact that men often have status and power outside family life and if women at home have no economic independence, can we then describe their power as real. Thus we need an analysis of interpersonal power that spans the public and the private domain.

Power in family therapy theories is defined as the relative influence of one person over another, based in differential access to socially valued resources. Williams and Watson's (1988) scholarly review of interpersonal power bases allows us to address the questions of differential access by gender to power bases, the qualitative differences between them and whether the presence or withdrawal of interpersonal power affects the processes of family negotiation. The power bases identified by Williams and Watson (1988) are domestic, affective, relational, reproductive, sexual, economic, ascribed, physical, contractual, informational and language. Williams and Watson argue that women have greater access to the first five and men have greater access to the last six power bases. Drawing on their account, a brief description of each power base will follow.

Domestic power is derived from the provision or threat of

withdrawal of domestic services, for example cooking and cleaning. This is a source of women's power hidden within the private world of the family, and arguably a weak power source since it carries with it the risk of being replaced. Affective power is often assigned to women as they are seen to be the 'nurturers' of family relationships, taking responsibility for family members' emotional well-being (Baker-Miller 1976). Baker-Miller has warned that the use of this power base carries the threat of being construed as being manipulative at best or taken as evidence of pathology at worst.

Relational power is based on connectedness between people, within and outside the family. For example, an alliance between a parent and a child could increase bargaining power in the face of opposition. Reproductive power may be a diminishing resource for women as the value of children as an economic resource declines. Sexual power is described by Schwendinger and Schwendinger (1983) and Llewelyn and Osborne (1990) as a frequent focus of major power struggles between men and women. It is seen by some men as their 'right' to have a sexual relationship with women and as such is a highly socially valued power base. It is inside the family that women exercise this power base largely by withholding sexual relationships.

Economic power is arguably the major power base in our society. Women's work within the home is mainly unwaged and outside the home women constitute the bulk of the workforce in lower paid service industries, often in part-time work below the threshold for employment protection (*Social Trends* 1990). Ascribed power is not earned, it is given to people on the basis of some characteristic or attribute, such as race, class and sex. It is used to legitimise the position of men as 'natural' head of the household. Physical power or the threat of its use is largely available to men because of their greater physical size. Dobash and Dobash (1987) point out that most women who are physically abused and raped are done so inside the family. It is only recently that the Metropolitan Police have been prepared to intervene in domestic violence, thus challenging this abuse of male power, previously legitimised by lack of legal protection for women. Contractual power is the ability to leave the relational field, most often noted by family therapists with their difficulties in convening and engaging men (O'Brien 1988). Goldner (1985) found that contractual power was often associated with money. She investigated the financial standing of men and women one year post divorce and found that men's economic well-being had risen by 42 per cent, whilst women's had fallen by 73 per cent. Thus low-income single-parent women have less access to this power base. Informational power or an expert base of social power values knowledge and skills as resources and varies according to the value system of the social group. It is argued that in our culture men hold valued information about the public world and women hold less valued information about the private world of the family, for example, parenting skills. Finally, the power of language refers to a power base that names and describes experience and reality (Henriques *et al.* 1984). Spender's (1980) research has supported the argument that men's experience and knowledge is over-represented in language, thus supporting and perpetuating a patriarchal social system.

Men and women have traditionally had differential access to types of power and the means of access have largely been determined by sex-role expectations and stereotypes. Women have tended to influence others using their own personal qualities and interpersonal relationships, whereas men have used a different set of resources, which emphasise strength, skill, knowledge and instrumentality. Thus according to this analysis sexual inequality is found within private and public worlds, perpetuated by unequal access to differentially valued power bases.

ENGAGING MEN IN THERAPY

The Hite report (1988) stated that women were profoundly dissatisfied with the quality of their intimate relationships with men. Of 4,500 women interviewed in the USA, 98 per cent said their biggest problem was a lack of emotional closeness in these relationships. Gurman and Kniskern (1981) in a clinical audit of American child and family therapy clinics found that men tended to be absent from consultations and that women more frequently approached the helping agencies. O'Brien (1990) in her work in Britain reported the same impression. Why might this be so? Gurman and Kniskern found the reason most often given by men for their absence was a time conflict between work and therapy and Briscoe (1982) found that women tended to seek and organise help at an earlier stage of perceived distress than did men.

Walters (1987) noted that when a therapist meets a couple, it is more often the woman who can acknowledge and express her feelings and engage in the process of therapy. Walters is concerned that this may lead therapists to ally with the woman and, by relying on her capacity to bring about change, thereby give the woman major responsibility. She comes across men who do not accept that what is happening in the relationship is anything that involves responsibility on their part and also therapists who are afraid of driving these men away if they challenge them too strongly.

Family therapists make theoretical assumptions about the relationship factors underpinning individual distress and believe in the value of shared responsibility for child care. There is no doubt that we need to engage men. So, how can we engage them differently? Brannen and Collard (1982) found that men preferred therapy sessions where they received more structured advice and engaged in goal setting. Similarly Bennun (1989) found that men in family therapy favoured a therapist style that was active, competent and goal setting and that they were more likely to stay in therapy when the therapist was optimistic about outcome and showed a positive liking for the family. In an investigation of structural family therapy, Russell, Atilano, Anderson, Jurich and Bergen (1984) found that fathers preferred enactments of parent–child interaction and manoeuvres that altered family members' proximity, whereas mothers preferred relatively less active interventions such as tracking and positive connotations. It could be argued that the use of active methods in therapy help to integrate the father back into the parental subsystem and enhance feelings of self-esteem as a father, thus reducing feelings of inadequacy and helplessness often thought to be associated with peripherality as a father (Minuchin 1984).

Women have often reported preferring therapy which gives them the opportunity to talk about their emotional reactions to family life in an open-ended way (O'Brien 1988) and it may be that men's apparent dislike of this rests on a fear that it could lead to discussion of power relations, control and decision-making in the marriage. On a more optimistic note, Hunt (1985) found that men who persisted in individual counselling soon came to value 'just talking'. The implication for family therapists is clear. Acknowledgement of both the positive motives of men and women in coming to the session as well as some of the personal costs to them of their present living arrangements may help in the initial joining process.

GENDER-SENSITIVE FAMILY THERAPY

It is not suggested here that we abandon our general systems-based family therapies but rather that we examine our theories and practices to incorporate gender and generation as two fundamental organising principles of family life. Every family therapy session we conduct is about both the politics and meaning of growing up and the politics and meaning of gender. So what might gender-sensitive family therapists do?

As described at the beginning of this chapter, gender-sensitive family therapy is not a set of skills or techniques, it is a process between the therapist and the family which provides an opportunity for all family members to negotiate their individual and system needs. The processes of gender-sensitive family therapy incorporate many factors, some of which will be detailed here.

1. Family therapists need to be aware of their own values regarding gender as they are expressed in therapy and supervision. Examination is needed of the extent to which our ideas about differences between men and women are based on sexist stereotypes. For example, Wheeler, Avis, Miller and Chaney (1989) suggest we broaden our conceptualisation of family life-cycle theory to include other choices available, such as remaining single and establishing an intimate social network, marrying and choosing not to have children, choosing to be a single parent, choosing homosexual/heterosexual cohabitation with or without children, and so on, thus releasing us from discussion of family life in terms of stereotypic roles, for example courtship, marriage, birth of first child, and so on.

2. Family therapists need to examine how gender roles and stereotyping affect each individual in the family, relationships between family members, relationships between family members and social institutions, and relationships between family members and the therapist. Such examination emphasises the social context as an important systemic determinant of behaviour and recognises that men and women face unique problems as a result of their socialisation.

3. Family therapists ask questions that make explicit the issues, decisions and behaviours that demonstrate to what degree equality and reciprocity exist between men and women in the family. For example, we might ask of a couple, how did you decide who would work and who would rear the children; how

much flexibility do you feel you have in these arrangements; how satisfied are you with these arrangements; who benefits most and who carries most cost?

4. Family therapists examine differentials in power between men and women. Williams and Watson's (1988) analysis of inter-personal power bases is helpful in formulating questions of how the presence or withdrawal of these sources of power affect everyday family processes, such as decision-making, negotiation and conflict resolution.

5. Family therapists can use positive reframing and relabelling to shift the conceptual and emotional perspective on an individual or a relationship, for example what may have been seen as personal inadequacy can be reinterpreted as socially pre-scribed. This can be achieved by exploring with women what they have been taught about being women in comparison to their actual competencies, interests and needs. Or by exploring with men what they have been taught about being men, or what they have been taught about women. A geneogram is a useful means of exploring these issues (Lieberman 1979).

6. Family therapists facilitate consideration of a wider range of perspectives, behaviour and solutions, that are less constrained by more traditional definitions of roles and personal identity; for example, when discussing parental teamwork and shared responsibilities, paying attention to the implications for both partners by checking that the woman is willing to share parental responsibility, and has other means of expressing her compe-tence and that the man is willing to bear the cost in the work place of being more involved with his family. The assumption is that the allocation of roles solely on the basis of gender is to be minimised.

7. Family therapists use their 'gendered selves' in therapy in a therapeutic manner, for example by modelling alternatives to traditional roles. Male and female therapists can exercise authority, show competence and draw and underline boundaries whilst at the same time offering empathy, respect and careful listening. Similarly mixed co-therapy pairs provide opportunities to model different styles of communication and negotiation between men and women.

8. Family therapists work outside the family, using their networking and organisational skills, for example helping fami-lies join and create social support networks, securing access to

child-care facilities, working in Social Services-funded family resource centres, and so on.

Thus, gender-sensitive family therapy constitutes a political awareness within the practice of family therapy which informs those questions we ask of family members and the understandings we obtain.

AN EXAMPLE OF GENDER-SENSITIVE FAMILY THERAPY

In order to illustrate the foregoing points, I shall use an example from our current work with families. I work as a clinical psychologist in an NHS locality based Child and Family Service in which I convene a regular family therapy workshop which has a training function. Our work, whilst integrating theory, is largely informed by Minuchin's Structural Family Theory and Therapy (Minuchin 1974; Minuchin and Fishman 1981). Our work with the S family is used to illustrate our attempts both to be aware of gender issues and to address them as sensitively as we know how. Consequently the commentary is less about the details of our structural interventions and more about how our interventions were guided by our gender awareness.

Mrs S referred herself and her family to our family therapy team asking for help with the management of her 7-year-old son's behaviour at home. A meeting with Mrs S and her son, James, revealed more widespread difficulties in the family, particularly at the interface between the world of family and the world of work, than had been indicated in the initial referral. Despite our request, Mr S did not attend the first meeting, according to Mrs S, because he could not get the time off work and more importantly for her, rearing the children was her responsibility. The other children (son of 4 years, daughter of 10 years) did not attend because Mrs S could not see their presence as relevant to our proceedings. At this meeting we gathered information about James' behavioural problems, the previous solutions tried by the parents and the impact of these problems on family members' relationships. We affirmed those strategies that seemed to contribute to positive changes in James' behaviour. Finally we explored with Mrs S the reasons why we would find it helpful to meet with all family members present. She agreed to speak to her husband and we followed up with a complementary letter.

The whole family arrived for our second meeting in which the nature of Mr and Mrs S' marriage became more explicit. We characterised it as a 'corporate marriage', following the work of Goodrich and her colleagues (1988) who note that such marriages are coming to the attention of family therapists increasingly often. Mr S was a high status executive with a national corporation and was the sole wage earner. Mrs S assumed sole responsibility for the care of the children and household management, and in such a way that she promoted and displayed her husband's employment success. She reported no significant interests or friendships outside the family.

Within our structural family therapy model, we explored their experience of and commitment to parental teamwork in their management of James' behaviour. It seemed both Mr and Mrs S were highly identified with their respective roles, precluding parental teamwork, and their extreme role differentiation even extended to include those personality attributes assumed to accompany their roles. For example, Mr S asserted his pride in his independence and strength, whilst enjoining his wife to be more assertive and confident and less dependent. Thus when dealing with James' disobedience, Mr S reported no difficulty. Mrs S reported she was not able to maintain control and guidance of James. When Mr S was at home he would leave Mrs S to deal with James and would intervene and 'take over' if he believed Mrs S was unsuccessful, leaving her feeling deskilled. Mrs S resisted and resented offers of help from Mr S, thus reinforcing their role split. Mrs S similarly reacted with overt distress to our exploration of their parenting and Mr S with frustration and a belief that nothing would change, especially by talking.

We had a number of questions that we wished to explore with the family at this point. How had Mr and Mrs S made decisions about who nurtured and socialised the children, who provided the family's income, and so on? How much flexibility in the discharge of these tasks did they think they had? How satisfied were they with their present arrangements overall? Who benefited the most and who carried the most costs, in social exchange theory terms (Nye 1982)?

Our discussion revealed that the distribution of interpersonal power bases (Williams and Watson 1988) in the family favoured Mr S, and Mrs S appeared not to challenge this dominant/subordinate structure directly, so that conflict was rarely expressed overtly. Further, we discovered that the corporation employing Mr S placed gendered constraints on their marriage. For example, the corporation dictated where the family would live and when they would move and required and received from Mr S his loyalty, energy and time, leaving little spare for himself and his family. We did not challenge directly the corporation as the organising principle of their marriage, but with the use of questions helped them to discover and reassess the basis of their family life. For example, frequent relocations had meant that Mrs S had little opportunity to develop a supportive social network, and the personal costs to Mr S of loyalty to the corporation were high in terms of lack of involvement in child rearing and a mutually satisfying marriage. The latter point was particularly painful for Mr S and he dropped out of therapy midstream for a few weeks, accusing his wife of using the sessions as an excuse to divorce him.

However, from our second meeting we progressed by exploring ways to promote mutuality in the marriage, with a particular focus on parental issues. In early sessions we were able to create rapport by positively connoting their behaviour as taking a real interest in each other and by joining with both of them in some enjoyable and non-gender-stereotypic aspect of their lives, for example Mrs S' interest in learning another language and Mr S' wish to learn to paint. Eventually these developed into active interests in which they both began to develop other circles of acquaintances besides the ones prescribed by the corporation.

As discussed earlier, gradually we made explicit the shaping force of the corporate culture on their marriage, without challenging directly Mr S' loyalty to and identification with the company. Exploration of the differences between working for a corporation and being married to someone who works for a corporation in terms of the personal costs and benefits and available options led on to two significant events in the therapy.

Mrs S soon found it possible to take part in parent–child enactments of problematic interactions with James which in the re-enactment allowed her to develop a teamwork approach with her husband in mutual decision-making and jointly executing those decisions. The couple continued to test and develop their team-working between sessions. Mrs S reported subsequently that our earlier discussions had made this shift possible for her as she became aware of options and opportunities previously thought to be unavailable.

However, the development of complementarity of function in their parental roles was not without hiccups. This leads on to the second significant event in therapy. There were still difficulties in the relative influence exercised by both Mr and Mrs S in other areas of their marriage and we negotiated some separate marital sessions. It was at this point that Mr S dropped out of therapy saying that it was too painful for him to acknowledge the costs of investing so highly in his career. We acknowledged his distress and left them the choice of when to return and continue. Mrs S was articulate in her desire to return and when they did so in a few weeks' time it was to tell us of their decision for Mr S to take a lower paid less senior position within another company, which released some of his time during the evenings and at weekends.

We are still working with this couple. Their decision to alter their lifestyle was not easy to take, neither is dealing with its many consequences and ramifications. Mr S struggles to identify and express his feelings while Mrs S struggles to make her expectations of marriage and family life explicit and overt. It is difficult to talk in terms of positive outcomes in such work. Both Mr and Mrs S recognise the complexity of their losses and gains and remain strengthened in their commitment to each other.

TRAINING ISSUES

The training of gender-sensitive family therapists takes place within a gender-bound culture; hence our training also needs to be gender-sensitive. This view has implications for the context in which training takes place, the content of the training programme and the relational processes between trainer and trainee. Just as we argued that gender is not to be treated as a 'special issue' in discussions of family theory and therapy, so it is important that gender not be relegated to a one-off workshop or seminar during training. Here too, gender operates as a structural and organising variable.

The context of training

Caust, Libow and Raskin (1981) suggest that traditional sex-role training, family members' and supervisors' expectations, and patriarchal institutional structures pose particular problems for the female family therapy trainee. Female trainees are characterised as tending to avoid confrontation, to downplay their authority, to use covert power strategies and to relate to their supervisors in stereotyped, submissive ways. The authors draw on Baker-Miller's (1976) analysis of subordinate–dominant relationships in which these behaviours are described as survival strategies for subordinates; whereas when women are not subordinates, for example with their own children or in role as teachers, they display the opposite behaviours, thus making the point that women's ability to be authoritative and confrontative depends in part on the demand characteristics of the setting. Thus the hierarchy in the institution offering the training programme and in the training programme itself needs to be continuously scrutinised and studied in an attempt to specify its impact on the training and the relationships taking place within its remit. Caust and her colleagues call for measures which make the context safe for women to experiment with a wider range of behaviour, such as teaching assessment and intervention skills not only in small family systems but in larger organisational structures.

The content of training

Structural family therapy techniques require therapists to be active, directive and competent. Great emphasis is placed on the therapist's ability to join with and engage each family member in therapy. Tomm and Wright's (1979) model of family therapy skills is a useful framework for structural family therapy trainers who are striving to make such training gender sensitive. The model specifies the necessary perceptual, cognitive and executive skills. Broadly defined these refer to the therapist's capacity to make relevant and accurate observations, to attribute meaning to the observations, and the therapist's action or response to these observations. Tomm and Wright's emphasis on theory–practice linking is best expressed in Cleghorn and Levine's (1973) definition of executive skills as the ability 'to influence the family to *demonstrate* the way it functions' and to 'influence the family's sequences of transactions so as to *alter* the way it functions' (emphasis added). Executive skills, according to Tomm and Wright, have two components, i.e. the actual overt intervention made by the therapist and the therapist's constructive use of their own emotional reactions by channelling them into specific therapeutic activity. This emphasis on the ability to elicit and share emotional responses is of particular significance to gender-sensitive family therapists, since structural and strategic therapists have tended to emphasise instrumental problem-solving, while neglecting the role of emotion in bringing about change. Goodrich, Rampage, Ellman and Halstead (1988) offer the somewhat daunting challenge to gender-sensitive family therapy trainers to teach feminist theory to trainees to provide them with the concepts needed to perform a gender role analysis. They draw on the pioneering work of Wheeler, Avis, Miller and Chaney (1985) in drawing up a useful checklist of supervision and training experiences, which includes:

a) helping trainees to develop both empathic responses and instrumental skills, such as giving clear directives, taking an authoritative stance, and so on;

b) teaching trainees to use their emotional reactions as cues to the type of intervention needed or to the processes between family members or between the therapist and family members;

c) teaching trainees to explore with family members their decisions about the division of labour, power and rewards in the family as influenced by gender stereotypes;

d) encouraging trainees to examine the implications of their own gender role stereotypes for themselves and for their interactions with family members. Uncovering the ways in which these lessons are learned in our families of origin helps trainees to maintain a perspective on their families as also part of the larger social system; and

e) teaching trainees to examine the impact of their gender on the process and outcome of family therapy.

Wheeler, Avis, Miller and Chaney (1989) provide an extensive checklist of gender-sensitive therapist behaviours, that includes skills for developing and maintaining a working alliance with the family, skills for defining the problem and skills for facilitating change in family members' attitudes, beliefs and behaviours. The checklist was developed within Tomm and Wright's (1979) framework for training perceptual, conceptual and executive skills in family therapists.

The work of Warburton, Newberry and Alexander (1989) has been helpful with regard to the last point above. In a series of studies of functional family therapy (Alexander and Parsons 1982) they looked at the effects of therapist and client gender on the therapy process. The structural and strategic family therapy training literature (for example, Haley 1976; Haley and Hoffman 1967; Minuchin and Fishman 1981; Selvini-Palazolli *et al.* 1978) suggests that male and female therapists can join families and conduct family therapy in the same way; whereas Warburton and her colleagues (1989) have shown that male and female therapists have different experiences in family therapy. Overall, male and female trainees can expect parents of the same sex to attempt to ally with them and parents of the opposite sex to be more defensive. Although it would seem that female trainees experience more defensiveness from family members than their male colleagues. The implications for female therapists are that they must work harder to find ways of joining with a potentially more defensive father without alienating or losing the support of the mother.

Warburton and her colleagues (1989) have developed some guidelines to help beginning female therapists overcome these difficulties. They suggest developing an active style (along with empathy and a relational focus) that helps deal with power issues overtly, for example by establishing interaction rules early on in the therapy, or by minimising the use of qualifiers when interviewing, such as 'perhaps', 'I'm not sure', and so on. This active style is to be promoted in the context of greater awareness of the interaction of gender differences between family members and therapist and by dealing directly with the different gender experiences of men and women in their family therapy training.

The process of training

Warburton's guidelines for training combine content and process issues. They are informed by the respect that obtains between trainees and supervisors. Such respect is evident in practice which teaches theory clearly; which identifies and affirms progress and competence; which supports the development of individual style; which allows trainees time to join with families before intervening; which explains the rationale for the timing and type of supervisor intervention; and finally which challenges each member of the training group to come up with ways of being both supportive and authoritative.

CONCLUSION

In my own clinical experience, feminist ideas have been slow to be incorporated into the family therapy mainstream. So it is exciting to see that these issues are now being addressed on this side of the Atlantic, as exemplified by the first publication of a book on gender and power in families (Perelberg and Miller 1990) based on a series of workshops in the Women's Project in Family Therapy Conference.

I feel sad that I have to agree with the lament of Barry Mason and Ed Mason (1990) that apart from a few exceptions, such as the work of Morris Taggart (1985), too little attention has been given by men to the examination of what it means to be a man in relation to women, and vice versa, as compared with the increasing output of women. (See Frosh, Chapter 7, in this volume for another exception!)

Family therapists have not deliberately promoted sexist beliefs and practices, but by failing to take account of differences in status and power between men and women in our society they have allowed gender to remain a hidden dimension of family life (Goldner 1985; Hare-Mustin 1978; Taggart 1985). Gender-sensitive family therapy attempts to address and reverse this far-reaching oversight. Thus a feminist analysis of family work encourages us to see families as they are, to explore all living arrangements for their creativity, potential and competence, and to support each family member's needs rather than trying to preserve one particular form of family life. Now that more women are active members of the paid workforce and more men are looking for greater involvement in parenting, our therapy needs to be flexibly responsive to the greater variety of family forms and the unprecedented dilemmas now facing men and women. I agree with Goldner (1985) that feminist analyses of family therapy need to be rescued from their peripheral status as 'special' topics. It is hoped this chapter goes some way towards encouraging a greater awareness and practice of gender-sensitive family therapy.

ACKNOWLEDGEMENT

Thanks to Charlotte Burck for her comments on an earlier draft of this chapter.

REFERENCES

Alexander, J. F. and Parsons, B. V. (1982) *Functional Family Therapy.* Monterey: Brooks/Cole.

Avis, J. M. (1985) The politics of functional family therapy: a feminist critique. *Journal of Marital and Family Therapy*, 11: 127–138.

Baker-Miller, J. B. (1976) *Toward a New Psychology of Women.* Harmondsworth: Penguin.

Bennun, I. (1989) Perceptions of the therapist in family therapy. *Journal of Family Therapy*, 11: 243–255.

von Bertalanffy, L. (1956) General System Theory. *General Systems*, 1: 1–10.

von Bertalanffy, L. (1968) *General System Theory.* Harmondsworth: Penguin.

Brannen, J. and Collard, J. (1982) *Marriages in Trouble.* London: Tavistock.

Briscoe, M. (1982) Sex differences in psychological well-being. *Psychological Medicine*, Monograph Supplement 1, Cambridge University Press.

Carpenter, J. and Treacher, A. (1989) *Problems and Solutions in Marital and Family Therapy.* Oxford: Blackwell.

Caust, B. L., Libow, J. A. and Raskin, P. A. (1981) Challenges and promises of training women as family systems therapists. *Family Process*, 20: 439–447.

Cleghorn, J. M. and Levine, S. (1973) Training family therapists by setting learning objectives. *American Journal of Orthopsychiatry*, 43: 439–446.

Dobash, R. E. and Dobash, R. P. (1987) Violence towards wives. In J. Orford (ed.), *Coping With Disorder in the Family.* London: Croom Helm.

Eisenstein, H. (1983) *Contemporary Feminist Thought.* Boston: Hall.

Friedan, B. (1963) *The Feminine Mystique.* Harmondsworth: Penguin.

Gale, A. and Vetere, A. (1987) Some theories of family behaviour. In A. Vetere and A. Gale, *Ecological Studies of Family Life.* Chichester: Wiley.

Goldner, V. (1985) Feminism and family therapy. *Family Process*, 24: 31–47.

Goodrich, T. J., Rampage, C., Ellman, B. and Halstead, K. (1988) *Feminist Family Therapy: A Casebook.* New York: Norton.

Gurman, A. S. and Klein, M. H. (1984) The family: an unconscious male bias in behavioural treatment? In E. Blechman (ed.), *Behaviour Modification With Women.* New York: Guilford Press.

Gurman, A. S. and Kniskern, D. (1981) *Handbook of Family Therapy.* New York: Brunner Mazel.

Haley, J. (1976) *Problem-Solving Therapy.* San Francisco: Jossey Bass.

Haley, J. and Hoffman, L. (1967) *Techniques of Family Therapy.* New York: Basic Books.

Hare-Mustin, R. T. (1978) A feminist approach to family therapy. *Family Process*, 17: 181–194.

Hare-Mustin, R. T. (1987) The problem of gender in family therapy theory. *Family Process*, 26: 15–27.

Henriques, J., Hollway, W., Urwin, C., Venn, C. and Walkerdine, V. (1984) *Changing the Subject.* London: Methuen.

Hite, S. (1988) *Women and Love: A Cultural Revolution in Progress.* London: Viking Press.

Hoffman, L. (1981) *Foundations of Family Therapy*. New York: Basic Books.

Hunt, P. (1985) *Clients' Responses to Marriage Counselling*. National Marriage Guidance Council, Rugby, Research Report 3.

Jacobson, N. S. (1983) Beyond empiricism: the politics of family therapy. *American Journal of Family Therapy*, 11: 11–24.

Lieberman, S. (1979) *Transgenerational Family Therapy*. London: Croom Helm.

Llewelyn, S. and Osborne, K. (1990) *Women's Lives*. London: Routledge.

McGoldrick, M., Anderson, C. M. and Walsh, F. (eds), (1989) *Women in Families*. New York: Norton.

Mason, B. and Mason, E. (1990) Masculinity and family work. In R. J. Perelberg and A. C. Miller (eds), *Gender and Power in Families*. London: Routledge.

Mintz, S. and Kellogg, S. (1987) *Domestic Revolutions: A Social History of American Family Life*. New York: Free Press.

Minuchin, S. (1974) *Families and Family Therapy*. London: Tavistock.

Minuchin, S. (1984) *Family Kaleidoscope*. Cambridge, Massachusetts: Harvard University Press.

Minuchin, S. and Fishman, C. (1981) *Family Therapy Techniques*. Cambridge, Massachusetts: Harvard University Press.

Minuchin, S., Montalvo, B., Guerney, Jr., B. G., Rosman, B. L. and Schumer, F. (1967) *Families of the Slums: An Exploration of their Structure and Treatment*. New York: Basic Books.

Minuchin, S., Rosman, B. and Baker, L. (1978) *Psychosomatic Families: Anorexia Nervosa in Context*. Cambridge, Massachusetts: Harvard University Press.

Nye, F. I. (ed.) (1982) *Family Relationships: Rewards and Costs*. Beverley Hills, California: Sage.

Oakley, A. (1974) *Women's Work: The Housewife, Past and Present*. New York: Pantheon.

O'Brien, M. (1988) Men and fathers in therapy. *Journal of Family Therapy*, 10: 109–123.

O'Brien, M. (1990) The place of men in a gender-sensitive therapy. In R. J. Perelberg and A. C. Miller (eds), *Gender and Power in Families*. London: Routledge.

Parsons, T. (1964) Age and sex in the social structure. In R. L. Coser (ed.), *The Family: Its Structure and Functions*. New York: St Martin's Press.

Perelberg, R. J. and Miller, A. C. (1990) *Gender and Power in Families*. London: Routledge.

Rich, A. (1976) *Of Woman Born: Motherhood as Experience and Institution*. New York: Norton.

Russell, C. S., Atilano, R. B., Anderson, S. A., Jurich, A. P. and Bergen, L. P. (1984) Intervention strategies: predicting family therapy outcome. *Journal of Marital and Family Therapy*, 10: 241–251.

Schwendinger, J. R. and Schwendinger, H. (1983) *Rape and Inequality*. London: Sage.

Selvini-Palazolli, M., Cecchin, G., Prata, G. and Boscolo, L. (1978) *Paradox and Counterparadox*. New York: Jason Aronson.

Social Trends (1990) London: HMSO.

Spender, D. (1980) *Man Made Language*. London: Routledge & Kegan Paul.

Taggart, M. (1985) The feminist critique in epidemiological perspective: questions of context in family therapy. *Journal of Marital and Family Therapy*, 11: 113–126.

Tomm, K. M. and Wright, L. M. (1979) Training in family therapy: perceptual, conceptual and executive skills. *Family Process*, 18: 227–250.

Vetere, A. (1987) General System Theory and the family: a critical evaluation. In A. Vetere and A. Gale, *Ecological Studies of Family Life*. Chichester: Wiley.

Wachtel, E. F. and Wachtel, P. L. (1986) *Family Dynamics in Individual Psychotherapy*. New York: Guilford Press.

Walsh, F. and Scheinkman, M. (1989) (Fe)male: the hidden gender dimension in models of family therapy. In M. McGoldrick, C.M. Anderson and F. Walsh (eds), *Women in Families: A Framework for Family Therapy*. New York: Norton.

Walters, M. (1987) Seminar presentation, Institute of Family Therapy, London, June.

Warburton, J., Newberry, A. and Alexander, J. (1989) Women as therapists, trainees and supervisors. In M. McGoldrick, C. M. Anderson and F. Walsh (eds), *Women in Families: A Framework for Family Therapy*. New York: Norton.

Wheeler, D., Avis, J. M., Miller, L. A. and Chaney, S. (1985) Rethinking family therapy training and supervision: a feminist model. *Journal of Psychotherapy and the Family*, 1: 53–71.

Wheeler, D., Avis, J. M., Miller, L. A. and Chaney, S. (1989) Rethinking family therapy training and supervision: a feminist model. In M. McGoldrick, C. M. Anderson and F. Walsh (eds), *Women in Families: A Framework for Family Therapy*. New York: Norton.

Williams, J. and Watson, G. (1988) Sexual inequality, family life and family therapy. In E. Street and W. Dryden (eds), *Family Therapy in Britain*. Milton Keynes: Open University Press.

Chapter 7

Masculine ideology and psychological therapy

Stephen Frosh

THE SUBTLETIES OF SEX

The abstractions of gender dissolve, leaving concrete precipitates: amongst the speakers in this book, mine is the only male voice. Ironically, I am allowed in not because of any representativeness of my point of view, but precisely because it might not be representative, might not be 'masculine' in the terms given by the ordinary bipolarities of psychology. The women here allow me some feminist credentials because I do not take issue with them in their work to undermine the sexism of psychology, I do not say 'Stay at home, your place is in the kitchen, nurturing man and child, biologically predisposed to do the ironing and the hoovering'. After all, Kristeva (1974) says we can all be part of the semiotic, the fluid – we can all be pregnant with ideas. But this is not entirely so: we know who it is that really gives birth. Those of us who are men must overcome our envy of women's specific sphere of production and learn that our place is to help. As feminists struggle to produce a new, sparkling life, we men can only offer support, whispering gently, 'Breathe deep and slow, allow the pain to go'.

It is not really to do with what we do, it is rather what we are. More fashionably, it is the position from which we speak, the point from which our discourse erupts. What psychology has gone for is the action, a standard masculine technique. What differentiates male and female behaviour? How aggressive are boys, how much do girls like dolls (the hidden text being, 'How much are girls like dolls?')? Can we predict what each of them will do and is it biology or social conditioning that makes them so? On the whole, as it happens, we can say that there are some small differences and that there are some establishable influences which may lie at the source of these, influences such as differential parental responses to boys and girls from infancy onwards. But that is not the point, or not the whole or important point, or only one point amongst many. Psychology shows how much it is infiltrated by standard masculine practice when it adopts the following strategy: instead of looking inside, at emotions and feelings, at the subjective structures of the self, it looks at action alone, it measures and calibrates and avoids the issue. 'Hard' and 'soft' we go: hard–soft, tight–loose, rigid–pliable, dry–fluid, objective–subjective, masculine–feminine. Why are these oppositions so poignant, why do they speak so loud? Perhaps because it really is all about speech, about how we articulate what we are about. That is, after all, the Foucaultian message: discourse is what we are in and this discourse has some very specific properties.

> Femininity and masculinity are ideological practices all the more effective because they appear as natural and inevitable results of biology or experience. The appearance of something coherent which could be explained as the property of the individual is precisely the effect of this ideological movement.
>
> (Wetherell 1986: 77)

Femininity and masculinity are ways of experiencing the world. They are constructions which are built around anatomical difference, signifying only because they are given significance in the context of the power relations that constitute the social environment. Masculinity and femininity are subjective positions, central to our concepts of self because we are constructed in a world divided along gendered lines, but in principle they are just positions, ways of seeing and speaking about what we see. In practice, however, they become fixed: the realities of power bolster the reduction from subjective to objective, from psychological to physical, from gender to sex. In Lacanian terms, we live in the Imaginary; the phallus, fetishised, becomes the penis.

The lists of oppositional terms are hard to displace. Masculine, active, instrumental; feminine, passive, emotional. Contemporary feminism even adopts this stance, albeit with a reversal of sign, so that the previously disparaged becomes the valued half. Try rigid (masculine) versus fluid (feminine) in this luxurious sentence by Hélène Cixous.

She has never 'held still'; explosion, diffusion, effervescence, abundance, she takes pleasure in being boundless, outside self, outside same, far from a 'centre', from any capital of her 'dark continent', very far from the 'hearth' to which man brings her so that she will tend his fire, which always threatens to go out.

(Cixous 1975: 91)

The feminine luxuriates in one long, flowing sentence (in French it is softer). It cannot be pinned down, it flows and flies; it accepts and enjoys. How different from the male fantasy, the fascism of control. Here is (the man) Klaus Theweleit on the proto-Nazis of Weimar Germany:

The monumentalism of fascism would seem to be a safety mechanism against the bewildering multiplicity of the living. The more lifeless, regimental and monumental reality appears to be, the more secure the men feel. The danger is being-alive itself.

(Theweleit 1977: 218)

There is something to be said for this reading of masculine armour defending desperately against feminine energy: such celebrations of femininity oppose masculine ideology in a creative way, validating poetry over prose, understanding and ebullience over control. But they do not deconstruct the masculine order, they affirm its truth while contesting its power to decide what is valuable and what is not. They say, 'You are right to differentiate between masculine and feminine, between rationality and intuition, singularity and plurality, instrumentality and emotion. All you are wrong in is what you think best; actually, the feminine is worth most. Better never to hold still than to become a monumental fascist.' But this does not really contest the phallic power of masculine ideology, it accepts its terms and tries to be a strong female, to resist the controls of the man – to keep away from the hearth. It strives for the phallus, forgetting that the phallus is a fraud. I write in this book, but I am no female after all.

Before turning to the practice of clinical psychology, a few more lists are relevant. The masculine–feminine oppositions have become so 'real', so embedded in all our subjectivities, that they can be found everywhere, in clinical psychology no less (perhaps more) than in other engagements of people with one another. But in psychology they are scientised – made fraudulently scientific, another strategy of control. So, recognising masculinity as a social construct competing for power, let us recall its procedures and techniques, its methods for governing the other. All these are present in the operations of psychology; that is, psychology is infiltrated by masculine ideology. This ideology operates by reifying masculinity and femininity, making what are essentially social readings of the significance of anatomical difference into concrete things with specific attributes, usually valued in particular ways. Moreover, this ideology can be seen not only in the content of the individual terms, masculine and feminine, but also in the enthusiasm with which these terms are opposed: that is, it is the very act of opposing masculine to feminine – of constituting the one by means of contrast with the other – that ensures the continuation of their dichotomous relationship. So here, again, are the oppositions:

strength–weakness
control–understanding
independence–dependence
achievement–acceptance
abstraction–concreteness
behaviour–experience

How do you oppose an opposition? Not necessarily by choosing and fighting for one of its terms over the other ('weakness is better than strength, understanding than control'), but by shifting levels, by becoming what systemic therapists call 'meta' to the bind: by finding alternative constructs that subsume the opposition, revealing it as farce. Remembering that the context here is psychological therapy, any possible 'meta' terms need to convey both concern and force, both dependence and strength. I suggest these two as tools for exploring and dissolving the effects of masculine ideology on psychological therapy:

reverie
empowerment

EXPERIENCE

Within psychology, the hard–soft opposition has its own way of operating (see Ussher, Chapter 2 in this volume). 'Hard' psychology is experimental, clear on statistics and the purity of research, concerned largely with part processes, physiology, cognitive science. It is less concerned with subjectivity, with people's experience and its meaning, and less still with the subjectivity of the researcher – with the psychologist's response to the other. The observer and the observed remain in separate worlds. 'Soft' psychologists are more phenomenological, exploring self and social context, taking seriously what individuals say and trying to relate their psychological work to the lives and narratives of the people with whom they come into contact. On the whole, but not by any means entirely, clinical psychology is more soft than hard, particularly in its therapeutic guise. It has its hard elements: neuro-psychology and behaviourism, for example. But the major project of clinical work, the helping encounter of one with another, is soft and, in the terms of the opposition, feminine in tone. It takes the other and her or his distress, explores, restructures, tries to ease the pain.

This work can be done in various ways, some on the pole of control, some on that of understanding and interpretation. It can and is done by men and women, but mostly women – although the positions of power are still largely occupied by men. In the structures of the profession, men operate as men and women as women; they all compete, the fast and the slow. Much can be written about the gender components of this social structure of the psychology profession; some of the essays in this book are focused precisely on that (e.g. Nicolson, Chapter 1 in this volume). But my target is what happens in therapy, in the moment of encounter between psychologist and patient; and in particular, what happens when the psychologist is a man. What is going on, and what is possible, when the man takes on the 'soft' role, becomes the nurturing other who can take on the sufferer's pain?

Let me make what I am exploring clearer by polarising the therapeutic endeavour, by making the therapeutic process as 'soft' as possible. I think successful, meaningful therapy arises out of a quite specific stance of the therapist, what Bion calls 'reverie'. In the developmental context,

> Reverie is that state of mind which is open to the reception of any 'objects' from the loved object and is therefore capable of the reception of the infant's projective identifications whether they are felt by the infant to be good or bad.
>
> (Bion 1962: 36)

It is a kind of dreaming state, a receptiveness to all experience, to everything that the child can offer; this is also, according to Symington's (1985) gloss, the state of receptivity to be sought by the therapist (in his context, the psychoanalyst), basically an openness to being changed by the patient's experience.

> A conscious state of not-knowing underpinned by a preconception stance seems to be what Bion recommends. Through the analyst's being a container. . .it is possible for a transformation to occur in the patient, from a means of communicating through projective identification to one where there are dream thoughts. This explains the paradox that when a patient has a dream, a phantasy or a thought about a particular thing it means that the thing is already within manageable proportions and can be so dreamed, phantasised or thought about. What had been got rid of through projective identification has now been reintrojected in a modified form, so can be dreamed about.
>
> (Symington 1985: 293–294)

Taking in, holding, making sense, giving back – this is the process of containment resulting from the state of reverie. From the point of view of the patient, the experience of being contained in this way is of having one's fragmented self, with all its destructive elements, accepted, tolerated and made manageable, alongside an awareness that this beneficial cycle arises from the presence of a reliable and stable other. According to psychoanalysts, its closest parallel, indeed the originating experience that makes reverie a possibility throughout life, is that of successful mothering. The Kleinian argument (e.g. Klein 1957) is that the mother acts as a receptacle for the infant's destructiveness as well as for her or his loving impulses; she takes these in and, by surviving them and continuing to be available to her infant, she communicates the possibility of acceptance and integration. The infant, consequently, experiences her or his destructiveness as managed and therefore manageable, thus becoming more able to tolerate it as an aspect of self. In therapy, what goes on is something similar: the articulation of pain and anxiety, and the projection of destructiveness into the therapist, creates a tension which can result in greater integration or in a more desperate splitting. Where therapy is successful, this account suggests, it is through the therapist's ability to 'hold' these projections, to recognise and respond

to them without retaliating or falling apart. Thus it is that the
patient experiences containment, the sense that something – some
reparation – can be made of what might otherwise be viewed as
inner waste.

The imagery here, the imagery of holding and containing pain,
is explicitly the traditional imagery of mothering. What has this to
do with masculinity, at least as it is systematically constructed in
Western culture? The therapeutic situation is one in which emotion surfaces as the fundamental currency; words and ideas, the
conventional medium of masculine expression, are of value only to
the extent that they convey or influence emotion. There are a
variety of possible responses to this situation which differ from the
focus on reverie outlined above. Reverie involves a balanced openness to all the projections of the patient. But one can refuse them:
it is possible to close the channels of emotional communication, to
be sympathetic but firm, to make suggestions but not really to
receive communications. Many interventionist procedures in psychological therapy work in this way, sometimes successfully. They
offer ways of managing distress which, from the point of view of
both patient and therapist, may be less stressful, less emotionally
intrusive than the open receptiveness of reverie. To some extent,
one can see these as masculine responses: the father comes in,
breaks into the unity of one and other, mother and child, says 'No'
to its all-absorbing properties, takes control and exerts his power.
As will be described below, this has in it some productive, empowering elements, but it can also be an avoidance of the maternal
hold, a way in which intense emotion is refused.

Something else might also operate here. The emotional
intensity of the therapeutic contact can be enormously enticing
and exciting in a voyeuristic way: it offers the intense emotional
experience of entering another's life in a highly charged environment, but it is also chaste, bounded, kept in its place and under
control. There is the stimulation, penetration of the emotional
centre, without the personal and emotional cost. If it is truly the
case that men tend towards emotional illiteracy (Seidler 1985),
that we find intimacy difficult but also alluring, then one of the
masculine infiltrations of the therapeutic situation is precisely this:
to use it to experience intimate, emotional contact, within bounds
which are given from outside, which reduce the personal load and
make the encounter safe. Thus, we may enter fully into the session
and yet not fully mean it; psychological therapy may meet some of

the needs of the therapist by offering an intense encounter – an experience of mothering – at minimal personal cost.

Elsewhere, I have suggested that the emotional illiteracy of men connects with the predominance of men amongst sexual abusers of children (Glaser and Frosh 1988); I have also suggested that one response to this for male workers is to become involved in therapeutic work with the victims of child sexual abuse, as a kind of reparative or perhaps counterphobic measure (Frosh 1987a). Perhaps, however, this is a more general masculine mechanism: for those men trying to convert masculinity into something more whole, less abbreviated, one attraction of therapeutic work is that it offers a situation in which emotion can be talked about with the safeguard that, as it is primarily other people's emotion, it can also be kept at bay. The session is bounded in time and place, it ends and so does the emotional demand. We do not have to take it home.

This should not be made into too much of a caricature. Most actual encounters between male psychologists and their patients are too complex to be understood just as an opportunity for the therapist to experience some vicarious emotion. Indeed, in the case examples given in the article on child sexual abuse mentioned above (Frosh 1987a) there is considerable evidence of a 'spilling over' of the emotion from the sessions into the external world of the therapist – as well as it also being clear that the therapeutic contact was being used to work through some difficult issues surrounding masculinity and sexual abuse. Conversely, it is probably also the case that women working in this area use the therapeutic situation to deal with some of their own unconscious conflicts. However, in this chapter it is the systematic contributions of gender which are under examination and it is in that context that I am claiming a connection between male involvement in psychological therapy and men's often unmet needs for intimacy with the other. At its extreme, what is being pursued is the fantasy of reabsorption in the mother, a regressive urge to re-enter the all-encompassing 'monad' (Grunberger 1989) from which the male feels himself to have been untimely ripped. More prosaically, masculine infiltration of the therapeutic situation can be seen in the way psychological therapy sometimes becomes a struggle for mastery between psychologist and other, reflected, as noted above, in some of our 'techniques'.

All this material suggests that masculinity intrudes upon the therapeutic process, never advancing it. If that is so, one wonders if there is any future for male clinical psychologists and other male therapists. But this is not the entirety of my argument; infiltration of psychological therapy by 'masculine ideology' means the debasement of the therapeutic encounter, but it is not all that happens or might possibly happen when the male therapist connects with the patient or, more symbolically, when the 'Other' enters the room. To explain and explore what I mean by this, I want to discuss the imagery of therapeutic power.

POWER, POWERLESSNESS, EMPOWERMENT

The traditional fantasy of power is one in which power is possessed by one person or group and used over and against another. Foucault's analyses of cultural history, particularly the cultural history of sexuality (Foucault 1979), demonstrate the inadequacy of this notion of power and the comparative utility of a view of power as something created through all the networks of force relations which arise between people.

> Relations of power are not in superstructural positions, with merely a role of prohibition or accompaniment; they have a directly productive role, wherever they come into play.
>
> (Foucault 1979: 94)

The point here, for our purposes, is that despite the wider differences between the power of men and women as social groups, demonstrated in the historical and contemporary oppression of women, each actual encounter is one in which specific relations of power and resistance are engaged with, re-negotiated, and reborn. Power, therefore, is not something which remains with the man and can only be opposed or acknowledged, any more than it is some concrete entity inherent 'in' the therapist. Power differentials certainly exist – white male psychologist and black female patient do not have the same starting point – but something can potentially be made of this in the therapeutic setting. Power can be an object of investigation and a means through which the 'subjectification' (Banton *et al.* 1985) of the individual occurs – that is, a means whereby the patient can move towards the discovery of her or himself as subjected to a complex variety of inner and outer forces.

A useful psychoanalytic perspective is brought to bear on this from the work of Lacan. Lacan's emphasis on the status and symbolic functions of the phallus has led to accusations of phallo-centrism and, indeed, of straightforward sexism and misogyny on his part. These accusations may be well-founded in themselves (see Gallop 1982; Irigaray 1977) and there are certainly instances of anti-feminist provocation on Lacan's part which deserve, and have received, scathing repudiation (see Frosh 1987b, 1989 for dis-cussions of the debates on Lacanian views of femininity). However, many of Lacan's ideas are particularly productive in relation to thinking on sexual difference, power and therapy. The one I want to mention here concerns the fictitious, or rather 'Imaginary', status of the phallus. The phallus, taken as an emblem of patri-archy, apparently dividing and ruling the world, is fantasised by people as a real entity, a unity of purpose and power. In the end, it is usually understood as, or reduced to, a kind of 'guarantor' of sexual difference ('Of course men and women are different – you only have to look to see') and its power is invested in men as bearers of a bodily organ mistakenly taken for the phallus – the penis. But the phallus is not real and it is not the penis; nor is it something, the possession of which will provide all the answers, will give power to her who has not. What the phallus 'actually' is, is a reminder that there is no real oneness, no absolute power at all.

> It is an essential element in Lacan's theory that there is no complete unity or Otherness that inhabits the universe; there is only the search for this Other that reflects and constructs the absences each individual feels inside and which are fantasised as fulfilling the desires that have to be repressed at the insistence of the castration complex – the desire to be the object of the mother's desire.
>
> (Frosh 1987b: 198)

The phallus functions as an imaginary cover for loss and dis-ruption; it represents power, but it has no real power in itself. One of the goals of therapy, it might be said, is to discover this – to discover that there is no single answer to everything, no 'Other' to which all questions may be referred. An argument that can be made here is that discovering the fictitious nature of the 'mastery' of the therapist can be entwined with exposure to the gender difference of male psychologist/female patient so common in the clinical psychological environment. That is, the lack of mastery of the supposed 'master' – the expert – is potentially a liberating experience, allowing the patient to hear her own voice rather than taking on some fantasy of the Other.

It is the typical encroachment of masculine ideology to act as if the phallus is real, as if there is mastery, an answer, which can be imposed or delivered from without. Then a kind of dance develops, in which the male psychologist depends on the female patient to allow him to demonstrate his mastery and expertise, while the patient, aware only of her distress and loss, needs the therapist to tell her what to do. Each bolsters the other and sometimes change occurs and both are satisfied; more commonly, however, all that changes is in the Imaginary – each partner is confirmed in their fantasy of self and other. It is the classic Master–Slave dialectic, found commonly in the relationship of expert to client, and perhaps especially doctor to patient (Banton *et al.* 1985): Master and Slave need each other. Reflecting the wider social associations of masculinity and mastery, femininity and slavery, in relations between male therapist and male patient the blocks to progress come from a more cautious dialectic, shown perhaps in some shadow-boxing and avoidance, perhaps in some shuffling around of the cards of power without any being played.

Where there is a recognition of the reality and limits of power, however, there is also the prospect for change. What this means is that claims to mastery can be punctured, power subverted, the subjected individual empowered. This links with the advocacy of reverie, given earlier, in that reverie is a total acceptance and holding of the other, not a means of imposing prestructured knowledge and expertise. There is considerable technique involved in maintaining the attitude and stance of reverie, but the technique is not the essence; the essence of reverie is an ability, as therapist, to be centred enough in oneself for it to be possible to incorporate fully the projections of the patient without being fragmented and destroyed. By its very nature, this is an approach opposed to 'mastery' and power; it allows the patient to use the therapist as a container for what is otherwise experienced as un-contained – for pain, anger, rage and despair. The therapist, however, does not 'solve' the problem presented by the patient; the therapist just survives it, in the process allowing the patient to discover her own ability to survive. The man who can do that subverts the imagery of the phallus – the notion of the masculine order as in control.

This idealised picture may be unbelievable in its extreme form, but I think small instances of such empowerment occur quite frequently in practice, even if they are only partial and confused. Here is one such small example, from a brief piece of work with a family referred to me in the setting of a child and family therapy clinic, a family whom I shall call the M family.

The referral to the clinic was made by Mrs M, on the advice of her child Mary's school. Mary, aged six, was compulsively masturbating, constantly rubbing herself against tables. She used to do this at home but had recently stopped. The rubbing was so severe that Mary made herself very sore and had bruises in the genital area. There had been considerable involvement in the family from their health visitor and general practitioner, who did not believe that Mary was being sexually abused – the GP reported that he had seen Mary regularly and that the soreness occurred only during the school term time and was consistent with Mrs M's story.

The family was made up of Mr M (aged 35), Mrs M, (aged 33), who had worked in the same office as her husband, but was now at home with the children full time, Mary and three other children – Rose (8), Paul (4) and Damian (1). The case was taken on by myself and a female psychiatric social worker with whom I had never previously worked.

In the first session, Mrs M was very dominant. Mr M was quiet and took no initiative with respect to the children, although when his wife told him to do something he was quite effective. Mrs M was very aggressive towards us – an aggression perhaps symbolised by the fact that she brought her knitting to the session, which coincided with the anniversary of the French Revolution. She confronted us, demanding explanations for her child's behaviour, but she also made fun of us – for instance, saying about me, 'he just sits there and takes it all in'. She described how Mary used to masturbate at home but stopped when she was firm with her and shouted at her. She said that the school refused to be firm in the same way – the teacher tried it once and Mary 'crumpled' so badly and seemed so frightened that the teacher felt unable to be severe with her again. Mrs M described her husband in an angry and derogatory way, particularly for being unavailable for the children or her. She said that he spends his time in the garden shed, leaving her to do everything in the house. He is quiet, she talks. Mary was described as reasonably assertive at home, but she was noticeably passive and frightened in the session, while her siblings took easy control of the room. Mrs M told us that she intercedes for Mary at home, because Rose is always taking her things or hurting her and there is a great deal of competitiveness between them.

The second session began in the same way. Mrs M told us she was appalled that we had discussed Mary in front of her – she claimed that the school and the health visitor were equally critical of us. She doubted our ability to do anything and had brought her knitting again so as not to waste the time. Mr M sat quietly, answering questions asked of him but saying little else. My colleague and I were acutely aware of Mrs M's sardonic glances at us. We felt antagonistic towards her, wondering how the children could manage to survive – it was not surprising, we thought, that Mary was in such a state. Her masturbation was the same as ever, almost constant at school (confirmed by a telephone call to the teacher). Mrs M got annoyed when we asked if she ever went into school, saying that the other mothers did, but how could she when she had the boys to look after at home? She challenged my silence, asking if I had anything to offer her at all. I responded with a very direct intervention, developing and verbalising a hypothesis there and then, suggesting that Mary found school harder than people realise, that she knew her mother could not come in to help her as she does at home unless something really extreme happens, and that she had realised that her constant rubbing was just such an extreme thing. Mrs M suddenly began to listen, seeming very engaged in what was being said. We left the family to think about this hypothesis, also asking Mr M to take more control.

This last section of this session proved to be a turning point in our work with the family; subsequently, Mrs M, whilst still provocative and demeaning of her husband, worked hard with us to understand her child and to help her. Indeed, following a visit to the school, Mary's compulsive rubbing ceased with no particular intervention on our part, and the focus of the sessions shifted to Mrs M's anger at the lack of support she felt herself to be receiving from her husband – in particular his lack of emotional responsiveness.

There are obviously a number of reasons why the changes which occurred in this family may have come about, some at least of which might have been located outside therapy, for instance in changes in the schoolteacher's perception of Mary. Moreover, this was by no means a perfect piece of family therapeutic work, nor does it have perfectly non-sexist credentials. Perhaps character-istically for a male psychologist, my focus was not on the male patient; indeed, it may have been that the relative insignificance of my female colleague in this session was due to my usurpation of her isometry with Mrs M – we both competed for the ear of the woman. Change came about, but as usual through the mother: the opportunity to challenge the father's secure unavailability to his wife and children was left unrecognised. Some shadow-boxing, a few suggestions, but not too much conflict or pain. Or maybe there is another, partially contradictory source to this overdetermined sequence: by not challenging the male but focusing on changes in the woman, we men are in a happy identificatory collusion. After all, structuralists claim the woman to be the object of exchange between men. Also, of course, my potency as therapist has its competitive edge with my 'colleague'; when the male takes over, the professional voice is heard. We all wait to see what rabbit the expert male will pull out of his hat.

But I want to find something positive in this, and to focus on just one element in the family–therapy relationship, the meaning of the therapy for Mrs M. There appeared to be a 'transformational moment' in the second session, when, riled by Mrs M's challenge, I managed to offer something which both surprised and engaged her. Some of it may have had to do with the content of the 'hypothesis' about Mary's behaviour, which seemed to make sense to Mrs M. But I think something else happened too. With her husband, the pattern was for his withdrawal to be reinforced by her aggressive attacks – her withering, emasculating remarks. Alongside this dynamic, I think Mrs M actually felt terrible about what Mary was doing, believing that it indicated a severe failure on her own part, for after all she was charged with – and had taken on for herself – complete responsibility for all that happened with her children. In addition, she felt strongly identified with Mary, seeing Mary's personality as just like her own. I think that this combination of factors, plus other elements in Mrs M's history, led her to feel quite desperate about herself, overwhelmed both by anger and by an intolerable sense that Mary, by damaging herself, was actually damaging her. That is, Mrs M's identification with her daughter was such that she felt Mary's self-injuring actions to be attacks on her. My response, in most respects quite accidentally, broke into this vicious cycle. First, the content of it was not blaming of her. More importantly, however, its context was as a response to Mrs M's challenge; it was animated by my own sense of being disturbed by her, but it was not an aggressive assault. As a man, I

had neither withdrawn nor exploded, but had unconsciously cued
into her own emotional tone – desperation and rage rather than
violence – and made something of it.

I was not particularly full of reverie that day, but perhaps just
enough to register the message underneath the words. Moreover,
it was important, I am sure, that it was I rather than my female
co-worker who hit upon this response. The sexual challenge in Mrs
M's behaviour was strong, as perhaps it was too in her daughter's
behaviour – which may have been an unconscious echo of Mrs M's
own sense of the destructiveness of her own sexuality. In any event,
my maleness was significant to her, both in traditional trans-
ferential ways (her relationship with her father and her husband
were constant themes in her talk in later sessions) and as a specific
marker of difference. I was not identified with her, was not 'same'
like her daughter, so my recognition of her emotional state came
from somewhere else than her, broke into her consciousness to
turn things around. My difference from her made my apparent
understanding of, and sympathy for, her that much more un-
expected and therefore powerful. My masculinity was a challenge
to her, which is why she challenged me: she had to triumph. But
when we escaped this dance, this symmetry, it was a difference that
helped her renew herself.

It is here that what some psychoanalysts (e.g. Grunberger 1989)
refer to as the Narcissus–Oedipus opposition enters, an opposition
which is built around the polarity of same and different. Much
feminist psychology and psychoanalysis has been concerned particularly with a revaluing of mothering. This can be seen especially
clearly in feminist uses of object relations theory (e.g. Chodorow
1978; Eichenbaum and Orbach 1982; Ernst and Maguire 1987),
which has resulted in a serious and challenging exploration of
mother–daughter relationships and of the identification
mechanisms whereby internalisations of assumptions and attitudes
towards femininity occur. One of the things that is intriguing
about this, however, is that it contrasts, at least in part, with the
celebrations of femininity as heterogeneity so characteristic of
what might be called the radical feminist position within recent
psychoanalytic thinking. In the quotation from Cixous (1975),
given earlier, for example, the emphasis is on the multifariousness
of femininity; Irigaray (1977), exiled from Lacanianism on this
very issue, famously celebrates the multiple nature of femininity,
claiming feminine sexuality as a mystery which is always plural – at

least two, never subject to the singularity of the penis. It is the female body that speaks of this: the woman is always touching herself autoerotically, the lips of the vagina rubbing and embracing continually.

> The woman does not have a sex. She has at least two of them, but they cannot be identified as ones. Indeed she has many more of them than that. Her sexuality, always at least double, is in fact plural.
>
> (Irigaray 1977: 102)

The 'otherness' of woman resides in her inconstancy, her multiplicity and flux, which functions subversively to undermine masculine attempts at control, at holding things in their place. What is particular about feminine sexuality, according to Irigaray, is that it is not any one 'particular' thing, not located in any one bodily part, nor constrainable into any singular form.

Despite the many differences between object relational and post-Lacanian accounts of femininity (see Frosh 1987b), there is a shared perspective here of some importance, a perspective which might be called narcissistic. This is that the woman creates herself; through the cycle of mothering she forms a closed community of women, self-sustaining, rooted in the body and in the particularity of non-masculine states of feeling – semiotic states, rhythmic rather than semantic, not pinned down to a system of phallic mastery and control. This is a double-edged sword with which to fight masculine ideology, however. On the one hand, as emphasised earlier in this chapter, femininity expressed as multifariousness, as 'infidelity' (Gallop 1982), subverts the masculine attempt to homogenise and constrain experience into easily manageable units. On the other hand, however, it romanticises women in remarkably traditional ways – as intuitive, inconsistent, unreliable, with a less bounded sexuality than that of men. Certainly these groups of feminists produce a different valuing of this polarity: it is better to be joyously heterogeneous and intuitive than rigidly straight and scientific. But they do not, on the whole, oppose its terms: femininity is still, by nature, different from masculinity, in well recognised and ideologically accepted ways.

There is a broader point here concerned with the narcissism issue. The focus on mother–infant relations so characteristic of both object relational and psychological literature on development, has its counterpart in approaches to psychological therapy that emphasise support and nurture – the reconstruction of what Grunberger (1989) calls the 'monad', the post-natal protected environment supplied by the mother to her child. The danger of this position is that it can be a regressive one, offering the fantasy of wholeness or oneness as a possible escape from reality into the confirming circularities of empathy. The feminine orientation of therapy here can support this circularity, by making an enclosure in which the structuring realities of the external world are bracketed out, and self and other unite. The contrast with this is what Lacan terms the 'Name-of-the-Father', the Oedipal contradiction that shatters the imaginary unity of self and other by introducing the workings of the Other, the systems of Law through which culture operates – the third term in the Oedipal matrix that determines the possibility of functioning of the other two. The desire of child for mother is forbidden by an outside force; analogically, the cosy unity of patient and therapist is undermined by the dimension of difference which appears across the boundary of sex.

Somewhere in this material lies a starting-point for a revaluation of the masculine position in psychological therapy. Its drawbacks have been described in detail earlier: attempts at control, vicarious emotionality, power-manipulation and exploitation of the other in the service of the self. But the productive side of it is the introduction of difference, the realisation that therapy is not just about self-confirmation but is also about challenge. In work with women, acceptance of the other and refusal of mastery intersects with the confrontation implicit in speaking from the position of otherness – encouraging an expectation of difference but also subverting its presumed content. In work with men, the 'mothering' stance of empathic reverie combines with the power of sameness to confuse the accepted categories of what is appropriate to masculine speech and modes of interrelationship. In both instances, there is the potential for psychological therapy to be a creative struggle, in which the ability of the therapist to be at one with the other also allows articulation of critical challenges and a breaking out from the circle of sameness into which gender so often forces us. All of this is about sexual difference after all, and making a difference is what psychological therapists are supposed to be trying to do.

REFERENCES

Banton, R., Clifford, P., Frosh, S., Lousada, J. and Rosenthall, J. (1985) *The Politics of Mental Health.* London: Macmillan.

Bion, W. (1962) *Learning from Experience.* London: Maresfield.

Chodorow, N. (1978) *The Reproduction of Mothering.* Berkeley: University of California Press.

Cixous, H. (1975) Sorties. In H. Cixous and C. Clement, *The Newly Born Woman.* Manchester: Manchester University Press.

Eichenbaum, L. and Orbach, S. (1982) *Outside In. . .Inside Out.* Harmondsworth: Penguin.

Ernst, S. and Maguire, M. (eds) (1987) *Living with the Sphinx.* London: Women's Press.

Foucault, M. (1979) *The History of Sexuality,* Volume 1. Harmondsworth: Penguin.

Frosh, S. (1987a) Issues for men working with sexually abused children. *British Journal of Psychotherapy,* 3: 332–339.

Frosh, S. (1987b) *The Politics of Psychoanalysis.* London: Macmillan.

Frosh, S. (1989) *Psychoanalysis and Psychology.* London: Macmillan.

Gallop, J. (1982) *Feminism and Psychoanalysis.* London: Macmillan.

Glaser, D. and Frosh, S. (1988) *Child Sexual Abuse.* London: Macmillan.

Grunberger, B. (1989) *New Essays on Narcissism.* London: Free Association Books.

Irigaray, L. (1977) *This Sex Which is Not One.* Ithaca: Cornell University Press.

Klein, M. (1957) Envy and gratitude. In Klein, M. *Envy and Gratitude and Other Works.* New York: Delta.

Kristeva, J. (1974) *Revolution in Poetic Language.* New York: Columbia University Press.

Seidler, V. (1985) Fear and intimacy. In A. Metcalf and M. Humphries (eds), *The Sexuality of Men.* London: Pluto.

Symington, N. (1985) *The Analytic Experience.* London: Free Association Books.

Theweleit, K. (1977) *Male Fantasies.* Cambridge: Polity Press.

Wetherall, M. (1986) Linguistic repertoires and literary criticism: new directions for a social psychology of gender. In S. Wilkinson (ed.), *Feminist Social Psychology.* Milton Keynes: Open University Press.

Chapter 8

Working with socially disabled clients

A feminist perspective

Rachel E. Perkins

INTRODUCTION

This chapter will consider, from a feminist perspective, gender issues in relation to working with severely socially disabled people: people who are unable to cope with the demands of everyday life without a great deal of help, support and shelter. It is not the intention to consider particular diagnostic groups, or to consider the aetiology of different types of problems. Rather, attention will be directed towards the resulting social disablement with a focus on those severely disabled as a result of major mental health problems: people who have the serious disturbances of cognition, affect and behaviour that have been called 'schizophrenia', 'manic-depressive illness' and the like. Although consideration will centre on this type of social disablement, the majority of issues raised also apply to people who are seriously socially disabled as a consequence of various forms of brain injury, learning difficulties, or senile and pre-senile dementias. There are an estimated 40 million people worldwide who are severely socially disabled by mental health problems (World Health Organisation 1973, 1987; Cohen 1988). However, whilst gender issues in relation to people with problems that are less disabling have received a great deal of attention over the last two decades from both psychologists and feminists (e.g. Chesler 1973, 1989; Penfold and Walker 1984; Brodsky and Hare-Mustin 1984; Blechman 1984; Mowbray, Lanir and Hulce 1985), this has not been the case for those whose difficulties are more long-lived or profound. Severely socially disabled women remain largely invisible, 'lost' amongst the 'Forgotten Millions' described by Cohen (1988). Clinical psychologists' work with severely socially disabled people almost invariably involves more than working with individual clients. It involves the planning of services, the definition of service needs of populations and individuals, the evaluation of services, the teaching of other professionals, and support/help for other carers, all of which are intimately related. Therefore both service provision and individual care will be considered.

THE NATURE OF SOCIAL DISABLEMENT

Psychologists have long eshewed the 'medical' model and have replaced concepts of disease with ideas about faulty learning, dysfunctional cognitions and intra-psychic conflict. However, research and interventions remain largely 'cure' based in terms of time-limited interventions directed towards the modification of dysfunctional thoughts, feelings and behaviour, or the resolution of intra-psychic conflicts. The bulk of clinical training is directed towards such endeavours, and there has been relatively little consideration of concepts of disability in thoughts, feelings and behaviour. Feminist theorists have also rejected the medicalisation of distress and the psychiatric enterprise as a means of patriarchal control. It has been variously argued that 'mental illness' is invented by, or caused by patriarchy (e.g. Showalter 1987; Chesler 1973, 1989; Penfold and Walker 1984). On the one hand, 'mental illness' has been seen as a means of oppressing women who deviate from their traditional role: women who do not define themselves in terms of men and service men in the manner expected are defined as 'mad'. Undoubtedly this has occurred and some of what has been called 'hysteria' and 'personality disorder', and most, if not all, 'sexual dysfunction' might be seen in these terms. On the other hand, psychological distress has been viewed as a product of oppression. The stresses imposed by oppression can, and undoubtedly do, precipitate socially disabling disorders of cognition, affect and behaviour (e.g. Brown and Harris 1978; Garner *et al.* 1980; Garfinkel and Garner 1982) and much of what has been labelled depression, anxiety-based disorders, eating disorders and alcoholism might usefully be understood in these terms. A third strand has been the romanticisation of madness as some state of 'heightened awareness' in which the person is in touch with their 'real self': a state of 'enhanced creativity'. Whilst this approach has at various times been popular, it is almost impossible to believe in ideas about 'heightened awareness' and 'creativity' when faced with the reality of the disability and distress of someone whose internal world is chaotic and disorganised, who experiences a grossly distorted reality, and who suffers 'high levels of stress and anxiety as they struggle to negotiate between the world as others know it and the world of their inner reality' (Hatfield 1989: 1,142).

> Schizophrenia is painful, and it is craziness when I hear voices, and when I believe people are following me, wanting to snatch my very soul. I am frightened too when every whisper, every laugh is about me; when newspapers suddenly contain curses, four-letter words shouting at me; when sparkles of light are demon eyes. Schizophrenia is frightening when I can't hold on to my thoughts . . . My existence is undefined – mere image that I keep reaching for but never touch.
>
> (McGrath 1984: 638)

Romanticisation may make others feel better but it does little for the women concerned: it merely renders them more isolated in their distress (Ussher 1991; Sedgewick 1982). In general both psychologists and feminists have tended to deny the existence of serious disability and have assumed that all problems are essentially remediable with the correct therapeutic approach, the elimination of patriarchal oppression, or both. Whilst it is undoubtedly the case that many difficulties are remediable and that oppressive political structures generate much distress and disability, the assumption that all difficulties are an invention or product of oppression seems dangerous. Within existing patriarchal structures profound social disablement does exist. It is impossible to say how much there would be in a different political setting. However, I cannot understand the processes or mechanisms via which all severe disturbances of cognition and affect (or learning difficulties, brain injury or dementia) will be eradicated along with patriarchy. It is my contention that there is nothing sacrosanct about thoughts feelings and behaviour that somehow render them immune from disability. Probably the most useful framework for understanding severe social disablement comes from the work of the social psychiatrists (Wing 1962, 1963, 1967, 1978; Wing and Morris 1981). A person is defined as socially disabled if they are unable to perform socially to the standards expected by themselves, people important to them, or society in general (Wing and Morris 1981). 'Their difficulties can be best understood as failure to be able to cope in various everyday roles'

(Shepherd 1984: 22). Just as the person with physical disabilities is unable to negotiate the physical world without help, aids and assistance, so the socially disabled person is unable to negotiate the social world without special supports. Such social disablement is seen as a consequence of three interrelated sets of factors:

1. Primary impairments which comprise the disturbances of cognition, affect and behaviour that characterise the disorder itself. The inability to organise one's thoughts; to concentrate on, or attend to, anything for more than a few minutes; to be continually hearing voices talking about you; to know that everyone around wishes you malice: all of these present problems for the person in coping with everyday life that the non-disabled person does not experience.

2. Adverse personal reactions is the term used to describe the person's response to the experience of serious mental health problems. These reactions are not inherent in the disorders of cognition, affect and behaviour themselves, but instead comprise the way in which the person responds to or copes with the experience of such problems in our society. The experience of serious long-term mental health problems represents a major and extremely traumatic life event. Not only do people experience the primary impairments of cognition, affect and behaviour, but their life often changes in a number of negative ways: friends and family are lost, or relationships substantially altered; jobs are lost; homes are lost; indeed all that the person had previously taken for granted is jeopardised. 'These men and women have the awesome task of learning to accept that life is irrevocably different' (Hatfield 1989: 1,143). It is less than surprising then that people react adversely to the experience. Shepherd (1984) describes two typical 'adverse personal reactions': denial of any problems because the idea of 'mental illness' and its consequences is too terrifying to contemplate; or complete loss of confidence, and avoidance of stress of any kind for fear of exacerbating problems (Wing and Morris 1981). These reactions are not a feature of the disorder itself, nor some additional 'pathology'. They parallel those of non-disabled people to traumatic life events (e.g. Parkes 1972; Lazarus and Folkman 1984; Steptoe and Sullivan 1986; Taylor and Perkins 1991) and constitute a perfectly understandable response to the experience of major problems and the way in which these are

understood and managed within society. However, they make it difficult for the person to make the most of the skills and abilities that they do have (Wing and Morris 1981; Shepherd 1984).

3. Social disadvantages. The third contributor to social disablement is the various social disadvantages that either reflect pre-existing disadvantage, or are a consequence of the experience of serious problems with cognition, affect and behaviour in our society. Pre-existing disadvantages include, for example, poor education, living conditions, family relationships, and, specifically in relation to women, the oppression, violence, sexual abuse, subordination, and devaluation inherent in patriarchal oppression (Jeffreys 1990). As Bachrach (1988) stresses, women typically experience a variety of social disadvantages as a consequence of their oppression that contribute to their social disablement. Other social disadvantages may be seen as a consequence of the problems themselves: poverty, homelessness, stigmatisation, exclusion from many aspects of 'normal' life, and disrupted family and social networks are all ways in which those who do not 'fit in' as a result of cognitive, affective and behavioural difficulties are marginalised and rendered powerless.

These represent a major contributor to social disablement. I could not live on £43 per week in a high-rise flat in central London without a job, friends, family, and with the knowledge that everyone regarded me as the 'loony' next door and did not understand my experiences or distress. Nor could I live in a hospital or hostel on around £10 per week with people who I did not choose, often in fear of violence from others, never being able to call anything my own, having my few possessions stolen, being harassed for cigarettes or sex, and excluded from the outside world. Yet this is what we expect of some of the most vulnerable people in our society who are often least able to cope with the stresses that it imposes. The courage and determination of people in this position is amazing.

Whilst ideas about social disablement have been extant for nearly 30 years, it has always been assumed that such disablement is a 'given' and 'objectively' definable characteristic. However, it is evident from the very definition of social disablement that it represents a socially constructed phenomenon. The expectations of the individual, those important to them, and society in general (Wing and Morris 1981) are determined by the social/political structures in which the person functions. Different forms of political organisation determine the nature of the social world, what 'successful' negotiation of it involves, the nature of 'everyday' or 'normal' social roles, and the range of acceptable role performance.

From a feminist perspective, social disablement must be understood in the context of heterosexist patriarchal oppression. Within hetero-patriarchal organisation the roles of women are defined in relation to men. Thus social disablement is defined in terms of the extent to which the disabled individual is unable to perform adequately in male-defined roles. Clinical psychologists tend to avoid such political issues under the auspices of 'science' and 'outcome' research (see Ussher's Chapter 2 in this volume). Problems are individualised and personalised (Kitzinger 1987), and work with the socially disabled person is seen as a largely technical enterprise. The person's problems and needs are defined via a series of inventories (e.g. Brewin *et al.* 1987), and then interventions are directed towards changing the person by the most 'effective' means available. However, the 'outcomes' (and related methods) essentially involve political judgements. The effect of avoiding these is to design intervention, support, and continuing care services (and evaluate the 'effectiveness' of these) in terms of the extent to which they enhance the functioning of their recipients in 'normal', that is male-defined, roles: those very roles in which they have by definition been unable to perform adequately.

To illustrate with a case example. For years May had been coming in and out of hospital – always more in than out – with life-threatening periods of depression when she took to her bed; refused to eat, drink, go to the toilet, or speak; and if anyone approached her she would attack them. She was admitted when her husband could no longer tolerate her at home. In hospital she would improve with treatment, support and relief from her responsibilities as a wife. She would then be discharged home to resume her wife role (looking after the domestic arrangements of the house, and furnishing her husband with support and sex) with individual and family therapy to sustain her in this role. After increasingly brief periods at home she would relapse and require re-admission. It took 20 years before anyone seriously questioned the wisdom of this approach. What we did eventually was to discourage her from going home – suggest she remain in hospital. The result? For the next 3 years she never relapsed. She continued to see her husband – he visited her, she visited him – but she did not have to 'service' him. She still required considerable help and support with daily life, but, when relieved of much of the 'wife' role, she ceased to become profoundly depressed. She developed friends amongst other service recipients and, with the shelter of the hospital, was able to resume several interests and activities that she had long since ceased to perform. Clearly continued hospitalisation was not an ideal solution, but given the many constraints in the situation it was probably the best that could be achieved: the 'community' may not always be 'best'.

Severely socially disabled women represent a marginalised and powerless group who are often desperately trying to 'fit in' and belong. All too often the only opportunity for belonging comes via acceptance of the prescriptions of patriarchal roles and expectations. A striking feature of the effectiveness of women's oppression in general lies in its ability to cause the oppressed group to oppress themselves. Severely disabled women are no exception. Marginalised and excluded from patriarchal society because of their inability to perform socially to the standards expected of them they see their only hope of acceptance and value as lying in male-defined roles and expectations. It is a common clinical experience to find the majority of severely disabled female clients desperately want to look attractive to men, get married, have children and adopt a traditional female role: all aspirations that are reinforced by services. Work is typically seen as less important for women (Showalter 1987; Goering *et al.* 1988; Perkins and Rowland 1986, 1990). Instead, domestic pursuits are encouraged and a lot of what have been called 'women's groups' in psychiatric services spend an inordinate amount of time involved in make-up, nail polish and 'hair doing' sessions, recipients being praised when they 'look nice'.

The possibility of disabled women not defining themselves in relation to men and their traditional role in patriarchal society is rarely if ever considered. Indeed, it is almost impossible to be a lesbian with long-term social disablements. Whilst lesbianism is itself no longer proscribed within patriarchal psychiatry, lesbianism in the context of severe social disablement is almost invariably seen as a manifestation of disorder. For example, one severely disabled lesbian explained her lesbianism thus: 'When I was playing golf a ball hit my little finger and broke it: that's what made me lesbian.' Her lesbianism, together with the explanation for it, was written off as a delusional belief.

Likewise, the heterosexist practices of most facilities for the severely disabled completely omit consideration of the possibility that some of their users may not define themselves in relation to men. For example, one young woman gave up going to the day centre that she was supposed to attend 'because they are always trying to pair me up with men – I'm really not interested in men you know, I like women but at [the day centre] its always about men'.

Severely disabled women are unlikely to change the world – they make lousy revolutionaries! They often act alone according to rules that make no 'sense' and are contrary to those of our culture (Chesler 1973) and are too vulnerable to the rejection, exclusion and abuse that people attempting to change the existing order are likely to engender. Yet as they have manifestly been unable to cope in 'normal' roles it must be seen as the responsibility of services to consider the possibility of alternatives.

In considering gender issues in relation to clinical psychologists' work with severely socially disabled people, two interrelated areas are important: the philosophies guiding service provision and care, and specific models of intervention.

GENDER ISSUES IN SERVICE DEVELOPMENT: COMPETING PHILOSOPHIES OF CARE

Traditionally, severely socially disabled people have been excluded and marginalised from society: hospitalisation was intended to bring back into line those who deviate from prescribed norms, and excluded them from society and rendered powerless until such time as they conformed. The shortcomings of such institutions, isolated from everyday life with their 'rigid routines' and 'block treatment', and their depersonalising and handicapping effect on their residents are well documented (Barton 1959; Goffman 1961; Wing and Brown 1970), as is the sexist nature of treatment within them (Showalter 1987).

Ideas about institutionalisation and asylum for severely socially disabled people have now been replaced by concepts of deinstitutionalisation, normalisation and community care. These terms are often used interchangeably, but it is important to distinguish between them. The fundamental tenets of deinstitutionalisation are that most, if not all of the problems of patients in psychiatric institutions result from the institutional practices that occur within them, and that by removing people from such an environment their problems will disappear. These ideas proved very attractive to politicians who were becoming increasingly concerned about the expense of large psychiatric institutions. So what developed was a rather unholy alliance between what Bachrach (1978) has called 'therapeutic radicals and fiscal conservatives': a massive run-down in hospital populations ensued, together with attempts to avoid admission wherever possible. These deinstitutionalisation initiatives often had extremely deleterious effects upon the severely disabled women involved. Such women are particularly vulnerable to violence and sexual exploitation (Test and Berlin 1981), and there are suggestions that severe psychopathology is more widespread and intense amongst homeless women than homeless men (Bachrach 1985).

The deinstitutionalisation movement effectively denies the existence of severe social disablement as anything other than a product of institutionalisation. The folly of this assumption has been amply highlighted in the popular media by the various revelations of gross neglect and distress amongst those who have been discharged from psychiatric hospitals (e.g. Wallace 1987; National Schizophrenia Fellowship/Schizophrenia: A National Emergency 1988). However, a deinstitutionalisation philosophy still guides much service provision today. For example, there are large numbers of 'short-stay' hostels, sheltered working environments and day facilities that basically operate on a 'throughput' model. Such facilities purport to help the person to make the transition from hospital to community and essentially deny the existence of ongoing disability of cognition, affect and behaviour and consequent need for support and help without limit of time. To take a parallel with physical disability: if a person has no legs then no one would dream of setting a time limit on their use of a wheelchair, walking aids, or residence in a specially adapted environment. These would be seen as essential long-term supports and would be provided on an ongoing basis.

One consequence of deinstitutionalisation moves has been the invention of the 'revolving door' patient (Hoult 1986): the person who is hospitalised during periods of acute distress and disturbance when their symptoms can no longer be accommodated in the community. In hospital they are treated and discharged as soon as possible, generally with only minimal out-patient follow-up. Care is instead provided by 'the family' and there is a burgeoning literature on the 'family management' of such disorders as 'schizophrenia' (e.g. Leff *et al.* 1985; Falloon *et al.* 1987; MacCarthy *et al.* 1989). However, the reality is generally that care is transferred from hospital staff to female relatives – usually mothers. The burden of care on these women, and on others in the community, is increased. All they can do is to wait until the person's condition deteriorates to the point where re-admission is considered to be warranted by hospital services. The disabled person takes on the role of 'patienthood' and is marginalised in just the same way as happened in the traditional institution – but at less expense to the state.

Sheehan (1982) has described the experiences of one severely disabled woman's experience of the 'revolving door': a woman who never quite belonged in hospital or in the community and who was searching for a world in which she could be understood and accepted. The question is not simply one of 'protecting' women from unwarranted interventions by patriarchal psychiatry (e.g. Quinn 1985; Cook 1985) – it often becomes one of disabled women's rights to help and support.

It should be noted that the effects of anti-psychiatry, deinstitutionalisation ideas on severely disabled women have been largely similar to those of traditional psychiatry and institutionalisation. Such women are rendered marginal and excluded/removed from the male-defined roles in which they have been unable to perform adequately. 'Incarceration' and 'neglect'/'denial of disability' have similar consequences, but the latter is less expensive. A quite different approach can be seen in 'community care' and 'normalisation' approaches: that of supporting severely disabled women in 'normal' roles.

The philosophy of community care accepts that instead of preparing people for community living, the essence of services for the severely socially disabled person must be to sustain them in community living (Stein and Test 1980). The basic tenets of community care are that there is no treatment, intervention or support available within a hospital that could not equally well be provided outside, and that care provided outside hospital is preferable because it avoids the negative consequences of hospitalisation.

In contrast to deinstitutionalisation which involved the discharge of people from hospital, community care essentially involves the discharge of services and professionals from hospital to provide care for people in the communities where they live. 'Outcome' studies demonstrate that, if done properly (Bachrach 1989), community care 'works' (e.g. Keisler 1982; Stein and Test 1980; Hoult and Reynolds 1984). However, from a feminist perspective it is important to examine closely what 'working' means for severely disabled women.

In the development of community care services Bachrach (1984, 1985, 1988) suggests that prevailing assumptions about gender have had major implications in the design of programmes for severely socially disabled women in America. Programmes for men tend to be based on higher performance expectations and focus on their eventual readiness for open employment. By contrast, the stereotyping of women as passive, emotional and childlike has meant that programmes encourage severely disabled women towards relatively dependent roles and domestic pursuits. Women are generally regarded as less capable than men, therefore programmes tend to reinforce female recipients' helplessness and encourage dependence.

However, a focus on specific differences in service provision for men and women can obscure more fundamental problems. The essence of community care is to provide people with the support they need to sustain 'normal' social role functioning. As has already been argued, within patriarchy, this means functioning in relation to men. This can be seen in the emphasis placed on 'program issues' for severely disabled women such as family planning, child care, contraception, appearance and the like (Test and Berlin 1981; Bachrach 1985). A recent 'feminist' text contained the following recommendations in relation to severely disabled women for 'eliminating sexist treatment':

11. In treatment planning for severely disabled female clients, the treatment team should consider issues of sex education and birth control . . .
12. Mental health programs must be sensitive to the needs of chronically mentally ill women who are mothers, by providing a range of services to increase parenting skills and to cope with the stresses of parenthood . . .

13. Inpatient facilities and residential programmes should ensure females have easy access to essential personal hygiene supplies, e.g. soap, shampoo, deodorant . . .
14. Mental health programs, especially those for long-term mentally disabled women, should ensure that adequate assistance is given regarding hygiene and appearance . . .

(Mowbray, Lanir and Hulce 1985: 116)

These recommendations make it clear that services for women clients were seen in terms of supporting hetero-patriarchal imperatives. Severely socially disabled women have by definition been unable to cope in such roles – hence their need for services. Exclusive focus on maintaining them in such roles is inherently oppressive.

Whilst community care is probably the philosophy guiding most current service developments, it is often intermingled with ideas originating in the learning difficulties field about normalisation. This is a popular, if controversial, set of ideas that have enjoyed a very rapid rise in popularity since their initial exposition (Wolfensberger 1970). Indeed, the term 'normalisation' is to be found 'liberally scattered through current policy documents' (Garety 1988), such as the House of Commons Social Services Committee Report on Community Care (1985).

At first sight the liberal, campaigning, flavour of normalisation sounds quite attractive. Advocates argue that part of the oppression of disabled groups is their invisibility: the medical model serves to differentiate devalued clients from society by presenting them as diseased, impaired, incompetent and passive. They argue that the 'sick role' is accorded to people who are no 'sicker' than most of the population, and they are interpreted as 'sick' by association with medically trained staff; the use of names such as 'hospital' and 'clinic' for the places where they live, go to school and work; and every conceivable activity of life is interpreted as some form of therapy (work therapy, self-care therapy, gardening therapy, etc.) (Wolfensberger and Tullman 1982). Normalisation is essentially an anti-professional movement directed towards valuing deviant groups and getting rid of psychiatrists, psychologists, hospitals and so forth.

However, from a feminist point of view, there are serious problems with this approach. According to its prime exponent Wolfensberger (1970) the principal of 'normalisation' is 'deceptively simple' and basically involves enabling the 'deviant person to function in ways considered to be within the acceptable norms of his [sic] society'. He further goes on to argue that this normal functioning should be achieved as far as possible by 'culturally normative' means. That is, 'deviant persons should be exposed to experiences that are likely to elicit or maintain normative (accepted) behaviour'.

In subsequent writing these ideas have been 'dressed up' a little (Wolfensberger 1972, 1980) and the term 'socially valued' has replaced 'socially normative'. There have even been attempts to change the term 'normalisation' itself to 'social role valorisation' (Wolfensberger, 1983). However, none of these developments change the basic premise. As with community care, the aim is to maintain functioning in 'normal'/'valued'. Burns and Roberts (1988) have argued that normality and value within patriarchal politics are inherently oppressive for women, and to encourage women to aspire to man-made models is a strategy identical to that of traditional psychiatry. However, under the auspices of anti-psychiatry, normalisation goes even further. Severely disabled people should not be incarcerated in psychiatric hospitals, or given specialist community services. Instead they should be exposed to the same contingencies for deviant behaviour as the rest of the population, as and indeed they are; for example, alarmingly high rates of sexual exploitation and violence, diversion into the criminal justice system, homelessness, and the like (Bachrach 1984) – the 'socially normative'/'valued' contingencies within hetero-patriarchy for deviant behaviour. The popularity of ideas about 'normalisation' is probably not unrelated to the expense involved in the provision of specialist community services.

Thus there has been a shift from marginalising and removing severely disabled women from 'normal' roles towards sustaining them in male-defined roles, with or without specialist community care services. Such roles are inherently oppressive for women; thus to sustain them in such roles may actually contribute to their social disablement by increasing the social disadvantages that they face (Bachrach 1988) and exacerbating their cognitive and affective disabilities. Stressful events can exacerbate florid symptomatology (Stone and Eldred 1959; Brown and Birley 1968; Brown, Birley and Wing 1972). The stresses imposed by oppression are therefore likely to exacerbate primary impairments.

It could be argued that the last 30 years of moves away from institutionalisation have actually disadvantaged women by depriving them of even the limited and unsatisfactory opportunity of asylum from servicing men that the hospital to some extent afforded.

From a feminist perspective, the patriarchal political context of the philosophies of service development is central to an understanding of gender issues in relation to work with severely socially disabled people. In particular it is relevant to ask whether the preservation of 'normality' or the enhancement of 'quality of life' are the key goals of services. There is a growing literature advocating optimisation of 'quality of life' as a conceptual and organising framework for long-term care (Strauss 1985; Lehman 1983; Thapa and Rowland 1989). However, there seems to be the implicit assumption that by establishing and maintaining 'normal' social roles 'quality of life' is automatically increased. Whilst under patriarchy this may be true for severely disabled men, it is almost certainly not for severely disabled women. That which is 'normal' often does not enhance 'quality of life' for severely disabled women, any more than it does for the non-disabled woman. Friedan's (1963) interviews with 'normal' suburban housewives amply demonstrate this: she identified much discontent and desperation in the lives of 'normal' women.

If services are to be developed that improve the quality of life for severely disabled women, then one consideration might be the provision of some form of 'asylum' from male-defined roles and servicing of men. 'Asylum' can be offered in ways other than the psychiatric institution and does not have to involve 'psychiatry' or 'professionals'. There are a variety of ways in which relief from various domestic and sexual roles in relation to men could be achieved.

Consideration of political issues concerning goals and styles of service provision are important to clinical psychologists in their role in the development of services: service planning, assessment of population 'needs', and evaluation of services. However, they are also important in working directly with individuals and their families, and in planning care for individuals.

GENDER ISSUES IN WORKING WITH THE INDIVIDUAL: CHANGING THE INDIVIDUAL OR THE SOCIAL ENVIRONMENT?

A 'psychological' approach to distress and disability is characteristically an individualised and personalised affair, as is the 'psychological' approach to other areas (see Kitzinger 1987). Problems are located within the individual in whatever terms: faulty learning, dysfunctional cognitions, lack of assertiveness, skills deficits, intra-psychic conflicts, etc. Time-limited interventions are then employed to change the individual, resolve their problems. The various 'feminist' alternatives in the form of 'feminist therapies' are really no different in these regards, and neither differ markedly from traditional 'medical' models. The ways in which problems are formulated, the mechanisms of individual change invoked, and the methods used to achieve that change vary markedly, but the aim remains 'cure' based in terms of problem removal via change within the individual. The concept of enduring disability is absent.

Clinical psychologists have developed a few interventions aimed directly at decreasing the primary impairments of major cognitive disturbance (Watts, Powell and Austin 1973; Allen, Halperin and Friend 1985; Done, Frith and Owens 1986; Fowler and Morley 1989). However, the major emphasis has been on various 'functional' or 'skills' approaches (e.g. Anthony and Margules 1974; Anthony 1977; Anthony 1979). These move away from a focus on 'symptom' removal: the central question is not what a person cannot do, but what they need to be able to do. Once a skills deficit has been identified, intervention proceeds in the form of behaviourally based skills training to help the person to acquire the necessary skill. Such models are extremely popular and widely used, and indeed work with severely disabled people is often seen as synonymous with skills training.

However, it is important to note the model of disability that such approaches imply: it is certainly not one that parallels the use of the term in the physical arena. It is assumed that the person is socially disabled because they have lost certain skills, or never acquired them in the first place, and that all the necessary skills can be taught and acquired by the person. In the case of physical disability, interventions to help a person who is blind are not geared around helping them to gain the skill of sight; neither are interventions to help a person with paraplegia geared towards helping them acquire the skill of walking.

However, in the case of social disablement the locus of problems is seen as residing within the individual and the solutions are seen in terms of change within the person: thus such approaches share all the difficulties of 'cure'-based approaches, whether they be pharmacological interventions or 'feminist therapy'. Essentially the existence of enduring disablement is denied and thus such frameworks offer no guidance for intervention if a 'cure' cannot be effected, or if a 'skill' cannot be developed.

Further, by locating problems within the individual and defining solutions in terms of individual change, it becomes the individual's responsibility to change. However, by implication, it is also their responsibility when they fail to change or develop the necessary skills (a not uncommon occurrence: Paul and Lentz 1977). This leads to further devaluation and hopelessness on the part of the individual, especially if this happens to be a disabled woman who has been socialised, unlike her male counterpart, to accept full responsibility for her own happiness (Penfold and Walker 1984).

Within a 'skills'-based approach it is only possible to consider those areas where there is a clearly identifiable mechanical skill that can be taught: self-care, cooking and using public transport are prime contenders. However, there is a danger of a type of 'naive materialism' when one moves away from such areas to, for example, social and emotional spheres. It has long been recognised, for example, that social competence involves more than the acquisition of skilled performances (Shepherd 1977, 1978).

Even at the level of mechanical skills, there are serious problems with the 'skills training' approach, and many gender issues to be considered. The skills that are considered important are, as one might expect, those that are necessary for 'normal' role performance. For women, this all too often means skills necessary for the successful execution of their functions in relation to men. Thus 'domestic skills', cooking and self-care training figure high on the agenda. However, it is perfectly possible for someone to be relieved of such responsibilities: there are such things as cafes, takeaway food purveyors and home-helps, all of which could be utilised, rather than expecting the person to perform these tasks unaided. These methods may be preferable if one considers what it must feel like for the adult concerned to be repeatedly taught to clean their teeth or bathe themselves. 'Star charts' are a not uncommon adjunct to such a process – with all the infantilisation and devaluation that they imply.

A question must be asked by any clinician working with a severely disabled client: Is the 'best' course of action to attempt to change the person, or to change the environment in which they function? Because of their emphasis upon changing the individual, clinical psychologists all too often resort to the former. 'Skills training' packages are designed to remove 'skills deficits'; behavioural programmes are designed to reduce 'dysfunctional behaviour'; counselling and therapy are offered to help the person (or their family) to accept and deal with the realities of their situation. In short we typically work very hard to change the disabled person so that they fit into a patriarchal social world and the acceptable roles for women that it implies. However, there are other approaches, and in this context it is appropriate to draw a parallel with physical disability. When someone is physically disabled the main focus of intervention is to adapt the physical world to the needs of that individual. Instead of 'skills training' the focus is upon adapting the physical environment (by the use of aids, supports and shelter) and relief from some tasks in order to enable the person to function.

In the context of social disablement, a parallel approach would mean that if the person were unable to cook, budget, perform domestic chores, look after themselves, or behave appropriately in social situations, the options would be to provide aids, help, shelter and support to facilitate performance, or relieve the person of some responsibilities completely.

The central question determining the choice between these, as with service development, concerns what services are trying to achieve for the individual concerned. That is whether the aim is to optimise and maintain male-defined role functioning or their quality of life. As the former is inherently oppressive for women, thus exacerbating their disablement, from a feminist perspective the latter 'quality of life' approach is preferable. Such an approach, combined with a focus on changing environments rather than individuals, has implications for the interventions employed, as well as the services developed.

The case of May (outlined above) serves as one illustration: the quality of her life was improved by relieving her of many of the components of the 'wife' role, with a commensurate decrease in her level of distress and improvement in her functioning. Likewise Mary is not untypical. She lived in a flat but she found managing her money impossibly difficult. This had resulted in her building up large debts that threatened her tenure in the flat. She was offered 'budgeting skills training', but this made her feel stupid: 'they treat me like I treated my son when he was little'. The training was ineffective and the debts continued to mount, she refused to go any more because she did not like it – and was deemed by services to lack the 'motivation' to change. A simple, effective, alternative was to set up systems to help her with her money management: someone else to pay her bills, begin to pay off her debts, and to give her each week only that which she could afford to spend. Mary welcomed this idea, and the problems are resolved – not by changing her, but by offering supports in her environment.

When I first met Jane she was 83 years old. She was living in a 40-bedded dormitory in a large 'old long-stay' psychiatric unit and had been doing so for the last 30 years. She was referred to me because of her 'disruptive' behaviour: she was described as be-having like 'lady muck', expecting everyone to do as she wanted, always complaining about the unit and the way it was run, denying that she had any problems whatsoever and demanding to be discharged, and was generally extremely abusive both to other residents and staff. No one knew anything about her life before she became a 'long-stay patient' – this had been lost in the mists of time and many volumes of 'psychiatric notes' gathering dust some-where. In fact the absence of this knowledge prevented any real understanding of her. For the majority of her life she had travelled the world as the first violinist with a show band. Indeed her life before hospital read rather like a glossy romantic novel. The gap between this and her life when I met her was astounding and her reactions to her situation fully understandable.

A typical clinical psychology intervention might have been 'therapy' to help her to 'come to terms with her situation' and a behaviour programme to promote 'pro-social' behaviour (problems and solutions located within her). However, another approach was to locate the problem in the world in which she was expected to function: after she moved to a small residential home for the elderly, with people to whom she could relate, her 'dis-ruptive behaviour' reduced, and she is a great deal happier with life.

CONCLUSIONS

The severely socially disabled person is unable to negotiate the social world without help, support and adaptation of that world: just as the physically disabled person is unable to negotiate the physical environment without aids and assistance. However, it is important to remember that definition of the social world, and hence of disablement within it, are political issues. The social world is defined in terms of the patriarchal and heterosexist forms of political organisation that prevail. Roles for women within such structures are inherently oppressive and thus exacerbate disabled women's handicap.

In considering gender issues in relation to work with severely socially disabled people, at both an individual and a service development level, key political questions are raised concerning the goals of services: what services are trying to achieve. Institutionalisation and deinstitutionalisation approaches both served to deal with those unable to perform adequately in 'normal' social roles by exclusion (incarceration or marginalisation and 'patienthood' in the community). Community care and normalisation approaches are designed to support people in 'normal' roles. Therapy and skills training approaches attempt to change disabled people so that they fit in, and continuing care services offer support to maintain role functioning.

It has been suggested that in designing both services and care for individuals within these, adoption of the organising principal of optimising 'quality of life' may be appropriate. However, it cannot be assumed that what is 'normal' or 'socially valued' is always that which enhances quality of life. For men in patriarchal society this may be the case: for women it almost certainly is not. Therefore it is proposed that efforts should be made to move away from supporting severely disabled women in those male-defined roles in which they have manifestly been unable to function adequately.

Further, in optimising quality of life, attention should focus not on ways in which the individual can be changed, but instead on how their environment can be modified. As in helping physically disabled people, emphasis should be placed on aids, supports, and shelter within the environment. Relieving socially disabled women of some roles or tasks, and the provision of various forms of asylum, may be an important factor in optimising quality of life. It is unlikely that the world will be changed by severely socially disabled women. However, it is possible for services and supports to be organised to provide some relief for these vulnerable groups rather than being exclusively directed towards helping them to 'fit in' to an inherently oppressive social world.

REFERENCES

Allen, A., Halperin, J. and Friend, R. (1985) Removal and diversion tactics and the control of auditory hallucinations. *Behaviour Research and Therapy*, 17: 267–282.

Anthony, L. A. (1977) Psychological rehabilitation – a concept in need of a method. *American Psychologist*, 32: 658–662.

Anthony, L. A. (1979) The rehabilitation approach to diagnosis. *New Directions in Mental Health Services*, 2: 25–36.

Anthony, L. A. and Margules, A. (1974) Toward improving the efficacy of psychiatric rehabilitation: a skills training approach. *Rehabilitation Psychology*, 21: 101–105.

Bachrach, L. L. (1978) A conceptual approach to deinstitutionalization. *Hospital and Community Psychiatry*, 29: 573–578.

Bachrach, L. L. (1984) Deinstitutionalisation and women. *American Psychologist*, 39: 1,171–1,177.

Bachrach, L. L. (1985) Chronic mentally ill women: emergence and legitimation of programme issues. *Hospital and Community Psychiatry*, 36: 1,063–1,069.

Bachrach, L. L. (1988) Chronically mentally ill women: an overview of service delivery issues. In L. L. Bachrach and C. C. Nadelson (eds), *Treating Chronically Mentally Ill Women*. Washington, DC: American Psychiatric Press.

Bachrach, L. L. (1989) The legacy of model programs. *Hospital and Community Psychiatry*, 40: 234–235.

Barton, R. (1959) *Institutional Neurosis*. Bristol: Wright.

Blechman, E. A. (ed.) (1984) *Behaviour Modification with Women*. New York: Guilford Press.

Brewin, C. R., Wing, J. K., Mangen, S. P., Brugha, T. S. and MacCarthy, B. (1987) Principles and practice of measuring needs in the long-term mentally ill: the MRC need for care assessment. *Psychological Medicine*, 17: 971–981.

Brodsky, A. M. and Hare-Mustin, R. (1984) *Women and Psychotherapy: An Assessment of Research and Practice*. New York: Guilford Press.

Brown, G. W. and Birley, J. L. T. (1968) Crises and life events and the onset of schizophrenia. *Journal of Health and Social Behaviour* 9: 203–214.

Brown, G. W., Birley, J. L. T. and Wing, J. K. (1972) Influence of family life on the course of schizophrenic disorders: a replication. *British Journal of Psychiatry*, 121: 241–258.

Brown, G. W. and Harris, T. (1978) *The Social Origins of Depression: A Study of Psychiatric Disorder in Women*. London: Tavistock.

Burns, J. and Roberts, T. (1988) A Feminist Perspective on the Normalisation Principle. Paper presented at the BPS Conference, Psychology of Women Section Symposium, April 1988.

Chesler, P. (1973) *Women and Madness*. New York: Avon Books.

Chesler, P. (1989) Twenty years since *Women and Madness*: Toward a feminist institute of mental health. In P. Chesler, *Women and Madness*. New York: Harcourt Brace Jovanovich.

Cohen, D. (1988) *Forgotten Millions*. London: Paladin.

Cook, G. (1985) Psychiatry as male violence. In D. Rhodes and S. McNeill (eds), *Women Against Violence Against Women.* London: Onlywomen Press.

Done, D. J., Frith, C. D. and Owens, D. C. (1986) Reducing persistent auditory hallucinations by wearing an ear-plug. *British Journal of Clinical Psychology,* 25: 151–152.

Falloon, I. R. H., McGill, C. W., Boyd, J. L. and Pederson, J. (1987) Family management of schizophrenia: social outcome of a two year longitudinal study. *Psychological Medicine,* 17: 59–66.

Fowler, D. and Morley, S. (1989) The cognitive-behavioural treatment of hallucinations and delusions: a preliminary study. *Behavioural Psychotherapy,* 17: 267–282.

Friedan, B. (1963) *The Feminine Mystique.* Harmondsworth: Penguin Books.

Garety, P. (1988) Housing. In A. Lavender and F. Holloway (eds), *Community Care in Practice.* Chichester: Wiley.

Garfinkel, P. E. and Garner, D. M. (1982) *Anorexia Nervosa.* New York: Bruner/Mazel.

Garner, D. M., Garfinkel, P. E., Schwartz, D. and Thompson, M. (1980) Cultural expectations of thinness in women. *Psychological Reports,* 47: 483–491.

Goering, P., Cochrane, J., Potasznik, H., Wasylenski, D. and Lancee, W. (1988) Women and work: after psychiatric hospitalisation. In L. L. Bachrach and C. C. Nadelson (eds), *Treating Chronically Mentally Ill Women.* Washington, DC: American Psychiatric Press.

Goffman, E. (1961) *Asylums.* Harmondsworth: Penguin Books.

Hatfield, A. (1989) Patients' accounts of stress and coping in schizophrenia. *Hospital and Community Psychiatry,* 40: 1,141–1,145.

Hoult, J. (1986) Community care of the actively mentally ill. *British Journal of Psychiatry,* 149: 137–144.

Hoult, J. and Reynolds, I. (1984) Schizophrenia: a comparative trial of community oriented and hospital oriented psychiatric care. *Acta Psychiatrica Scandinavica,* 69: 359–372.

House of Commons Social Services Committee (1985) *Community Care with Special Reference to Mentally Ill and Mentally Handicapped People, Second Report from the Social Services Committee.* London: HMSO.

Jeffreys, S. (1990) *Anticlimax.* London: The Women's Press.

Keisler, C. A. (1982) Mental hospitals and alternative care. *American Psychologist,* 37: 349–360.

Kitzinger, C. (1987) *The Social Construction of Lesbianism.* London: Sage.

Lazarus, R. S. and Folkman, S. (1984) Coping and adaptation. In W. D. Gentry (ed.), *Handbook of Behavioral Medicine.* New York: Guilford Press.

Leff, J., Kuipers, L., Berkowitz, R. and Sturgeon (1985) A controlled trial of social intervention in the families of schizophrenic patients: two year follow-up. *British Journal of Psychiatry,* 146: 594–600.

Lehman, A. F. (1983) The well-being of chronic mental patients: assessing their quality of life. *Archives of General Psychiatry,* 40: 369–373.

MacCarthy, B., Kuipers, L., Hurry, J., Harper, R. and Lesage, A. (1989) Counselling relatives of the long-term mentally ill. I. Evaluation of the impact on relatives and patients. *British Journal of Psychiatry*, 154: 768–775.

McGrath, M. E. (1984) First person accounts: Where did I go? *Schizophrenia Bulletin*, 10: 638–640.

Mowbray, C. T., Lanir, S. and Hulce, M. (eds) (1985) *Women and Mental Health.* New York: Harrington Park Press.

National Schizophrenia Fellowship/Schizophrenia: a National Emergency (1988) *Mental Hospital Closures.* Surbiton, Surrey: NSF.

Parkes, C. M. (1972) *Bereavement: Studies of Grief in Adult Life.* London: Tavistock.

Paul, G. L. and Lentz, R. J. (1977) *Psychosocial Treatment of Chronic Mental Patients: Milieu vs. Social-learning Programs.* Cambridge, Mass.: Harvard University Press.

Penfold, P. S. and Walker, G. A. (1984) *Women and the Psychiatric Paradox.* Milton Keynes: Open University Press.

Perkins, R. E. and Rowland, L. A. (1986) Planning Community Services for People with Major Long-Term Needs: The Maudsley Experience. Paper presented at the National MIND/District Services Centre, Maudsley, Joint Conference, London.

Perkins, R. E. and Rowland, L. A. (1990) Sex differences in service usage in long-term psychiatric care: are women adequately served? *British Journal of Psychiatry*, 158 (supplement 10): 75–79.

Quinn, K. (1985) The killing ground: police powers and psychiatry. In C. T. Mowbray, S. Lanir and M. Hulce (eds), Women and Mental Health. New York: Harrington Park Press.

Sedgewick, P. (1982) *Psychopolitics.* London: Pluto Press.

Sheehan, S. (1982) *Is There No Place On Earth For Me?* Boston: Houghton Mifflin.

Shepherd, G. (1977) Social skills training: the generalisation problem. *Behaviour Therapy*, 8: 100–109.

Shepherd, G. (1978) Social skills training: the generalisation problem – some further data. *Behaviour Research and Therapy*, 116: 287–288.

Shepherd, G. (1984) *Institutional Care and Rehabilitation.* London: Longman Applied Psychology.

Showalter, E. (1987) *The Female Malady.* London: Virago.

Stein, L. I. and Test, M. A. (1980) Alternative to mental hospital treatment. I. Conceptual model, treatment program, and clinical evaluation. *Archives of General Psychiatry*, 37: 392–397.

Steptoe, A. and Sullivan, J. (1986) Monitoring and blunting coping styles in women prior to surgery. *British Journal of Clinical Psychology*, 25: 143–144.

Stone, A. A. and Eldred, S. H. (1959) Delusion formation during activation of chronic schizophrenic patients. *Archives of General Psychiatry*, 17: 177–179.

Strauss, A. (1985) *Chronic Illness and Quality of Life.* St Louis: Mosby.

Taylor, K. E. and Perkins, R. E. (1991) Identity and coping with mental illness in long-stay psychiatric rehabilitation. *British Journal of Clinical Psychology*, 30, 73–85.

Test, M. A. and Berlin, S. B. (1981) Issues of concern to chronically mentally ill women. *Professional Psychology*, 12: 136–145.

Thapa, K. and Rowland, L. A. (1989) Quality of life perspectives in long-term care: staff and patient perceptions. *Acta Psychiatrica Scandinavica*, 80: 267–271.

Ussher, J. M. (1991) *Women's Madness – Misogyny or Mental Illness*. London: Harvester Wheatsheaf.

Wallace, M. (1987) A caring community? *Sunday Times Magazine*, 3 May 1987.

Watts, F. N., Powell, G. E. and Austin, S. V. (1973) The modification of abnormal beliefs. *British Journal of Medical Psychology*, 46: 359–363.

Wing, J. K. (1962) Institutionalism in mental hospitals. *British Journal of Social and Clinical Psychology*, 1: 38–51.

Wing, J. K. (1963) Rehabilitation of psychiatric patients. *British Journal of Psychiatry*, 109: 635–641.

Wing, J. K. (1967) The concept of handicap in psychiatry. *International Journal Psychiatry*, 3: 243.

Wing, J. K. (1978) Clinical concepts of schizophrenia. In J. K. Wing (ed.), *Schizophrenia: Towards a New Synthesis*. London: Academic Press.

Wing, J. K. and Brown, G. W. (1970) *Institutionalism in Schizophrenia*. Cambridge: Cambridge University Press.

Wing, J. K. and Morris, B. (1981) Clinical basis of rehabilitation, in J. K. Wing and B. Morris (eds), *Handbook of Psychiatric Rehabilitation*. Oxford: Oxford University Press.

Wolfensberger, W. (1970) The principle of normalisation and its implications to psychiatric services. *American Journal of Psychiatry*, 127: 291–297.

Wolfensburger, W. (1972) *The Principle of Normalisation*. Toronto: NIMH.

Wolfensburger, W. (1980) The definition of normalisation: update, problems, disagreements and misunderstandings. In R. J. Flynn and K. E. Nitsch (eds), Normalisation, Social Integration and Community Services. Baltimore: University Park Press.

Wolfensberger, W. (1983) Social role valorisation: a proposed new term for the principle of normalisation. *Mental Retardation*, 21: 234–239.

Wolfensberger, W. and Tullman, S. (1982) A brief outline of the principle of normalisation. *Rehabilitation Psychology*, 27: 131–145.

World Health Organisation (1973) *The International Pilot Study of Schizophrenia*. Geneva: WHO.

World Health Organisation (1987) *Report on Pilot Projects*. Geneva: WHO.

Chapter 9

Feminism, psychoanalysis and psychotherapy[1]

Janet Sayers

INTRODUCTION

Sexual[2] difference and inequality, as demonstrated throughout this book, are central to mental illness and its treatment. Yet, as I shall explain these issues are regularly overlooked in psychoanalysis – a subject now increasingly adopted by both feminist theory and therapy. Not that psychoanalysis has always overlooked sexual difference as I shall indicate by outlining Freud's theory of the castration complex and its restatement by feminists influenced by the work of the French psychoanalyst Jacques Lacan. Paradoxically, however, it is the work of the British psychoanalyst Donald Winnicott, despite its neglect of sexual difference, that is now much more widely used by feminists and others in therapy. It is on his work, and the need to attend to sexual difference and inequality in clinical practice that I shall therefore concentrate, illustrating these points throughout by reference to my own work as a clinical psychologist.

FOREGROUNDING SEXUAL DIFFERENCE: 1 FREUD

To begin at the beginning. Freud insisted that the Oedipus complex – the child's incestuous desire for one parent in sexual rivalry with the other – is the 'kernel' of neurosis. Again and again he demonstrated that his adult patients' neuroses stemmed from this childhood complex still dominating their lives. Increasingly, as a result of his clinical work, he showed this complex to be mediated by sexual difference – by the child's construction of the girl's lack of a penis as signifying the father's power to punish the child's Oedipal desire with castration.

Little Hans, for instance, a five-year-old about whose agoraphobia his father consulted Freud, endlessly wanted to canoodle with his mother and, in this, to play with his penis. At this his mother warned, 'If you do that, I shall send for Dr A. to cut off your widdler' (Freud 1909: 171). Hans greeted the threat with disbelief until he saw his baby sister naked. At first he denied the evidence of his senses. She has a small penis, he told himself, that will get bigger as she grows older. Then, recognising that neither she nor his mother had a penis, he interpreted their lack as effect of the castration previously threatened him in the name of the doctor's patriarchal authority. It was the fear to which this gave rise that seemingly caused his agoraphobia in which he displaced this fear from patriarchal figures – his father – onto horses. Hence his unwillingness to go out lest he meet them on the street.

Similarly another of Freud's patients – the Wolf Man – dated his neurosis to early infancy when his nurse reprimanded his masturbation by telling him that children who did that got a 'wound' in that place (Freud 1918: 25). Again, like Hans, the three-year-old Wolf Man, now became preoccupied with sexual difference. At first, seeing his sister peeing, he denied her lack of a penis. Then, recognising phallic lack, he became fearful lest, were he to realise his Oedipal desire for his father, he would become likewise castrated as his mother seemed to be when he saw his father making love to her from behind so he could see she had no penis. His desire for his father – previously expressed in naughtiness designed to elicit beatings from him – became repressed. Instead it was expressed in disguised form – in obsessional religious subservience to God, and in constipation involving unconscious identification with his mother in anal intercourse with his father.

Generalising from such cases Freud argued that the boy abandons or represses his 'negative' homosexual Oedipus complex out of fear lest were his desire for his father realised he would become castrated as his mother seems to be. He likewise represses his 'positive' heterosexual Oedipus complex lest its realisation be punished with castration by the father. For, observed Freud, although this threat may be uttered by women as in the above cases it is the father who is located as its ultimate source. Nor, one might add, is this any surprise given that in male-dominated society sex and power are so readily vested in the father, whatever his actual attributes.

If sexual difference, construed in terms of castration, thus ends the boy's Oedipus complex it initiates it in girls according to Freud. Catching sight of the boy's penis, he claimed, the girl immediately wants one for herself and falls victim to penis envy. At first she interprets her phallic lack as the effect of castration, as a punishment peculiar to herself. Then she recognises her mother's phallic lack. The latter accordingly becomes devalued in her eyes. She blames her mother for failing 'to provide. . .the only proper genital' (Freud 1931: 383) and turns away from her with Oedipal desire for the father in the hope of gaining from him the now longed-for penis unconsciously equated with a baby.

It is no surprise to learn that feminists often reject this phal- locentric account of women's psychology – at least of the first dawning of their heterosexual and maternal desire. So too do many psychoanalysts. Yet in doing so they have opted for psycho- logical theories and therapies that assume and in the process overlook sexual difference and inequality, as I shall explain by reference to the work of Winnicott and its use by feminists in women's therapy. First, though, I shall outline an alternative feminist response to Freud put forward by those influenced by the work of the French psychoanalyst Jacques Lacan.

FOREGROUNDING SEXUAL DIFFERENCE: 2 LACANIAN FEMINISM

Illustrative is Juliet Mitchell's 1974 book *Psychoanalysis and Feminism*. Drawing on Lacan's 'return' to Freud via anthropologist Lévi-Strauss's account of patriarchal kinship relations and linguist de Saussure's account of words acquiring meaning through presence/absence of that which they signify, Mitchell argued the importance for feminism of Freud's theory of the Oedipus and castration complex in describing the way the child comes to situate itself, through recognition of the presence/absence of the phallus, in terms of the kinship law of patriarchal sexual exchange of women by men that the phallus represents.

Briefly, and as far as I understand it, Lacan (1949, 1953) argues like Freud that the baby is initially a welter of component sexual drives – oral and anal, masochistic and sadistic, voyeuristic and exhibitionistic – drives that are expressed towards both parts of itself and others. Eventually these disparate autoerotic impulses 'cathect' – libidinally invest – the body and self as a whole. The child falls in love, Narcissus-like, with itself.

Indicative of this process, says Lacan, is the fascination of six- to eighteen-month-old toddlers with their mirror image. An example from my own work is Robert whom I observed as part of my psychotherapy training. For weeks, at least since he started smiling, Robert had imitated and been imitated by his mother. By six months, when his mother first returned to work and Robert began attending a child-minder, his imitation included copying her waving 'Bye bye' by clenching and unclenching his fist – holding onto her, as it were, and letting her go. Six weeks later, in front of the mirror in which a month earlier he had been uninterested, he repeated the gesture. He clenched and unclenched his fist at his mirror image which he then seemed to regard as different from himself, just as Robert regards his mother. Certainly he crawled round the back of the mirror to look for his counterpart just as he looks for his mother behind the towel with which she covers her face in playing peep-oh. By nine months however Robert began equating his reflected image with himself just as, seeing his mother's image in the mirror, he turned round to check whether she was in the room as well as in the mirror.

It is this development that Lacan describes in his theory of the 'mirror stage'. The baby, he says, becomes captivated by its reflection because the latter provides an ideal image of itself as whole and coordinated in contrast to the fragmentary and unco-ordinated character of its sexual drives and attachments. Hence the lure of the mirror image which, in enabling the child to recognise itself in something outside itself, is a forerunner of being able to represent itself by the personal pronoun 'I' of language. More immediately the mirror stage also involves the child beginning to think about itself as reflected in its mother's eyes or, as Mitchell puts it, this stage enables the child to conceptualise itself through being mirrored back 'from the position of another's desire' (Mitchell 1982: 5). Just as the child 'misrecognises' itself in the mirror – in that it is not actually one with its mirror image which is both the same and outside itself – so the child likewise 'misrecognises' itself as one with the desire of the mother.

This 'imaginary' oneness with the mother is only severed, says Mitchell following Lacan, with discovery of the mother's phallic lack. This punctures the child's narcissism. In recognising her lack the child recognises it is not all in all with her, that no one can be this all now equated with the phallus the significance of which is only acquired with recognition of the possibility of its absence. Up till then the boy had not imagined being without the phallus and the girl had not known of its existence. Now she wants to have it – in the first place via the father – and the boy wants to be it. Five-year-old Hans, for instance, consoled himself, following discovery of his mother's phallic lack, not only with assurance of having a penis but also with the thought that one day it would be as big as that of his father.

The puncturing of the child's illusion of narcissistic union with the mother, according to this account, thus brings into being its desire – either to 'have' or 'represent' the phallus (Mitchell 1982: 7). This is akin to Freud's observation that babies only begin to know they need something once dreams give way to reality, once the hallucination of desire fulfilled is repressed into the unconscious through recognition that such hallucination does not bring about actual fulfilment of desire.[3]

Wakened from the illusion of unified wholeness with the mother through recognition of her phallic lack toddlers are thereby forced into recognising their separateness from her in so far as they construe her lack as signifying the father's power to punish union with her with castration. This in turn, according to Lacanians, enables children likewise to recognise the divisions of language – the fact that just as they are not one with the mother neither are words the same as the things they signify, signifiers not the same as their signifieds.

Not for nothing, it would seem from this account, Robert's parents identified his first word as 'Da', as signifying his father, the outsider to his relation with his mother – the one who most put the doting mutual admiration of this relation into words, while at the same time being sceptical of the potency his wife attributed to their son. One day she proudly anticipated Robert skiing whereupon his father scornfully retorted, 'He might be rolling over', and he doubted even that; 'but he can't even stand up yet'.

Putting experience into words – as Robert's father thus did – being able to thus distance ourselves sufficiently from experience to be able to verbalise and reflect upon it – is the *sine qua non*, according to Lacanians, of psychoanalysis as the 'talking cure' it was once dubbed by an early patient, Anna O. While language is thus the means of therapy, its aim, according to Mitchell, should be the reconstruction of 'the subject's construction in all its splits' (Mitchell 1982: 26). For Lacanians, as indicated above, the central split is that initiated by recognising and construing sexual difference in terms of patriarchal power. The child is thereby forever severed from the omnipotent mirror stage illusion of being one with the mother – an illusion that thereafter can only be fleetingly recaptured with the suspension in dreams and psychosis of conscious 'secondary process' thought.

But, although Mitchell is a psychoanalyst, she gives few leads as to how people are to be disabused of such illusions so as to begin to recognise the need to act on the world if they are to bring about actual fulfilment of their needs and wants. This is in keeping with her 1974 book in which, having demonstrated the value to the women's movement of Freud's work as a description of the child's initiation into patriarchal social relations, Mitchell singularly failed to spell out, except in the most general and utopian terms, its implications for feminist practice. Feminists have accordingly looked elsewhere for guidance in this matter. As regards psycho-therapeutic practice those persuaded of the value of psycho-analysis have looked particularly to the work of the paediatrician and psychoanalyst Donald Winnicott even though, as I shall explain, he overlooked the centrality to patients' problems of sexual difference and its patriarchal construction.

ASSUMING/IGNORING SEXUAL DIFFERENCE: FROM KLEIN TO WINNICOTT

While Freud focused on the way images of the father's sex and power stalk us even into adulthood and its neuroses, today's psy-choanalytic psychotherapy focuses much more on the maternal determinants of mental health and illness. As I have explained elsewhere (Sayers 1991), this volte face is largely attributable to the work of psychoanalysis's leading women pioneers – Helene Deutsch, Karen Horney, Anna Freud and Melanie Klein. Drawing on their own mothering experience – as daughter, and as mothers to their own and others' children – and drawing on their patients' experience of them as mother-figures, all four women drew atten-tion to the importance of the early mother–child relation in shaping our psychology.

In the process they often assumed that the individuation of self from other is innate, not formed through patriarchal construction of sexual difference as Lacan insists. While Freud and Lacan em-phasise the child's understanding of sexual difference in terms of phallic lack in the mother, Horney (e.g. 1930) and Klein (1928) emphasise the child's image of the mother as plenitude – as full of milk, feces, babies, and penis too – as only becoming depleted, and that only in fantasy, through the infant's hatred, envy and greed, not through any intervention by the father. This goes along with assuming that our psychological sense of ourselves as male or female is innate, that sexual difference is a pre-given of our psychology not, as Freud and Lacan insist, acquired and then central to our subsequent complaints and disorders. In the process the significance to the patient of the analyst's sex was also overlooked, even though it was precisely patients' experience of women analysts, by virtue of their sex, as mother-figures that brought about the changeover from the father-centred theory and therapy bequeathed by Freud to its current mother-centred focus whereby analysts, whatever their sex, often view their function as essentially maternal (see e.g. Winnicott 1971; Bion 1967). This approach arguably reached its apotheosis in the work of Klein's sometime pupil, Donald Winnicott.

Briefly Winnicott argued that the baby initially has no sense of itself as psychically separate from the mother – a hypothesis subsequently thrown into question by infant observation (see e.g. Stern 1985). In the absence of such data Winnicott insisted that the newborn has no sense of being anything but one with the mother. Similarly, he wrote, the 'good enough mother' likewise experiences herself as one with her baby as a result of the 'primary maternal preoccupation' brought about by pregnancy. She is thereby able to anticipate and meet her baby's needs before they break up its continuity of being, its fragile beginning sense of self – its ego. She thus brings external reality – the breast say – into accord with the baby's internal world – its hallucination of the breast when hungry. The baby's ego is thereby enriched with details of external reality. In the process the mother fuels the baby's omnipotent fantasy of creating whatever was wanted. Alternatively, if the mother resists identifying with her baby, she may instead interpose her own needs such that the baby, in order to survive, has to acquiesce with what she wants – the baby's 'true self' accordingly going into hiding behind a compliant 'false self' facade.

If all goes well, however, and the mother meets the baby's needs and thereby strengthens its sense of self – its ego – then the baby will thereby develop the cognitive ability internally to represent the external world including the mother. This enables it to brook lapses in her care and attention. The stage which Winnicott terms 'absolute' or 'double' dependence thus gives way to the stage of 'relative' dependence whereby the baby begins to take on board the fact of the mother's separateness and of its dependence on her. That is, according to Winnicott unlike Freud and Lacan, recognition of separateness from the mother is solely the product of maternal care, not of the father's intervention – of construction of sexual difference as signifying the power of the father to punish union with the mother with castration. Indeed Winnicott so ignores sexual difference that he describes the father's function as essentially one of mothering the mother.

Not that the baby does not need help negotiating the transition from the illusion of oneness with the mother to the reality of separation from her. Winnicott points out that this dawning gap is often bridged by the baby clinging to a much thumbed and handled piece of cloth, blanket, or other 'transitional object' suffused with subjective sense of oneness with the mother while also recognised as separate and external – an object on which the baby particularly depends when actually separated from the mother as in going to sleep.

Winnicott arrived at this account of the baby's initial sense of oneness with and subsequent recognition of separateness from the mother, through lapses in her care, as a result of his clinical work with children and adults. He writes of patients experiencing the therapist as anticipating and meeting their needs as they arise, of their experiencing well-timed interpretations as almost self-created, as the baby supposedly experiences the breast when it arrives just as the baby hallucinates its appearance (see Phillips 1988). And Winnicott (1971) likens patients' response to felt lapses in the therapist's care to the baby's response to lapses in maternal care. He also suggests that patients often use therapy as a 'transitional space' – as both suffused with subjective feeling while also recognised as objective and external.

This process is seemingly illustrated by one of my clinical psychology patients, Kevin. He feels his mother never understood him – that she was blinded to his individuality, to his own needs as they arose, by the general prejudices and dogmas of her fundamentalist religion. By contrast he idealised me as someone well attuned to his feelings, even to those welling up inside him but not yet expressed. He told me, 'Sometimes you say things in a couple of sentences that summarise what I've been feeling but not been conscious of . . . you understand what's going on inside me'. He said I turned his words into thoughts at which I was reminded of the Kleinian analyst, Wilfred Bion's (1967) claim that mothers make the baby's thoughts thinkable.

At other times Kevin was acutely aware of lapses in my attention, as he was of those of his girlfriend Avril and of his mother long ago. He reported how Avril used to give him all her time – listen to him a lot – and how disruptive it had been to discover that she also had her own, different agenda for their relationship. This went along with noticing my separateness – that I seemed to be drifting off. In turn he was put in mind of his loss of trust in Avril after discovering her keeping things from him for herself just as he described his ex-wife witholding herself from him in sex.

Although he knew that they and I have a separate life – indeed he saw me in town with my family – Kevin arguably used therapy as a transitional space in which he both did and did not know of my separateness. Referring to a phone on the desk, for instance, he emphasised he could not bear it to ring. Its never ringing sustained the illusion that I had no other concern but him although, as indicated, he also knew full well I had other calls on my time. Likewise another patient, Susan, told me she thinks of me through holiday breaks as still there for her in our therapy room.

Such idealisation of the therapist as a mother, ever attentive and available to meet the patient's need, is a far cry from Freud and Lacan's account of women as phallic lack. No wonder therefore feminists often prefer Winnicott's more positive approach to mothering, as I shall now illustrate.

WINNICOTT, MOTHERING AND WOMEN'S THERAPY

Within feminist theory, US feminist Nancy Chodorow's (1978) use of Winnicott's work has been particularly influential. She uses it to explain the reproduction of our currently unequal sexual division of labour whereby women mother while men work. She argues that this division is reproduced psychologically by the way girls remain much more psychically merged than boys with their mothers. Since girls are the same sex as their mothers, Chodorow writes, they feel less pressure to separate psychologically from the mother. Boys, by contrast, feel the need to divorce themselves from initial psychological merger with the mother's femaleness in order to forge a different male identity. The end result, according to Chodorow, is that boys thereby become psychologically suited to the differentiated and impersonal demands of work, women to the more merged relations implied by Winnicott to be necessary to early mothering.

Paradoxically, however, in the very process of seeking to incorporate sexual difference Chodorow assumes and thereby loses sight of it. Just as Winnicott assumes a pre-given sense of self – of the 'true self' – in seeking to explain its coming into being as separate and individuated from the mother, so Chodorow assumes a pre-given sense of sexual identity and difference in seeking to explain its genesis. She assumes that from earliest infancy girls and boys know their sex – as same or different from the mother – in identifying with, or differentiating from her in developing an identity as female or male.

Nevertheless it is true that women stereotypically feel more emotionally involved – fused even – with others than men (see e.g. Ernst 1987). Perhaps this in part reflects women's maternal situation in which, while capitalist development has progressively freed men to sell their labour on an individual basis, it has not traditionally accorded the same privilege to women. Instead they remain hemmed in by family ties and obligations. Even today women are still often condemned as selfishly individualistic for working especially if they have young children or other dependent relatives needing their care (Ussher 1989).

Society may accord boys the right of separating from and surpassing their mothers through school and work achievement. But it enjoins women to become mothers themselves. Their self-liberation as individuals therefore often involves sloughing off and refusing to become one with their mother's destiny. And this can involve struggling against the mother's unwillingness to let her daughter go, in so far as society offers her little beyond mothering in which to realise herself.

Although some feminists celebrate women's sense of unity with each other through mothering (e.g. Irigaray 1980), securing separation from the mother is often a central goal of women's therapy, as Sheila Ernst (1987) points out (but see Apter 1990). Ernst illustrates this point by reference to three women still unconsciously wedded to their mothers' image of them as babies. Angela continues to identify with her mother's picture of her as there solely to satisfy and meet her needs. Mary likewise still feels herself to be her 'mother's little girl', specifically the very distressed woman her mother became in giving psychotic vent to the family's stresses and strains on emigrating to this country. Lastly Evelyn is still imprisoned within her mother's image of her as a 'sick little girl', this seemingly being the only way her mother felt able to tend her as a baby.

Ernst describes how all three women initially longed to be understood by her without their having to explain or tell her anything, just as Winnicott describes the baby in the stage of absolute dependence as unaware of its dependence on the mother, of the need to communicate with her as a separate being. Ernst's patients also sought to accommodate – 'false self' style – to what they thought she wanted, just as they had long sought to accommodate to their mothers' needs. Slowly, holding onto therapy as a transitional space between their infantile sense of omnipotence – Angela's illusion, for instance, of mothering and thereby controlling Ernst – and the vulnerability involved in recognising the separation and boundaries between them, each began 'to unravel the entangling strings which prevented her from existing separately' (Ernst 1987: 106). This included recognising that the therapist could survive their anger, that however powerful their internal experience of rage it was separate and distinct from its external effects on Ernst qua mother-figure in therapy. Therapeutic progress also included growing trust in the therapist such that the patient felt more able to be playful, with all the separateness this involves. So too separation and becoming independent involved dealing with fear of the mother's resulting envy.

I have experienced just the same in working with women patients. Kate, for instance, has several children. She is terrified of becoming the same as her mother. As a child she felt her mother's critical and envious looks could kill, that she stared at Kate with laser beam intensity and destructiveness. Kate however remains seduced yet horrified by the idea of being her mother. She tries on her dead mother's clothes, while fearing becoming mentally ill like her. She is preoccupied with her health, as her mother must have been through the fatal disease that eventually killed her. And she experiences me as though I were a mirror in which she sees herself – as likewise a wife and mother who makes the same feminist demands on her as she does on herself.

Winnicott and many other post-Freudian analysts suggest that separation from such fusion with the mother – and all the anxieties it involves, including those resulting from hatred, envy and jealousy – can be achieved through the maternal function of the therapist in adapting to the patients' needs, holding patients in mind and containing their anxieties, and providing a transitional space whereby patients can brook lapses in their ersatz maternal adaptation.

Much is made of interpreting, often in these maternal terms, the patient's response to gaps between sessions, holiday breaks and the ending of therapy. Kate, for instance, who as a child fled her mother whenever she could and built up an internal image of herself as perfection itself unneedful of any outside help or provision, tells me she only remembers sessions by writing them down on a general household memo pad, as though she cannot bear to acknowledge any personal dependency on me. Often she arrives late and takes ages to come to the point. But as the end of each session approaches she bursts into tears as if, only with the imminence of actual separation, can she acknowledge her need of me, just as she felt this most acutely as a child on the eve of her mother's hospitalisation.

Similarly Vanessa was always very loathe to leave at the end of sessions. She would spin them out and forestall parting by making a great to-do of putting on her hat and coat, and gathering up her things. She found it almost unbearable to attend our last session so much did she want to avoid experiencing my loss, just as she had previously fled from emotionally working through her mother's death some years previously.

Recognition of separation from the mother is not, however, the mother's doing alone. It is not solely the effect of gradual lapses in her care, culminating in physical separation and death. For this leaves intact the illusion that, but for her absence, mother and child could be all in all to each other. This illusion is only disabused, and, with it, separation of self from mother only achieved, through the intervention of the father, as I shall now explain in returning to sexual difference and its centrality to patients' problems, so often ignored in Winnicottian therapy – feminist and non-feminist alike.

INDIVIDUATION THROUGH SEXUAL DIFFERENCE

Whatever the focus of post-Freudian psychoanalysis on separation and individuation through the mother's presence and absence, patients often feel that only the father has the power ultimately to bring about such independence. Kate complains her father did nothing to help free her from tantalising identification with her mother. 'My father's was more the sin of omission when I was a child,' she says. 'He didn't do anything to help . . . I wish he'd let me in on his side.' Meg, trammelled up in self-destructive identification with her adoptive mother who beat her, likewise bemoaned her father's failure to intervene, his seemingly turning a blind eye both to his wife's abuse of their daughter and to the latter's misery. Similarly Anna felt hopelessly entangled with her mother, not least because she felt handed over to her by her father as sacrificial lamb to staunch her mother's grief at the death of her mother just as, when Anna was a child, her father seemingly all too willingly vacated the matrimonial bed for Anna to have her mother to herself. Anna likewise felt disappointed at being handed over by a male consultant to me, a woman therapist: 'I wouldn't have got into all these messy things [her enmeshed relation with me and others] with a man as I do with you,' she maintained.

It is a measure of the power exercised by men in our male-dominated society that, whether or not the father aspires to patriarchal authority, he is looked to – as by Kate, Meg and Anna – as the only figure potent enough to enable them to become their own person separate from, albeit interdependent with, others. The problems patients bring to therapy often turn on the illusions of patriarchal power fostered by the all too real power of men in our sexually unequal society. It is these illusions that also need dismantling in therapy. And this entails drawing attention to sexual difference so readily overlooked in therapy as in society generally, so much is it in men's interests, as Karen Horney once observed, to conceal the social inequalities therein involved. Moreover, just as attention to sexual difference and inequality depends not solely on theory but also on practice – on the consciousness raising whereby women became aware of, and shared with each other, their immediate day-to-day experience of sexual inequality – so too in individual therapy attention to sexual difference depends on patients becoming aware of it, and of its disavowal as manifested in their day-to-day experience of the therapist. Again I will illustrate this point by reference to some of the patients I have worked with as a clinical psychologist, beginning with the women.

As a young woman Vanessa trained to be an opera singer. Now she often imagines herself as a prima donna – the diva – divine in her aesthetic sensibility, way above the mundane concerns of other mortals – of her neighbours – whom she describes as spending their days trimming their gardens and preparing freezer food. More often, however, she is sunk into paralysing depression by this omnipotent illusion's obverse – her sense of herself as damaged – as 'phallic lack' as Freudians might put it (as explained above). She complains of her lopsided body, of it not even being properly feminine, of being ever more crippled by arthritis and its sequelae. Nor does she feel she amounts to anything socially – just a pathetic old woman reduced to nothing in being abandoned by her husband leaving her wholly beholden for any self-esteem to other men – her elderly widowed father who lives with her, her doctor, and famous tenors on whom she dwells.

Crucial to Vanessa gaining some sense of herself as neither nothing nor everything was the interpretation of her early sense of me, qua woman, as likewise nothing – as in no way able to help as she felt my male colleagues could. Also important was her movement from this sense of herself and me as nothing as women toward recognising that we each amount to something, albeit not everything, that I provided her with some help as a patient, just as she increasingly recognised her helpfulness to the children in her part-time care.

Anna's therapy, by contrast, was more concerned with deconstructing her illusion both of herself and me as androgynous masculine woman. She saw me, for instance, as her critical father, to whom she enviously ascribed all creativity, and her jealous mother combined. She imagined herself penis-like emerging between labial lips. In this she was like the women Freud described as retaining the illusion of having a penis; an image that for Anna only became disassembled through interpreting, in terms of sexual difference, her constant need to surround herself with images of women, to reassure herself of being a woman and not also a man, and her need to have men lovers to whom to escape from otherwise seemingly drowning in a sea of femininity in which she believed she entirely created and manipulated others, just as she also felt created by them, the product of women alone. It was her all too precarious sense of boundary – marked not only by my presence and absence within and between sessions but also by sexual difference, by the fact I am a woman not also a man – that was central to the transference and to the work of therapy in enabling her to individuate from remaining embedded within an otherwise all-encompassing seeming maternal matrix.

Illusions of omnipotence were more rare in Kevin. Not that he did not sometimes bask in the illusion of saving the world from ecological disaster as though, single-handed, he could create the universe anew. This alternated with feeling full of unbridled anger, just as his father seemed on his infrequent visits to Kevin's childhood home when he engaged Kevin in intimidating rough-house play ending with abrasive unshaven hugs, kicking the furniture and beating up Kevin's mother. More often Kevin felt empty. He experienced others – particularly women, myself included – not himself as the seat of all potency, as able both to provide ever-attentive mothering while also draining him of whatever phallic potency he might otherwise have. In this he disavowed sexual difference. He told me it was no matter I am a woman not a man – I had no sex. Indeed it did seem as if I figured as neuter – as phallic mother, man and woman combined – in his internal world. He complained that I penetrated his inner self with my interpretations, drained him of his sexual desire, yet that I also understood him as his mother never had. Similarly he conjured up his girlfriend Avril's maternally attentive qualities while also telling me she threatened him with sharp knives in leaving them in the washing-up water. He likewise recalled his ex-wife selling his tools along with their car – an injury to his masculinity he underlined by saying, 'Your husband could tell you how he'd mind you doing away with his car tools. They take so long to amass.' It was to woman as phallus – to another girlfriend with her cigarettes he so deplored – that he looked to make the first move. It was his fantasy of all us women as 'phallic mother' – as though we parthenogenically created and sustained his being without need of paternal intervention – that needed interpreting and undoing by reference to sexual difference for Kevin to gain a sense of his own potency as neither nothing nor all-encompassing world saviour either.

Lastly Pete whose usual sense of himself, quite unlike Kevin, is of complete self-sufficiency. An artist, and formerly a high-up dignatory in the Church, Pete disavows his father's potency even though, like himself, his father was also a senior Church figure and sees himself, and is seen by Pete's mother and siblings, as very much the patriarch. Pete, by contrast, tells me his father had none of the authoritative masculinity of his senior colleagues' annual synods. When he was eight Pete reacted to his father's then desertion of his childhood home by appropriating, in fantasy, the latter's power to himself (cf Chasseguet Smirgel 1981). He created, in paint, his own world, peopled with the figures of his own imagination and control. His sex life is similarly self-created. He masturbates to images of himself upright benignly caring, mother and father combined, for a child – also himself – ejaculating and thereby seemingly out of control. Embodying as it were everything – the phallus both erect and detumescent – Pete experiences me as woman as nothing, as knowing nothing say of painting or of Church affairs. As therapy has progressed however he has begun to glimpse that I might not be so deficient. And with this comes painful recognition of the want of something outside himself if he is actually to father a child, as he has so long imagined doing.

CONCLUSION

In a sense this is the general aim of psychoanalytic therapy – to bring about just such longing. Therapy seeks to undo the om-nipotent illusion on which our self-realisation at work and at home so often becomes beached. For only by knowing we want and need something outside ourselves, that we are not self-sufficient, can we begin to change the world so as to realise ourselves actually and in fact. All too often this project is stopped in its tracks by the infantile illusion of already being at one with the world – with the mother in the first place. Undoing this illusion is achieved not only through recognising lapses in maternal care reflected in the thera-pist's presence and absence in and between sessions as described by Winnicott. It also involves undoing, as I have sought to explain by reference to the work of Lacan, the illusions fostered by patri-archy that we can realise ourselves as women and men through having or being the ideal phallic man. In this, therapy is one with feminism in seeking to expose such illusions and the sexual inequalities therein involved, so we can begin to challenge them and bring about a world that more nearly meets our needs in all the similarities and differences of our sexual and social being.

NOTES

1 My thanks to students, patients, and baby Robert from whom I have learnt so much. All identifying details have been changed to preserve their anonymity.
2 The psychological ill-effects of sexual inequality, illustrated in this chapter, result primarily from discrimination exercised against women as a sex and only secondarily from associated gender

expectations regarding psychological femininity and masculinity. Hence my use of the term sex, not gender (see also Sayers 1989).
3 In his early theory of mind Freud (1911) distinguished two principles of mental functioning: primary process, unconscious thought which he hypothesised characterises the developmentally earliest form of thought dominated by the pleasure principle, consisting of hallucinated wish-fulfilments, and characterised by considerable fluidity of meaning as evident in the condensation and displacement involved in dreams and psychosis; and secondary process, conscious thought, a developmentally later form of thought involving language, and recognition of the need to take account of reality if our wishes are to be fulfilled actually and in fact, rather than in the merely illusory, hallucinatory form afforded by the unconscious.

REFERENCES

Apter, T. (1990) *Altered Loves: Mothers and Daughters During Adolescence.* Hemel Hempstead: Harvester Wheatsheaf.
Bion, W. I. (1967) *Second Thoughts.* London: Heinemann.
Chasseguet Smirgel, J. (1981) Loss of reality in perversions. *Journal of the American Psycho-Analytic Association*, 29: 511–534.
Chodorow, N. (1978) *The Reproduction of Mothering.* Berkeley: University of California Press.
Ernst, S. (1987) Can a daughter be a woman? In S. Ernst and M. Maguire (eds), *Living with the Sphinx.* London: Women's Press.
Freud, S. (1909) Analysis of a phobia in a five-year-old boy. In Penguin Freud Library, 8. Harmondsworth: Penguin.
Freud, S. (1911) Formulations on the two principles of mental functioning. In Penguin Freud Library, 11. Harmondsworth: Penguin.
Freud, S. (1918) From the history of an infantile neurosis. In Penguin Freud Library, 9. Harmondsworth: Penguin.
Freud, S. (1931) *Female Sexuality.* Harmondsworth: Penguin, Penguin Freud Library, 7.
Horney, K. (1930) The distrust between the sexes. In *Feminine Psychology.* New York: Norton, 1967.
Irigaray, L. (1980) When our lips speak together. *Signs*, 6, 1: 66–79.
Klein, M. (1928) Early stages of the Oedipus conflict. In J. Mitchell (ed.), *The Selected Melanie Klein.* Harmondsworth: Penguin.
Lacan, J. (1949) The mirror stage as formative of the function of the I as revealed in psychoanalytic experience. In *Ecrits.* London: Tavistock, 1977.
Lacan, J. (1953) Some reflections on the ego. *International Journal of Psycho-Analysis*, 34, 1: 11–17.
Mitchell, J. (1974) *Psychoanalysis and Feminism.* Harmondsworth: Penguin.
Mitchell, J. (1982) Introduction. In J. Mitchell and J. Rose (eds), *Feminine Sexuality.* London: Macmillan.
Phillips, A. (1988) *Winnicott.* London: Fontana.

Sayers, J. (1989) Goodbye sex, hello gender? *New Ideas in Psychology*, 2: 309–11.

Sayers, J. (1991) *Mothering Psychoanalysis*. London: Hamish Hamilton.

Stern, D. (1985) *The Interpersonal World of the Infant*. New York: Basic Books.

Ussher, J. (1989) *The Psychology of the Female Body*. London: Routledge.

Winnicott, D. W. (1971) *Playing and Reality*. Harmondsworth: Penguin.

Chapter 10

Feminist practice in therapy

Gilli Watson and Jennie Williams

INTRODUCTION

In the last two decades many feminists have been concerned with the mental health implications of sexual oppression, and much of the associated debate and development has focused on mental health services. Attention has been directed to a number of components of mental health care, including policy (e.g. Laing 1984; Walker 1984a), service development (e.g. Mowbray *et al.* 1984; Beckert 1987; Smith 1991) and training (Reiker and Carmen 1984b: Williams and Watson 1991b). The practices of traditional therapy have been fundamentally questioned (e.g. Chesler 1972), and feminists have sought ways of working that are sensitive to the influence of sexual inequality on the lives and experiences of women (Baker-Miller 1988; Sturdivant 1980; Dutton-Douglas and Walker 1988a).

In this chapter we review the emergence of feminist practice in therapy. Attention is given to the impact of feminist thought on the central principles and practices of therapy rather than its impact on specific therapies (Dutton-Douglas and Walker 1988b). It is acknowledged that feminist practice needs to be informed by an understanding of the psychological costs not only of sexual inequality, but of racial and other social inequalities. We emphasise that this knowledge needs to be integrated with an understanding of the societal and interpersonal processes that maintain these inequalities. We suggest that developing and working with this knowledge base within feminist practice is the major challenge for this decade.

THE EMERGENCE OF FEMINIST PRACTICE IN THERAPY

The context

The psychological costs for women of sexual oppression are now well documented (for review, Carmen *et al.* 1984; Williams 1984). Alongside this literature has evolved a growing critique of the role that the social and medical sciences have played in women's oppression. Feminist scholars have provided ample evidence (Fine and Gordon 1989) that these disciplines and professions protect the interests of men by generating ideologies that ignore, deny and obscure the existence of sexual and social inequalities. These ideologies, as a number of writers have noted (Chesler 1972; Smith and Siegal 1985; Penfold and Walker 1984; Caplan 1987; Caplan and Gans 1991), enable women's lives, despair and distress to be described in a language that does not invoke the concept of sexual inequality. This leaves many women coping with the consequences of sexual inequality without being able to name the real cause of their difficulties, and as Penfold and Walker (1984) observe 'When there is a disjunction between the world as women experience it and the terms given them to understand the experience, women have little alternative but to feel crazy' (55).

Male-serving ideologies and associated practices are also deeply embedded in the mental health professions and services. Largely well-intentioned mental health professionals locate problems within women and ignore or deny the socio-political factors that are the context, and frequently the source, of their distress (Ussher 1991). While the most compelling evidence for this can be found in the grim historical accounts of women's relationship with psychiatry (Showalter 1987), there are no reasons for believing that we have now entered a more enlightened era. For example, women's behaviour continues to be defined as pathological (Caplan 1987; Ussher 1991), women continue to be blamed for problems that occur within families (Williams and Watson 1988), and the mental health professions are still reluctant to recognise the psychological implications of sexual abuse and violence – the most explicit and direct expression of sexual oppression. Finally documentation of the sexual exploitation of women clients by male health professionals (e.g. Chesler 1972; Schoener *et al.* 1984; Bouhoutsos 1984) is a salutory reminder that not all mental health professionals are well intentioned.

The paradox for the mental health professions, as Penfold and Walker (1984) note, is that they serve a social function by helping to maintain sexual and other social inequalities and at the same time have the task of helping women cope with the personal consequences of these inequalities. The challenge for feminists working in the mental health professions is to develop ways of empowering women who are struggling to survive the effect of sexual and other inequalities on their lives.

Before considering the development of feminist practice in therapy it is important to acknowledge that not all feminists accept that the practice of therapy is compatible with the goals of feminism (e.g. Tennov 1973; Daly 1978). Tennov (1973), for example, described therapy as 'an unproven and expensive tyranny of one person over another' (107), and instead recommended women's self-help as a collective strategy compatible with feminism. While we share concerns about the limits of therapy, and would caution against therapy being seen as the primary solution to women's difficulties, our view, like other feminist practitioners such as Holland (1990), is that therapy forms a necessary part of a network of women-centred services.

Early principles for feminist practice

The development of feminist practice in therapy grew from women's personal and political dissatisfaction with their abuse and misrepresentation by psychiatry (e.g. Chesler 1972). Feminist practice was not developed from one particular theory of therapy: it originated from a new set of values, and a system for how these could be integrated into existing therapies. It represented an approach to therapy, a philosophy of practice, rather than a prescription of technique (Sturdivant 1980), and consequently many developments are considered relevant to both individual and group work. In a context of rapidly growing information about psychiatry's role in women's oppression, it is understandable that one of the dominant concerns in the early literature was to define principles which would safeguard the interests of women in therapy. There was a strong commitment to democratise therapy – to create a 'radical therapy of equals' (Walstedt 1971: 10.)

There are several good accounts of the early developments of feminist practice (e.g. Sturdivant 1980; Gilbert 1980; Butler 1985;

Cammaert and Larsen 1988). These suggest that three principles have remained central to the growth and development of feminist practice. Firstly, the commitment to equality within therapy, to an egalitarian relationship between client and therapist and to an open, explicit therapy process. As Brown (1985b) observed, power sharing is 'at the heart of feminist therapy' (303). Secondly, the commitment to bringing society into therapy, to working with women's experience of sexual inequality. This is contained in the assumption of 'dual causality': that women's distress has both societal and personal origins (Sturdivant 1980). Feminists argued that therapy could and should be informed by essentially political analyses of psychological distress, and were critical of the intra-individual preoccupations of traditional therapy. Thirdly, allied to power re-distribution in therapy was the commitment to power re-distribution within society: to political, economic and social equality between the sexes. Sexual inequality was assumed to have a major etiological role in women's psychological distress. Feminist practice was therefore committed to exposing, and re-dressing, the costs of sexual inequality. Personal change was not separated from social change. At the centre of the emerging feminist therapy was the strong commitment to bringing together 'the personal and the political' in social action as well as intro-spection. It was assumed that feminist practitioners and, ideally, also their clients would not only work to bring about personal change but towards establishing a social system consistent with feminist principles of sexual equality (Rawlings and Carter 1977; Gilbert 1980; Holland 1988).

The concerns which shaped the early development of feminist practice in therapy, also resulted in efforts to establish formal guidelines that would protect the interests of women by giving direction about the responsible use of power, and prohibitions against the abuse of power and privilege in therapy. Early guide-lines produced by the Feminist Therapy Collective (Fondi *et al.* 1977) were followed by ethical guidelines for therapy with women from the American and Canadian Psychological Associations (APA 1978; APA 1979; CPA 1980), an example that the British Psycho-logical Society has yet to follow. The development of guidelines for therapists has also been paralleled by the development of guide-lines attempting to define and authorise the rights of clients in therapy (e.g. National Organisation for Women 1978; National

Coalition for Women's Mental Health 1985). The ethics of feminist practice continues to be a source of concern, and more recent considerations can be found in the work of Brown (1982; 1985b; 1988a).

Re-defining the problem

Feminist critiques of the social sciences and psychiatry, and efforts to integrate feminist principles into therapy practice, were linked with attempts to re-define and review the difficulties women experience. New accounts of women's distress began to emerge that offered initial analyses of the effects of sexual inequality on women and their lives. For example, in 1978 a major report commented on 'the ways in which inequality creates dilemmas and conflict for women in the contexts of marriage, family relationships, reproduction, child rearing, divorce, ageing, education and work' (Carmen *et al.* 1984: 21). However, not all the concepts and analyses that were developed during this early period were helpful to women. Women were sometimes portrayed as victims, emotionally dependent, responsible for their own oppression, and responsible for creating dependency in their daughters. There was also considerable preoccupation with gender differentiation rather than gender stratification, for example the work on sex-typed traits (for review, Whitley 1983), sex roles (Marecek and Ballou 1981) and sex-role stereotypes (e.g. Franks and Rothblum 1983). These examples remind us that sexual inequality can be hard to 'see' and easy to perpetuate.

Re-defining the function of therapy

Attempts to offer alternative constructions of women's distress were accompanied by a re-definition of the function of therapy (Sturdivant 1980; Rosewater 1984). The primary goal of feminist practice in therapy was to help women overcome the effects of oppression in their own lives. The commitment was to change, not adjustment, and to client, not therapist, defined change. Furthermore, it was widely assumed, though somewhat idealistically, that women who engaged in this process of change were likely to become politically aware and involved in social action.

Feminist practice: the knowledge base

With the emphasis of feminist practice on the personal as political, women practitioners' own experience of oppression was recognised and valued as a knowledge base. The therapeutic work of many feminist practitioners was also informed by their own involvement in activities that challenged the sexual status quo, for example in consciousness-raising groups and campaign work; and by the continual evaluation of the effects of their own lifestyle, values and prejudices on the process of therapy (Butler 1985; Sturdivant 1980).

The emerging body of literature on the psychology of women (for review, Weisstein 1971; Parlee 1979), and feminist critiques of psychiatry (e.g. Chesler 1972; Broverman *et al.* 1970), constituted the beginnings of a formal knowledge base for the new feminist practice. It has been understandably argued that professionals unfamiliar with this information base are not qualified to work with women (Brown 1991). While this expanding literature addressed the psychological costs of sexual inequality for women, the focus has remained primarily within mental health and about white women. Indeed, the difficulties faced by black women (Sayal 1989; Holland 1990), by women of poverty (Belle 1984), by women with disabilities (Brown and Craft 1989) and by women with major mental health difficulties (Perkins 1991) have still not been substantially addressed. More recently, writings from women psychiatric and abuse survivors have begun to create a powerful knowledge base of women's experience (e.g. Chamberlain 1988; Poston and Lison 1989; Fraser 1989).

Feminist Practice: the process of therapy

We have seen that feminist principles for practice in therapy were established in order to create a qualitatively different therapeutic relationship, one not based on dominance and control. Traditionally, most therapy systems had been modelled on the adult(man):child(woman) relationship, and this was now rejected in favour of a model based on a relationship of equality between adults. It became a priority to establish a way of working in therapy – a practice base – that would promote equality and help to ensure congruence between theory and practice (Rosewater 1988). The development of this practice base occupied considerable attention in the early literature. The main strategies used to try to minimise inequality of power in therapy (Gilbert 1980; Sturdivant 1980; Brown 1982) are summarised below.

De-mystifying the therapy process

There was a strong commitment to reducing the power of therapy by exposing and making public the therapy process. This required therapists to be explicit about their work and to discuss the process of therapy with their clients.

De-mystifying the therapist

Similarly the power of the therapist was reduced by requiring practitioners to make explicit their personal and professional values, their training, areas of expertise and interests. Clients were encouraged to choose the person best suited to their needs, rather than the reverse.

Strengthening clients rights in therapy

The power of the client was strengthened by promoting clients' rights in therapy and publishing these in guidelines for clients (e.g. National Organisation for Women 1978).

Client as active participant in therapy

Emphasis was placed on the client's active participation in the process of therapy, e.g. in negotiations about the aims of therapy, in ongoing feedback to the therapist and in evaluating the outcome of therapy.

Client as expert

The position of therapist as expert about the client was replaced by the assumption that the client is the expert about herself and her life. This client-based information formed a major knowledge base for the therapist. Emphasis was placed on the client's strengths and abilities, not on pathology.

The therapist's use of power

In working to establish practices that promoted equality within therapy, differences in power and privilege between client and therapist were acknowledged, but emphasis was placed on not exploiting or maximising these differences. Inequalities were viewed as temporary. Client and therapist were accorded equal worth, if not equal power. The careful and conscious use of power and privilege was advocated. Power seeking techniques which stressed outcome over process were discarded in favour of techniques that enhanced client's personal power. Transference was particularly discredited in early feminist practice and replaced by client-centred concepts such as 'readiness' rather than the therapist-centred concept of 'resistance' (Brown 1982, 1984; Rosewater 1988).

Assumptions about change

Although no specific model of therapy was advocated, early practice showed a preference for an educative, skills-based model of change (Butler 1985; Cammaert and Larsen 1988). In contrast to interpretive ways of working, emphasis was given to counteracting sexual inequality through the development of autonomy, self-determination and independence in women. These were promoted largely on an individual basis by increasing individual women's skills, competence and decision-making through assertiveness training, consciousness-raising, access to information, resources and employment training. The focus of this early practice was on strengthening women's emotional, psychological, informational and economic independence. The skills-based approach advocated a consultative model of change in which women clients would be empowered to become their own agents of change. The therapist's function was primarily as an associate in this process, accompanying the client in her process of change (Sturdivant 1980). The use of appropriate self-disclosure by the therapist was advocated as a means of facilitating this by demystifying the therapist, and creating shared experience between the therapist and client as women.

Central to the process of feminist therapy was the legitimation of women's anger, 'perhaps the single most prohibited emotion for women' (Sturdivant 1980: 79). It was expected that in the process of differentiating internal from external sources of distress and discovering sources of oppression in their lives, women would experience rage and anger. This anger was seen as a rightful and appropriate response to oppression. Working with anger, with women's fear of anger as illegitimate and destructive, and enabling its safe expression, was seen as an essential part of feminist practice (Gilbert 1980; Kaplan *et al.* 1983; Sturdivant 1980).

The value of group work over individual work in reducing women's isolation and enabling women to develop mutual support was also acknowledged in early practice. In addition, therapy was usually not seen as a cure-all, and women were encouraged to gain strength from other sources. This was accompanied by a commitment to developing a sense of community between women, in order to confirm women's experience, develop a women-based value system, and collectively challenge inequality (Butler 1985).

Early practice: evaluation and review

Ten years later, these early principles remained the foundation of feminist practice. However, the emphasis given in early feminist practice to a linear, skills-based/educative model of change was beginning to be questioned. The inherent difficulties of this approach are identified by Fodor (1985) in her review of a decade of assertiveness training. Firstly, she questions the basic assumption that women have a 'deficit' in assertiveness which can be made good by learning appropriate behaviour. This assumption, she suggests, leaves assertiveness training open to criticism as yet another treatment directed at 'the victim of social injustice, placing the burden of change on the backs of individual women' (258). Fodor (1985) quotes Linehan and Egan (1979), who argue that 'when half the population is targeted as needing to change their behaviour in order to gain fair treatment by the system, we have to ask what system are those individuals trying to fit'. Secondly, Fodor (1985) takes issue with the assumption of assertiveness training that 'if individual women changed, societal attitudes towards them would change' (261). Fodor (1985) suggests this had not been the case, and cites follow-up research on assertiveness training programmes which indicate that there is a strong bias against assertive women. These concerns lead her to argue for moving beyond treating individual women towards challenging the continuing male monopoly of power in order to create an environment receptive to strong assertive women.

Fodor's 1985 article reflected the growing recognition that feminist practice now had to take into account men's reaction to women's new strength. There was increasing awareness of the potential and actual cost of change for women. Exposing sexual inequality had not dismantled it nor stopped it affecting the lives of individual women. Skills, resources and information alone were not sufficient to counteract the impact of inequality. Feminist practice now needed to be informed by an understanding of the processes maintaining sexual inequality. This resulted in an increasing interest within the theory and practice of feminist therapy on power, particularly on the power processes maintaining dominance and on the dynamics of change.

POWER AND INEQUALITY

Maintaining dominance: the abuse of power

The recognition that power is of central concern for feminist practice has been confirmed by increasing evidence of the violence and sexual abuse experienced by women and girl children. These figures render it impossible to view violence and sexual assault as exceptional ways of maintaining dominance.

Statistics from America indicate that between 1 in 3 and 1 in 2 families experience violence, that 1 in 4 women had been raped, and that 1 in 3 girl children and adolescents under 18 have experienced significant sexual abuse (Baker-Miller 1988). Baker-Miller concludes from these data that 'all women grow up in a context that includes the threat of violence particularly sexualized violence' (xxii). Incest and the sexual abuse of children are far more extensive than previously thought. Connections between abuse in childhood and subsequent abuse in adulthood have also become visible. Walker (1984b), in a survey of women who had experienced domestic violence in adulthood, found that 49 per cent had been sexually or physically abused as children. Similar figures have emerged in Britain, where it has been estimated that 1 in 7 women are raped in marriage (Hall 1986), that 1 in 5 households experience domestic violence (see Smith 1989), and that between 1 in 10 and 1 in 3 children are sexually assaulted in childhood (see Whitwell 1990). There continue to be reminders of the sexual abuse of women by mental health professionals (Bouhoutsos 1984).

These figures provide strong evidence that the subordination of women is not only maintained by the use of psychological and economic power, but by the all too frequent use of tyranny, torture, violence, sexual assault and rape. These processes of domination often commence in childhood and continue in adulthood. Recognition of the very damaging costs of sexual inequality for women and the way in which women's bodies – as adults and children – bear much of these costs, now must be taken into account in attempts to challenge the basis of this inequality.

The psychological implications of sexual abuse and violence, long obscured by the theory and practice of psychiatry, are also more visible. For example, recent research confirms the etiological role of sexual abuse in major mental health problems (see Whitwell 1990), and work by Rosewater (1985) suggests that women victims of domestic violence are at risk of being misdiagnosed as schizophrenic or personality disordered. Prolonged abuse, victimisation and tyranny carries major mental health costs for women.

There is also growing recognition that the mental health costs of racial oppression have been ignored, denied and obscured by, for example, theories of ethnic and racial 'vulnerability' (Sayal 1989). Studies also demonstrate a strong custodial bias in the response of the psychiatric services to black people. Afro-Caribbean people are 4–10 times more likely to be given a diagnosis of schizophrenia on first contact with psychiatric services (Littlewood and Lipsedge 1988; Errol *et al.* 1989), and black women are more likely than white women to be diagnosed as having a chronic rather than an acute mental health problem, and to be institutionalised for mental illness (Robinson 1983). The interactive and cumulative effects of racial and sexual inequalities carry high costs for black women in terms of poverty (Belle 1984), in the sanctioning of sexual abuse and rape of black women as a legacy of slavery (Robinson 1983) and in the expropriation of black women's history (Holland 1990).

Maintaining dominance: the dynamics of power

The documentation of these widespread power abuses has been paralleled by work exposing other costs for women of the processes maintaining sexual inequality. These were initially formulated by Baker-Miller in 1976, and this work remains a major resource for therapists concerned to connect socially structured sexual inequality with the lives of individual women. Central to her work is the observation that the power processes that maintain sexual inequality are similar in many important respects to those taking place in other inequitable social relationships. Using this comparison, Baker-Miller (1976) identifies some of the main processes by which one group maintains dominance over another, and the strategies used by the other to survive this domination. Critical to her analysis are the ways in which conflict about inequality is managed by a dominant group so that its position and advantages are protected. She notes that the interests of the dominant group are best served when open conflict about inequality is avoided and protest is driven underground. In these circumstances, subordinate group members are forced to resort to indirect challenges – hidden defiance, disguised conflict, winning by outwitting – patterns of protest which are well known to women and which can carry heavy psychological costs. Baker-Miller (1976) also identifies the risks for subordinate group members of engaging in direct conflict including, physical violence, social degradation, being labelled deviant, or becoming mad. This work laid bare two important sets of processes: the processes whereby inequality is legitimised and maintained over time, and the interactions that occur between individual members of dominant and subordinate groups to maintain inequality. By identifying these dynamics, Baker-Miller helped generate new ways of thinking about the psychological consequences of sexual inequality.

Smith and Siegel (1985) offer additional clarification of the use of power by women in the context of inequality. They describe the ways in which women exercise power while denying it so that 'he remains powerful and she remains safe' (15). They suggest that women use this 'underground power' or 'power of powerlessness' to resist or refuse, when overt refusal would invite retaliation. Retaliation could include physical violence, economic deprivation, or humiliation. In common with other writers (e.g. Cline and Spender 1988; Williams and Watson 1988), they draw attention to the costs of using power covertly by noting that tactics such as guile or helplessness contribute to perpetuating women's dependency and subordination.

Lerner (1983), using a similar analysis to Smith and Siegel (1985), argues that women's dependency is more apparent than real. She suggests that women's underfunctioning – keeping small so men are big – is part of the process maintaining inequality and as such cannot be seen in isolation from the system of inequality in which it is embedded. Men's dominance, she argues, depends on, and indeed requires, women to under-function. This is perpetuated by strong cultural injunctions. Women's strength and abilities are perceived as destructive and weakening to men and any move towards autonomy portrayed as betrayal and disloyalty. Lerner (1983) observes that women are offered myths as consolations, for example, that men's strength is really built on women's strength (the woman behind the man) and that men are in fact vulnerable, despite their apparent strength. Lerner (1983) argues that these injunctions which encourage women to under-function and thwart their own competencies are often a root cause of women's rage and anger. Bell and Newby (1976) in their article exploring the structural basis of power differences between women and men, offer a similar analysis of the deferential relationship between wives and husbands.

CURRENT CONCERNS: WORKING WITH POWER PROCESSES

Throughout the 1980s feminist practitioners working with families continued to 'name' domestic power processes (Goldner 1985a, 1985b; for review Williams and Watson 1988). Feminist practice began to work from the premise that sexual inequality is not temporary or historical – but stable and ongoing. Analyses of the dynamics maintaining subordination at an inter-personal level also offered an understanding of the way in which women are rendered powerless (Rosewater 1984). This was accompanied by a growing appreciation of the costs for women of challenging inequality, and with it an acknowledgement that the process of change itself needed to be contextualised (Goldner 1985a; Baker-Miller 1988).

This literature on power and inequality has enabled practitioners to become better skilled at identifying both the consequences of sexual inequality (the what) and the social and inter-personal dynamics which enforce and maintain sexual inequality (the how). It has strongly informed our own thinking and practice when we address the processes of empowerment and disempowerment for women. We would argue that much of the difficulty of working with empowerment arises from not addressing the continuing and systematic processes of disempowerment. We would now like to discuss these processes in relation to this literature and our own work with women.

Women's experience of power and power abuse

We would suggest that we cannot empower women without first understanding their individual experience of disempowerment. This requires listening well and carefully to women about their experience of power and power abuse as adult women and as children. These experiences – of violence or threat of violence; of racial abuse or exploitation; of sexual assault or incest in childhood; of rape or sexual assault in adulthood; of being silenced through fear or rage; of feeling unentitled to the ownership of our bodies or our lives – need to be well heard and understood. This forms the basis of understanding each woman's experience of power and powerlessness and of the strategies she has developed to survive. It is in this context – in the context of women's experiences of the use and abuse of power both as a child and adult – that the use of covert power by women can be understood. This is the starting point for work, and as such needs to be an integrated part of assessing and working with the needs of all women clients. The process of remembering and recounting experiences of power abuses may generate strong feelings of pain, fear or anger (Kaplan *et al.* 1983; Walker 1985; Hall and Lloyd 1989).

Symptoms of powerlessness

Knowledge of the power dynamics that surround sexual and other social inequalities provides important understandings of what is being communicated by women. One consequence of the process of maintaining subordination through strong paradoxical injunctions to women (e.g. 'win by losing') is that women frequently have to express their distress in hidden, masked and indirect ways. Careful understanding of the power processes involved and of the process of silencing is necessary in order to understand what is being spoken by the symptom and to establish a safe way to speak together. For example, eating difficulties may be a way of speaking about powerlessness; self-harm and substance abuse may be ways of managing huge anger and pain about abuse; madness/ psychosis a way of speaking the unspeakable without being held to account for what is said. Women's protest and distress may need to be conveyed in indirect ways in order to minimise retaliation – to signify without being seen. Understanding and translating this requires a preparedness to understand the processes that silence women, that make distress and protest difficult and unsafe to speak directly. This has been increasingly seen in relation to sexual abuse, where speaking of the abuse and naming the abuser may result in unknowable consequences. Instead women may speak, shout, scream of their abuse in silence (Janssen 1983). Orbach (1986) reconstructs anorexia as a hunger strike, a protest which cannot be named. Brown (1985a) suggests largeness is one way women can occupy space without forcibly having to take it. Women's bodies not only speak for women but also, as the frequent targets of abuse, may embody the distress, rage and pain. This embodied pain may manifest in physical symptoms, for example, gynaecological pain related to sexual abuse (Kitzinger 1990).

Empowerment

An understanding of women's personal experience of power and power abuses, and use of power in the context of sexual inequality, is the starting point of empowerment. Making explicit the social processes that delimit women's use of, and access to, power offers women a way of making visible these power processes. It may also lessen the shame or blame women may feel about the power they use – self-harm, alcohol, withdrawal. This can form the beginnings of identifying and valuing other sources of personal power they hold (Brown 1985a).

The process of empowerment is not about asking women to relinquish indirect power bases but about understanding their context and costs, and beginning to establish access to other forms of personal power. Emotional empowerment is central. Finding our own voice; feeling safe to speak; feeling well heard and understood; finding anger and managing rage in a safe way; lessening self-blame for abuse; establishing rights and entitlement; experiencing the pain and sadness of loss and abuse; feeling confirmed; all form the basis of what Laura Brown calls 'feeling at home in our own bodies' (Brown 1985a: 71).

This initial work provides the basis for acknowledging the risks of change. Relinquishing one form of power – even if self-damaging – before feeling protected by another may feel too disarming. It may not be possible for a woman to stop speaking through her body until she has found her voice and knows the risks of speaking more directly. It takes time to feel safe with, and know the cost of using, more direct forms of power. The risks involved for women of becoming bigger, stronger and taking up more space have to be considered and their options explored and rehearsed. This includes exploring the retaliation that may be expected, the form it might take (e.g. economic, emotional, physical), the practical and emotional preparations that can be made (e.g. forming an escape plan, Walker 1985), and identifying the sources of support that are available. It is important to remember that women themselves are the best judges of their safety, and that change needs to be in a woman's own timing, at her readiness (Rosewater 1988). Too often as workers we are puzzled by the apparent reluctance of clients to move forward. We forget that women whose lives have been at risk have reason for caution. We often need to work hard to hear the basis of this caution.

Empowerment also involves helping women find their own pathways to more direct forms of personal power. The resources needed to do this could include, for example, housing, employment training, self-defence training, and voice workshops. A major source of empowerment continues to be women's access to each other in workshops and groups, including incest survivor groups (Harflett and Scott 1987) and black women's history groups (Holland 1990).

For some women the risks of moving towards using more explicit power can be too great and they may choose not to, even if the costs to them in terms of self-harm or mental health difficulties are high. As a worker, witnessing this choice and accepting this decision is a painful and distressing reminder of the high costs of inequality for women.

CONCERNS FOR THE 1990s

As feminist practitioners committed to the development of a more effective feminist practice in therapy, we recognise that therapy is only one way of meeting the mental health needs of women, and rarely sufficient in itself. Other developments are needed to support individual women in change. It is important that as feminist practitioners we act on what we learn from listening to our women clients, and continually ask ourselves how we can add weight to, or initiate, the changes that need to take place. These ventures could include promoting the development of, for example, good legal and medical advice, better housing and child-care facilities, and opportunities for women to engage in collective support and action with other women. There are impressive examples in existence (Holland 1990) which can help us use our energy effectively. Legal action in America and in Britain has included campaigning for survivors of incest, and for changes in the law for rape and domestic violence (Rosewater 1984; Walker 1985; Hall 1986). The development of services for women has included refuges from domestic violence, rape crisis centres and therapy centres. Co-operation between women professionals and women psychiatric and sexual abuse survivors has led to the development of services (Women in Mind 1986) and advocacy campaigns such as the Scottish Action for Mental Health (1988) 'Why Women?' campaign. Women survivors have also fought for the resources to provide survivor-run services, including safe houses for women who have been sexually abused and self-harm telephone help lines. These innovations in service provision are often vulnerable because of their insecure funding, and working to ensure the financial viability of women-centred services can be a necessary and legitimate activity for feminist practitioners.

As feminist practitioners we also need to continue to find ways of informing our work with clients with an understanding of the impact of social inequalities on their lives. In particular, this means beginning to compensate for the failure of feminist practice in therapy to address the oppression of black women and women of poverty. In promoting the commonality of women's experience, the complexities of women's experience has been ignored and white, middle class, heterosexual, women's experience universalised (Bourne 1983; Murphy and Livingstone 1985). The impact of racism on black women's lives has been considered secondary to the impact of gender (Sayal 1989), and racism within mental health services, professions and training has yet to be seriously addressed (Holland 1990, 1991; Sayal-Bennett 1991). It is now essential that white feminist practitioners take responsibility for contributing to this situation, and take direction from existing critiques, research and models of service development (Robinson 1983; Belle 1984; Currer 1984; Holland 1990, 1991 and Chapter 3 in this text; Skodra 1989; and Brown 1990). It is also time to take action to compensate for ignorance about the needs and mental health service requirements of women with long-term psychiatric disabilities (Perkins 1991), women with learning disabilities (Brown and Craft 1989), and older women (Midlarsky 1988). The value of the scholarly and growing literature focusing on therapy and lesbian women (Sharratt and Bern 1985; Brown 1988a, 1988b; Siegel 1985) also needs to be more widely acknowledged.

Finally, it is important to be realistic about the difficulties that feminist practitioners are likely to encounter, particularly when working in statutory services. It is not easy to gain the knowledge and skills we need to work effectively (Williams and Watson 1991a), and when we do work from a feminist perspective we run the risk of being marginalised (Brown 1991). Women working in statutory services also have to contend with the pervasive effect of sexual and racial inequalities on their professional lives, for example on their supervision (Caplan 1985), and career development (Sayal-Bennett 1991). As a strategy for sustaining and developing feminist practice we would strongly endorse Walker and Dutton-Douglas (1988) and Rosewater's (1988) emphasis on the value of women's coalitions and networks. These can be a major source of strength, identification, support and enrichment, and of much needed opportunities for critique and challenge. This has certainly been our personal experience. Our own journeys have been strongly resourced by networks which have connected us with women from different working contexts and professional backgrounds, and by coalitions formed with women service users and survivors.

CONCLUSION

Early feminist practice was optimistic about the prospect of overcoming the effects of sexual inequality through empowering women with information, knowledge, and skills. This educative model of personal and social change mistakenly assumed that resourcing individual women would undermine socially structured sexual inequality. However, the greater emphasis in the 1980s on the dynamics of women's oppression has made it possible for feminist practice to be informed by a better understanding of power. There is now an established language for talking about power and power processes and a framework for addressing the strengthening of women's power. The increasing understanding of the basis of sexual inequality has enabled a major de-construction of psychiatric theory and the development of new analyses of the psychological difficulties women experience. Feminist practice now offers an approach to therapy based on principles of power sharing and a more comprehensive understanding of the processes and risks of change.

We have identified here the limitations within the feminist literature, most notably the dominance of white women's experience and preoccupations, and the tendency of some theorising to be women-blaming. These biases need to be redressed. The challenge for feminist practice is to develop perspectives that will enable us to work effectively with the psychological consequences of social structured inequalities based on race, class and disability. We need an elaborated understanding of the impact of gender, racism, poverty and disability on women's lives. The knowledge we use to inform our work needs to speak from all, and not just some, women's experiences.

Working explicitly with sexual inequality is challenging personally and professionally. It is neither easy nor comfortable to see more clearly the impact of inequality on women's lives. Nonetheless, it is empowering to participate in disentangling the processes that keep women small and to participate in the struggle to strengthen and enlarge women's lives and power.

REFERENCES

American Psychological Association Task Force on Sex Bias and Sex-Role Stereotyping in Psychotherapeutic Practice (1978) *American Psychologist*, 13: 1,122–1,123.

American Psychological Association, Division 17, Counselling Psychology (1979) Principles concerning the counselling and therapy of women. *Counselling Psychologist*, 8, 1: 21.

Baker-Miller, J. (1988) *Towards a New Psychology of Women*, 2nd edition. London: Pelican.

Beckert, A. (1987) Mental health: the Elizabeth Stone House alternative. *Women and Therapy*, 6, 1/2: 323–332.

Bell, C. and Newby, H. (1976) Husbands and wives: the dynamics of the deferential dialectic. In D. L. Barker and S. Allen (eds), *Dependence and Exploitation in Work and Marriage*. London and New York: Longman.

Belle, D. (1984) Inequality and mental health: low income and minority women. In L. E. A. Walker (ed.), *Women and Mental Health Policy*. London: Sage.

Bouhoutsos, J. C. (1984) Sexual intimacy between psychotherapist and clients: policy implications for the future. In L. E. A. Walker (ed.), *Women and Mental Health Policy*. London: Sage.

Bourne, J. (1983) Towards an anti-racist feminism. *Race and Class*, 15: 1–22.

Brodsky, A. M. and Hare-Mustin, R. T. (eds) (1980) *Women and Psychotherapy: An Assessment of Research and Practice.* New York: Guilford.

Broverman, I., Broverman, D. M., Clarkson, I. E. Rosenkrantz, P. S. and Vogel, S. R. (1970) Sex role stereotypes and clinical judgements of mental health. *Journal of Consulting and Clinical Psychology*, 34: 1–7.

Brown, H. and Craft, A. (eds) (1989) *Thinking the Unthinkable: Papers on Sexual Abuse and People with Learning Difficulties.* London: Family Planning Association Education Unit.

Brown, L. (1982) Ethical issues in feminist therapy: what is a feminist ethic? Presented at Advanced Feminist Therapy Institute, Washington, DC.

Brown, L. S. (1984) Finding new language: getting beyond analytic verbal shorthand in feminist therapy. *Women and Therapy*, 3, 1: 73–80.

Brown, L. (1985a) Women, weight and power: feminist theoretical and therapeutic issues. *Women and Therapy*, 4, 1: 61–71.

Brown, L. (1985b) Ethics and business practice in feminist therapy. In L. B. Rosewater and L. E. A. Walker (eds), Handbook of Feminist Therapy: Women's Issues in Psychotherapy. New York: Springer.

Brown, L. (1988a) Harmful effects of post-termination sexual and romantic relationships between therapist and their former clients. *Psychotherapy*, 25: 249–255.

Brown, L. (1988b) Feminist therapy with lesbians and gay men. In M. A. Dutton-Douglas and L. E. A. Walker (eds), *Feminist Psychotherapies: Integration of Therapeutic and Feminist Systems.* Norwood, New Jersey: Ablex.

Brown, L. (1991) Plus ça change . . . or, who writes the scripts for these guys anyway? *Feminism and Psychology* 1, 1: 89–92.

Brown, L. and Lerman, H. (1985) Feminist ethics. In L. B. Rosewater and L. E. A. Walker (eds), *Handbook of Feminist Therapy: Women's Issues in Psychotherapy.* New York: Springer.

Butler, M. (1985) Guidelines for feminist therapy. In L. B. Rosewater and L. E. A. Walker (eds) *Handbook of Feminist Therapy: Women's Issues in Psychotherapy.* New York: Springer.

Cammaert, L. P. and Larsen, C. C. (1988) Feminist frameworks of psychotherapy. In M. A. Dutton-Douglas and L. E. A. Walker (eds) Feminist Psychotherapies: Integration of Therapeutic and Feminist Systems. Norwood, New Jersey: Ablex.

Canadian Psychological Association (1980) *Guidelines for Therapy and Counselling with Women.* Ottawa: CPA.

Caplan, P. J. (1985) Sex-based manipulation in the clinical psychologist's workplace. *International Journal of Women's Studies*, 8: 175–182.

Caplan, P. J. (1987) The name game: psychiatry, misogyny, and taxonomy. *Women and Therapy* 6, 1/2: 187–202.

Caplan, P. J. and Gans, M. (1991) Is there empirical justification for the category of 'self-defeating personality disorder?' *Feminism and Psychology*, 1: 2.

Carmen, E. (Hilberman), Felip Russo, N. and Baker-Miller, J. (1984) Inequality and women's mental health: an overview. In P. Perri Reiker and E. (Hilberman) Carmen (eds), *The Gender Gap in Psychotherapy; Social Realities and Psychological Processes*. New York: Plenum.

Chamberlain, J. (1988) *On our Own*. London: MIND.

Chesler, C. (1972) *Women and Madness*. New York: Doubleday.

Cline, S. and Spender, D. (1988) *Reflecting Men at Twice Their Natural Size*. London: Fontana.

Currer, C. (1984) Pathan women in Bradford – factors affecting mental health with particular reference to the effects of racism. *The International Journal of Social Psychiatry*, 30: 1/2: 72–76.

Daly, M. (1978) *Gyn/Ecology: The Metaethics of Radical Feminism*. Boston: Beacon Press.

Dutton-Douglas, M. A. and Walker, L. E. A. (eds) (1988a) *Feminist Psychotherapies: Integration of Therapeutic and Feminist Systems*. Norwood, New Jersey: Ablex.

Dutton-Douglas, M. A. and Walker, L. E. A. (1988b) Introduction to feminist therapies. In M. A. Dutton-Douglas, and L. E. A. Walker (eds) *Feminist Psychotherapies: Integration of Therapeutic and Feminist Systems*. Norwood, New Jersey: Ablex.

Eichenbaum, L. and Orbach, S. (1983) *Understanding Women*. London: Penguin.

Errol, F., David, J., Johnson, N. and Sashidharan, S. P. (1989) Black people and psychiatry in the UK. *Psychiatric Bulletin*, 13: 482–485.

Fine, M. and Gordon, S. M. (1989) Feminist transformations of/despite psychology. In M. Crawford and M. Gentry (eds), *Gender and Thought*. New York: Springer-Verlag.

Fodor, I. G. (1985) Assertiveness training in the eighties: moving beyond the personal. In L. B. Rosewater and L. E. A. Walker (eds), *Handbook of Feminist Therapy: Women's Issues in Psychotherapy*. New York: Springer.

Fondi, M., Hay, J., Kincaid, M. B. and O'Connell, K. (1977) Feminist therapy: a working definition. Unpublished manuscript, University of Pennsylvania.

Franks, V. and Rothblum, E. D. (1983) *The Stereotyping of Women: Its Effects on Mental Health*. New York: Springer.

Fraser, S. (1989) *My Father's House. A Memoir of Incest and of Healing*. London: Virago.

Gilbert, L. A. (1980) Feminist therapy. In A. M. Brodsky and R. T. Hare-Mustin (eds), *Women and Psychotherapy: An Assessment of Research and Practice*. New York: Guilford.

Goldner, V. (1985a) Feminism and family therapy. *Family Process*, 24, 31–47.

Goldner, V. (1985b) Warning: family therapy may be hazardous to your health. *Networker*, Nov.–Dec. 19–23.

Hall, L. and Lloyd, S. (1989) *Surviving Child Sexual Abuse*. London: Falmer Press.

Hall, R. E. (1986) *Ask any Woman: A London Inquiry into Rape and Sexual Assault*. London: Falling Wall Press.

Hamerman Robbins, J. and Josefowitz Siegel, R. (eds) (1983) *Women Changing Therapy: New Assessments, Values and Strategies in Feminist Therapy*. New York: Haworth.

Harflett, G. and Scott, C. (1987). Breaking the silence. *Nursing Times*, 83, 37: 59–61.

Holland, S. (1988) Defining and experimenting with prevention. In S. Ramon and M. G. Giammichedda (eds), *Psychiatry in Transition: The British and Italian Experience*. London: Pluto.

Holland, S. (1989) Women and community mental health – twenty years on. *Clinical Psychology Forum*, 22: 35–37.

Holland, S. (1990) Psychotherapy, oppression and social action: gender, race and class in black women's depression. In R. Perelberg and A. Miller, *Gender and Power in Families*. London: Routledge.

Holland, S. (1991) From private symptoms to public action. *Feminism and Psychology*, 1, 1: 58–62.

Holroyd, J. (1976) Psychotherapy and women's liberation. *Counselling Psychologist*, 6: 22–28.

Janssen, M. (1983) *Silent Scream*. Philadelphia: Fortress Press.

Kaplan, A. G., Brook B., McComb, A. L., Shapiro, E. R. and Sodano, A. (1983) Women and anger in psychotherapy. In J. Hamerman Robbins and R. Josefowitz Siegel (eds), *Women Changing Therapy: New Assessments, Values and Strategies in Feminist Therapy*. New York: Haworth.

Kitzinger, J. (1990). Recalling the pain. *Nursing Times*, 86, 3: 38–40.

Laing, M. (1984) Summary and recommendations: advancing innovative mental health programs for women. In C. T. Mowbray, L. Lanir and M. Hulce (eds), *Women and Mental Health: New Directions for Change*. New York: Haworth.

Lerner, H. (1983) Female dependency in context: some theoretical and technical considerations. *American Journal of Orthopsychiatry*, 53, 4: 697–705.

Linehan, M. and Egan, K. (1979) Assertion training for women: square peg in a round hole? Paper presented at the Annual Meeting of the Association for Advanced Behaviour Therapy, San Francisco.

Littlewood, R. and Lipsedge, M. (1988) Psychiatric illness among British Afro-Caribbeans. *British Medical Journal*, 296: 950–951.

Marecek, J. and Ballou, D. J. (1981) Family roles and women's mental health. *Professional Psychology*, 12, 1: 39–46.

Midlarsky, E. (1988) Feminist therapies with the elderly. In M. A. Dutton-Douglas and L. E. A. Walker (eds), *Feminist Psychotherapies: Integration of Therapeutic and Feminist Systems*. Norwood, New Jersey: Ablex.

Mowbray, C. T., Lanir, S. and Hulce, M. (1984) *Women and Mental Health: New Directions for Change*. New York: Haworth.

Murphy, L. and Livingstone, J. (1985) Racism and the limits of radical feminism. *Race and Class*, 16, 4: 61–70.

National Coalition for Women's Mental Health (1985) *Women and Psychotherapy: A Consumer Handbook*. Tempe, Arizona State University.

National Organisation for Women (1978) *A Consumer's Guide to Non-Sexist Therapy*. New York: NOW.

NiCarthy, G., Fuller, A. and Stoops, N. (1987) Battering and abuse of women in intimate relationships. In D. S. Burden and N. Gottlieb (eds), *The Woman Client*. London: Tavistock.

Orbach, S. (1986) *Hunger Strike*. London: Faber & Faber.

Parlee, M. (1979) Psychology and women. *Signs: Journal of Women in Culture and Society*, 5: 121–133.

Penfold, P. S. and Walker, G. A. (1984) *Women and the Psychiatric Paradox*. Milton Keynes: Open University Press.

Perkins, R. (1991) Women with long-term mental health problems: issues of power and powerlessness. *Feminism and Psychology*, 1, 1: 131–139.

Poston, C. and Lison, K. (1989) *Reclaiming Our Lives: Hope for Adult Survivors of Incest*. Boston: Little, Brown.

Rawlings, E. I. and Carter, D. K. (1977) *Psychotherapy for Women: Treatment Towards Equality*. Springfield, Illinois: Charles C. Thomas.

Reiker, P. Perri and Carmen, E. (Hilberman) (eds) (1984a) *The Gender Gap in Psychotherapy: Social Realities and Psychological Processes*. New York: Plenum.

Reiker, P. Perri and Carmen, E. (Hilberman) (1984b) Teaching value clarification: the example of gender and psychotherapy. In P. Perri Reiker and E. (Hilberman) Carmen (eds), *The Gender Gap in Psychotherapy; Social Realities and Psychological Processes*. New York: Plenum.

Robinson, C. R., (1983) Black women: a tradition of self-reliant strength. In J. Hamerman Robbins and R. Josefowitz Siegel (eds), *Women Changing Therapy: New Assessments, Values and Strategies in Feminist Therapy*. New York: Haworth.

Rosewater, L. B. (1984) Feminist therapy: implications for practitioners. In L. E. A. Walker (ed.), *Women and Mental Health Policy*. London: Sage.

Rosewater, L. B. (1985) Schizophrenic, borderline or battered? In L. B. Rosewater and L. E. A. Walker (eds), *Handbook of Feminist Therapy: Women's Issues in Psychotherapy*. New York: Springer.

Rosewater, L. B. (1988) Feminist therapies with women. In M. A. Dutton-Douglas and L. E. A. Walker (eds), *Feminist Psychotherapies: Integration of Therapeutic and Feminist Systems*. Norwood, New Jersey: Ablex.

Rosewater, L. B. and Walker, L. E. A. (eds) (1985a) *Handbook of Feminist Therapy: Women's Issues in Psychotherapy*. New York: Springer.

Rosewater, L. B. and Walker, L. E. A. (1985b) Feminist therapy: a coming of age. In L. B. Rosewater and L. E. A. Walker (eds), *Handbook of Feminist Therapy: Women's Issues in Psychotherapy*. New York: Springer.

Sayal, A. (1989) Black women and mental health. *Clinical Psychology Forum*, 22: 3–6.

Sayal-Bennett, A. (1991) Equal opportunities – empty rhetoric? *Feminism and Psychology*, 1, 1: 74–77.

Schoener, G., Milgrom, Hofstee, J. and Gonsiorek, J. (1984) Sexual exploitation of clients by therapists. *Women and Therapy*, 3, 3/4: 63–69.

Scottish Action for Mental Health (1988) Atlantic House, 38 Gardener's Crescent, Edinburgh.

Sharratt, S. and Bern, L. (1985) Lesbian couples and families: a co-therapy approach to counselling. In L. B. Rosewater and L. E. A. Walker (eds), *Handbook of Feminist Therapy: Women's Issues in Psychotherapy*. New York: Springer.

Showalter, E. (1987) *The Female Malady*. London: Virago.

Siegel, R. J. (1985) Beyond homophobia: learning to work with lesbian clients. In L. B. Rosewater and L. E. A. Walker (eds), *Handbook of Feminist Therapy: Women's Issues in Psychotherapy*. New York: Springer.

Skodra, E. E. (1989) Counselling immigrant women: a feminist critique of traditional therapeutic approaches and re-evaluation of the role of therapist. *Counselling Psychologist*, 2, 2: 185–204.

Smith, A. J. and Siegel, R. F. (1985) Feminist therapy: redefining power for the powerless. In L. B. Rosewater and L. E. A. Walker (eds), *Handbook of Feminist Therapy: Women's Issues in Psychotherapy*. New York: Springer.

Smith, H. (1991) Caring for everyone? The implications for women of the changes in community care services. *Feminism and Psychology*, 1: 2.

Smith, L. J. F. (1989) *Domestic Violence: An Overview of the Literature*. A Home Office Research and Planning Report. London: HMSO.

Sturdivant, S. (1980) *Therapy with Women. A Feminist Philosophy of Treatment*. New York: Springer.

Tennov, D. (1973) Feminism, psychotherapy and professionalism. *Journal of Contemporary Psychotherapy*, 5, 2: 107–111.

Ussher, J. (1989) *The Psychology of the Female Body*. London: Routledge.

Ussher, J. (1991) *Women and Madness: Misogyny or Mental Illness?* London: Harvester Wheatsheaf.

Walker, L. E. A. (ed.) (1984a) *Women and Mental Health Policy*. London: Sage.

Walker, L. E. A. (1984b) Violence against women: implications for mental health policy. In L. E. A. Walker (ed.), *Women and Mental Health Policy*. London: Sage.

Walker, L. E. A. (1985) Feminist therapy with victim/survivors of interpersonal violence. In L. B. Rosewater and L. E. A. Walker (eds), *Handbook of Feminist Therapy: Women's Issues in Psychotherapy*. New York: Springer.

Walker, L. E. A. and Dutton-Douglas, M. A. (1988) Future directions: development, application, and training of feminist therapies. In M. A. Dutton-Douglas and L. E. A. Walker (eds), *Feminist Psychotherapies: Integration of Therapeutic and Feminist Systems*. Norwood, New Jersey: Ablex.

Walstedt, J. (1971) *36-24-36 Anatomy of Oppression: A Feminist Analysis of Psychotherapy*. Pittsburgh: Know.

Weisstein, N. (1971) Psychology constructs the female. In V. Gornick and B. K. Moran (eds), *Women in Sexist Society*. New York: Mentor.

Whitley, B. E. Jr (1983) Sex role orientation and self-esteem: a critical meta-analytic review. *Journal of Personality and Social Psychology*, 44, 4: 765–778.

Whitwell, D. (1990) The significance of childhood sexual abuse for adult psychiatry. *British Journal of Hospital Medicine*, 43, May: 346–362.

Williams, J. A. (1984) Women and mental illness. In J. Nicholson and H. Beloff, *Psychological Survey* 5. Leicester: British Psychological Society.

Williams, J. A. and Watson, G. (1988) Sexual inequality, family life and family therapy. In E. Street and W. Dryden (eds), *Family Therapy in Britain*. Milton Keynes: Open University Press.

Williams, J. A. and Watson, G. (1991a) Sexual inequality and clinical psychology training in Britain: survey report. *Feminism and Psychology*, 1, 1: 78–88.

Williams, J. A. and Watson, G. (1991b) Sexual inequality and clinical psychology training in Britain: workshop report. *Feminism and Psychology*, 1, 1: 96–109.

Women in Mind (1986) *Finding Our Own Solutions: Women's Experience of Mental Health Care.* London: MIND.

Name index

Subject index